THE POLITICS OF THE
EUROPEAN COMMUNIST STATES

THE POLITICS OF THE EUROPEAN COMMUNIST STATES

Ghiţa Ionescu

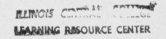

FREDERICK A. PRAEGER, *Publishers*

New York • Washington

BOOKS THAT MATTER

Published in the United States of America in 1967
by Frederick A. Praeger, Inc., Publishers
111 Fourth Avenue, New York, N.Y. 10003

© 1967 by Ghiţa Ionescu

Library of Congress Catalog Card Number: 67-24682

Printed in the United States of America

CONTENTS

ACKNOWLEDGEMENTS

This study is the fruit of two years of work undertaken under the auspices of the Nuffield Foundation and of the London School of Economics. A special grant from the former and the warm hospitality of the latter enabled me to conduct a seminar on 'The East European One-Party States' during the academic years 1964–5 and 1965–6. It is with great pleasure than I can now express publicly my gratitude to the Nuffield Foundation for its generous help.

Most of the work of research and consultation required by this present study was carried on in the seminar at the London School of Economics and Political Science. I want to thank Professor Michael Oakeshott, Professor Geoffrey Goodwin and most expressly Professor Leonard Schapiro for the help and advice they gave me during these two years. I am also grateful to all the other members of the academic staff of LSE and of other schools and colleges who participated in the seminar and in its two larger conferences.

I have also benefited from the advice of outstanding scholars on various aspects of my study. Thus I wish to record my thanks to Professors Giovanni Sartori, Bertrand de Jouvenel, Carl J. Friedrich, Richard Hofstadter and W. H. Morris-Jones who assisted me on the problems of political opposition; and to Professors Raymond Aron, Edward Shils, S. M. Lipset, Jovan Djordjević, J. Wiatr and Dr Anton Vratuša who discussed with me the problem of the party and of what I call the Apparat in the non-parliamentary states.

To three friends I owe a special debt of gratitude for reading, with difficulty, and correcting with enthusiasm the manuscript of this book. Professor Bernard Crick's incisive criticism helped me to see some aspects of the subject more clearly before, during and after the completion of this manuscript. Professor Ernest Gellner, both as a friend and as editor of this series, has had the burden not only of reading but of editing the manuscript, and the wealth of his observations on the subject would make up an entire other essay. I discussed with Dr Isabel de Madariaga all the ideas which went into this book, and she checked the numerous versions through which it went until it reached the present stage. But it is unnecessary to add that the many mistakes which remain are my own and should not be imputed to those who tried to help me.

To Miss M. Nicholson, my secretary, who typed this text many times I would like to express here my heartfelt thanks.

And to V. B. T., of course.

Highgate, 1967   GHITA IONESCU

THE POLITICS OF THE
EUROPEAN COMMUNIST STATES

INTRODUCTION

This is a book about the present relations between states and societies in seven countries: Bulgaria, Czechoslovakia, the German Democratic Republic, Poland, Rumania and Yugoslavia. Simplifying somewhat, the modern study of politics is about the relationship between state and society. As the title of this book is very condensed, it may be as well to examine beforehand the way in which the main terms contained in it are used.

Politics

In our generation the study of politics has been transformed by the new methods of political sociology and comparative politics. The stress is laid on political systems and societies as a whole, and modern studies endeavour to see how contemporary states do, or do not, correspond to their respective societies.

As a first approximation one might say that whereas the characteristics of the state are authority, unity and habitual obedience, those of society are diversity, internal contradictions and pluralism. A bad state tends towards more control, rigidity and coercion, and a bad society towards incoherence, dissolution and shapelessness. In other words, to return to the subject of this book, whereas the state has a functional tendency to become centralistic and monolithic, society tends to be decentralising and pluralistic. Indeed to speak of a monolithic society is a non-sense. Modern states can be classified according to the way in which they restrain and control the pluralistic forces of the societies over which, as it were, they preside.

For the purpose of this study, it is proposed to divide contemporary states, into, on the one hand, the pluralistic-constitutional states, to use Raymond Aron's particularly comprehensive formula; that is the states which by their charters and structures ensure the free manifestation of political pluralism. On the other hand, there are those states which are not pluralistic-constitutional and which can be grouped together by virtue of being oppositionless. We can thus take as our criterion the absence of political opposition.

But this emphasizes the importance of the concept of political opposition and it is therefore necessary to explain how it is used here.

The best way to proceed is to compare the widest and vaguest usage of the word opposition, with the most specific definition of the contemporary institution to which the words 'political opposition' could be applied. These then are the proposed definitions:

1. 'Opposition' in the broad sense is any concerted attitude or action, spontaneous or deliberate, sporadic or continuous, of anomic or associational groups or of individuals against the existing power[1] under any circumstances or by any means. In this sense opposition covers the entire range of motives and manifestations of political conflict in all societies. These are mostly to be found under two general headings: the conflict of interest which originates from the friction and rivalry between groups within the community (these activities are the causes of *political checks*[2] imposed on any government in any polity by interest groups, etc.); and the conflict of values, henceforth described as *dissent*, which originates logically from the incompatibility of opinions, outlook and beliefs among people of different allegiances and mentalities living together in the same community.

2. 'Political opposition' as an institution and as part of a constitutional political procedure is one party or more, or a coalition of political parties, which on the basis of a publicly proclaimed set of values present themselves to the electors as competitors for the established executive power and fail to command enough votes in an institutionalized consultation to enable them to claim to express the will of the sovereign people. Their role and function are then

---

[1] This shows that the definition does not apply to what anthropologists call 'acephalous' societies.

[2] The expression political *checks* has been chosen, after many other attempts, as against *control* (as used for instance by Karl Loewenstein in his *Political Power and the Governmental Process*, Chicago, 1957, by R. Dahrendorf in his works, and especially now by G. Bergeron in: *Fonctionnement de l'état*, Paris, 1965. Montesquieu called checks the *contre-pouvoirs* built into any polity against the *pouvoir*.

to criticize the existing government, its legislative and executive action, and the values upon which they are founded – in parliament or by any other constitutional means – with the object of influencing the government's action and legislation and eventually of replacing that government after further consultations,' or else of sharing power with it.

The first difference between opposition on the one hand, and political opposition on the other, is that the latter is institutionalized, recognized and legitimate. It is the essence of political opposition that it should function as such; this implies that the term political opposition should be used only in cases where it is not merely allowed to function but is able to do so. This is the second difference. Finally, political opposition, in contrast with the perennial 'opposition', is historical, in the sense that it appeared, at different times – and nowhere earlier than at the very end of the eighteenth and the beginning of the nineteenth centuries – in those polities in which a long historic evolution led to a broad institutionalization.

The functioning of political opposition is the supreme institution and the crowning of the entire political process.[3] History also records the appearance and disappearance of political opposition, as in Russia in the twentieth century, as well as intense periods of evolution towards the possible final appearance of political opposition in less politically developed societies, of which the outcome cannot be safely predicted.

But what happens in the sovereign and economically developed states, where political opposition does not fully function and therefore 'opposition', as inevitable here as in any polity, is reduced to inferior forms? Here political checks and political dissent provide, as far as is possible under coercive conditions, the outlet for the inherent conflict between the power holders and society.

Political checks, originating from conflicts of interest, and political dissent, originating from the conflict of values, replace in these countries the action which is best carried by and through political opposition. Indeed, no society, and especially no contemporary society, is so politically under-developed as not to contain, and reproduce within itself, the perennial conflict of

[3] For a fuller discussion of this point see: O. Hintze: *Staat und Verfassung*, Leipzig, 1943. R. R. Palmer: *The Age of Democratic Revolution*, 2 vols., London, 1964, A. S. Foord: *His Majesty's Opposition (1714–1830)*, Clarendon Press, 1964, and R. A. Dahl: *Political Opposition in Western Democracies*, Yale, 1966.

power. No contemporary society can, on the one hand, run all the complex activities of the state, political, cultural, social and economic, exclusively, by its own ubiquitous and omniscient servants, without collaboration and bargains with, or checks by, other interest groups.[4] And no contemporary society can be so efficiently policed as to prevent the perennial conflict of values, in the form of dissent, recurring again behind new chinks and through new loopholes. And affluence, while it renders dissent less violent, stimulates independence.

The political conflicts in non-opposition states form a continuum of sui-generis situations and phases. The intermediary situations may remain stationary for long periods. If, however, they were to be carried to the alternative ends of the continuum, they would lead in the event of political stability to the institutionalization of political opposition, and in the event of the accentuation of conflict to economic deadlock, revolution and, especially in the case of conflicts of values, civil war.

There are basically three main categories of sovereign oppositionless states:

1. Sovereign states in which the political opposition as an institution is not denied in principle by the power-holders, but does not exist in fact: Ethiopia, the states of francophone Africa, even some Latin-American states.

2. Sovereign states in which the political opposition as an institution is denied by the power-holders in the cause of pursuit of superior national goals: all military dictatorships from Franco to Nasser; and now Ghana, Nigeria, and all underdeveloped one-party states.

3. Sovereign states, called communist, in which the political opposition, as an institution, is denied by the power-holders in the pursuit of the ending of political alienation and of integration in the classless society.

The difference between category 1 and categories 2 and 3 of the non-opposition states is that the latter – to be called here: apparat states – also undertake a full mobilization of the national resources, the individual energies and the minds of the population towards some collective future aims. This means that in

[4] Talcott Parson's well-known phrase in his *Social System* (New York, 1957), that 'the processes of production require the "co-operation" or integration of different agencies' sums up this truism.

4

addition to denying political opposition these states also need, for the essential purposes of changing the unsatisfactory social and economic bases of the nation, to build and maintain an *Apparat*. The power-holders can thus ensure that the plans adopted and the decisions taken at the centre are implemented at all levels in all directions of the society thus organized.

Category 3 is divided in its turn into:

(*a*) Soviet Russia as an industrialized great power,
(*b*) China as a potential great power undergoing industrialization,
(*c*) the European communist states,
(*d*) the Asian communist states: North Korea and North Vietnam,
(*e*) Cuba.

European

The following sovereign states of Europe and full members of the United Nations Organization are communist: Albania, Bulgaria, Czechoslovakia, Hungary, Poland, Rumania and Yugoslavia; and also one territorial and political unit, East Germany, which is not a member of the United Nations, and whose sovereignty is not recognized by non-communist states. Yugoslavia and Albania are not members of the Warsaw Treaty Organization, headed by Soviet Russia. Russia is not included in the present list of small and medium states because it is a great power. Indeed there are many distinctions to be drawn, from this point of view, between Soviet Russia and the communist states listed above.

One minor distinction is the fact that while Soviet Russia defined in geographical terms is Eurasian, the states studied here are all exclusively European. To call these states – as is usually done – East European would help to distinguish them from the West European states, but it would not distinguish between them and Russia, which is also European, indeed East European. Moreover the delimitation between Eastern and Western Europe is very imprecise and is blurred by the existence of Central Europe (to which at least two of the states under study belong: East Germany and Czechoslovakia) – and by the fact that yet another delineation between Southern and Northern Europe, with important climatic and ethnical differences, cuts across the zone called Eastern

Europe in obvious ways. (So obvious that Yugoslavia and Greece, for instance, have more features in common than have Yugoslavia and Poland.) But whatever these secondary differences, the fact remains that these states are European because of their community of history with the rest of the continent of Europe; because they belong territorially only to Europe; because they are roughly the same in size and structure as other European states; and because of the cultural and economic links they have with them.

The second difference between Soviet Russia and the other European communist states lies in her status as a great power as opposed to theirs as small or medium states. This is a distinction which the rule of legal equality in international law did not recognize until it was embodied first in the Covenant of the League of Nations, and now specifically in the Charter of the United Nations. There is a difference in status between all the other member-states and the five great powers: Great Britain, the United States, Soviet Russia, France and China. It has been legalized in different ranks and privileges, the most striking one being that only five great powers have permanent representation on the Security Council.[5] Soviet Russia is, therefore, from all points of view, the Eastern European great power. This leads to substantial differences between Russia and the European communist states, which although obvious, must be briefly touched on.

As a great power Russia, under any system, has the means to keep her economy working by its own resources; moreover, like the United States, she is territorially self-contained and depends much less on overseas resources than the nineteenth century great powers, notably Britain and France. Two examples from such a recent period as Khrushchev's rule show the extent to which the leaders of Soviet Russia are conscious of this major fact of life. Khrushchev at first based his hope of solving the crisis in Soviet collectivized agriculture by cultivating the virgin lands of Kazakhstan and other Eastern provinces of this vast empire. His own references and indeed the references of all Soviet economists, during the discussion about the reorganization of COMECON[6]

[5] Lauterpacht: *Oppenheim's International Law*, Vol. I, *Peace*, London, 1947, p. 248-9.
[6] See especially Khrushchev's article of September 1962 in *World Marxist Review*.

stressed that Russia, as an economically self-contained great power, must play within COMECON an entirely different part from that of the other communist member-states.

Moreover, as a great power, Soviet Russia has a direct interest in world affairs, while the communist states have only limited, diplomatic and ideological, interests – and indeed many of these interests have been handed over to Soviet Russia as the leader of the bloc of European communist states. As a great power, too, she is able to organize the defence of her national territory by direct and indirect means. Not only does she take charge of the defence of the European communist states, she also organizes them from a strategic point of view as marches of her own defence. This also means that as a great power she is in a position to absorb them more or less into her own zone of influence or of imperial expansion; while they, so long as they remain sovereign states, have a distinct interest in maintaining their national and territorial integrity as intact as possible within the very relation shaped between each of them and Russia as a great power.

These differences are obvious and they are taken into consideration, implicitly or explicitly, in all serious studies of the Soviet bloc or of the communist states in general. But other differences are of even greater relevance to this study: differences in the age, origin and efficacy of the respective communist regimes. Soviet Russia, the direct successor of Tsarist Russia, has fifty years of experience as a vast federation of communist republics with a constitution and political structure given to her by the Russian Bolshevik Party. The European communist states, the successors of more or less successful democracies, started their existence after the Second World War by copying the constitutions and structures of the USSR and of the Communist Party of the Soviet Union. These have proved from the beginning to be irrelevant and unsuitable for the smaller European countries.

These differences between the political life of a great power and that of the smaller states are fundamental. Their neglect has distorted Western studies of the European communist states, a distortion which has been partially corrected only in the last five or six years. There was, first, the assumption that there was no difference between their internal political life and that of Soviet Russia, their societies being considered equally crushed under a totalitarian organization. But this was only part of the general assumption that their political structures, institutions and processes could best be explained by measuring them against those of their model, the USSR. This approach could have been justified so long as the new power-holders in these states, as they emerged after the Second World War, tried to reproduce in their constitutions and in their economic and social structures the features of the dictatorship of the proletariat, as embodied in Leninist-Stalinist Russia. It could also have been justified so long as the power-holders in these states claimed that the political evolution of the new states would follow and indeed imitate that of the USSR. But even by 1947–8 there were clear signs that some of the Communist Parties in power in those European states, when faced with the realities of their countries and the pressure of the peoples over whom they had to rule, had begun to disagree with certain of the formulae of the Russian blue-print.[7] This resulted in the open conflict in 1948 on basic questions of political and social-economic organization, between the Yugoslav League of Communists and the CPSU and the newly formed, and short-lived, COMINFORM. It led also to the formidable assertions of nonconformism represented by the Polish and Hungarian upheavals of 1956; and after that by the Albanian and the Rumanian open dissent of 1960 and 1963. This, together with the irresistible centrifugal force set up by the Sino-Soviet ideological conflict, led to the present polycentrism, or rather a-centrism, in communist ideology, in which the controversy over the present and future of the communist state and the society is one of the great divides.

The differences from this point of view between the European communist states and the great power, the USSR, are analogous in some respects to the differences between the political processes of the USA and those of some Latin-American states. The latter copied in their constitutions the main features of the American presidential system but applied them in characteristically different ways, or after a while gave up applying them. The assumption that the political systems of the European communist states can now best be interpreted in terms of the Soviet model only leads to confusion. (It is different when the projection upon the relevant

---

[7] Z. Brzezinski: *The Soviet Bloc*, New York, 1960, and my own: *The Breakup of the Soviet Empire in Eastern Europe*, London, Penguin Special, 1965, contain a more complete account of this first major split between some of the European Communist Parties in power and the CPSU.

Soviet institution or structure is made for historical reasons.) This does not mean that these states could not still one day become, in different international circumstances, part and parcel of the USSR, component republics of this vast federation, commonwealth or empire. But if this were to happen, they would not be, as they claim to be now, sovereign national states.

For one of the facts of political life of these countries *as* sovereign states which must be taken into account is that, precisely because a great power exerts a dominant influence in their part of the world, they are bound to try to maintain their sovereignty and their national and political identities in spite of her. They therefore feed into their own political institutions and systems some national, and if the expression can be used in this sense, popular substance. From this point of view the difference between the part played by the party in the shaping of the new political systems in the USSR and in the European communist states becomes again highly relevant.

In Soviet Russia at the beginning of the century the party was the exponent of an international doctrine. But this doctrine could serve also as the national ideology for a great power and a messianic people. The Bolshevik Party carried out the actual revolution on its own. It came to and remained in power by means of its own forces. In a state in which the institutions of representative, parliamentary democracy were practically unknown, it imposed the Marxist-Leninist dictatorship of the proletariat and the techniques of local government and therefore acted, long before it took upon itself the tasks of economic planning and social mobilization, as an educator and moulder of the new society.

In the European communist states, the parties before the war borrowed their ideology entirely, via the COMINTERN, from the CPSU. After the war, the party came to power either, in the exceptional case of Yugoslavia, as the political apparat and leadership of the Partisan Army, or, as in all the other six states, as the political organization chosen by the Soviet army to be installed in power. The parties were immediately faced with administrative and economic tasks which overshadowed ideological and historical considerations.

The second fact of political life which should not be forgotten when dealing with the politics of the European communist states, is that because of their entirely European tradition they show more and more obvious socio-economic pluralities and a faster tendency towards pluralization than Soviet Russia. In a sense the quasi-neutralist image of these states as a bridge between Russia and the West which their Communist Parties now so often project, with characteristic wishful-thinking, is inspired by this matter-of-fact consideration. Slavic or non-Slavic, the seven states are European. They have a historical and recent political past in which European political institutions and culture have been their main example and inspiration, and from most points of view they are Western – rather than Eastern-orientated.

Also, this latent pluralism was more vigorous in the European communist states because interest groups of every kind upheld an active *Bewusstsein*. The army, the civil service, the political police remembered in most of these countries the influence they had often exerted in politics. The army often acted in some of them as the ultimate umpire in major political crises; the political police often exercised a direct influence on governments. The churches in Poland, Rumania and Bulgaria served as the cradle of the political and national consciousness of these countries, so frequently over-shadowed in history. Since the nineteenth century the intelligentsia had played a very important national and social role in Poland, Hungary, Rumania, etc. The ethnic minorities, or national-administrative groupings (the federal republics) also used their traditional technique of political struggle and influence. The trade unions, and the working class in general, the managers and the leaders of technology have acquired a special status in the politics of their developing countries. It is on the study of the interior pluralistic forces of the societies of the oppositionless states that the analysis of this book will be based.

One final remark at this point. It will have been noticed that implicitly and explicitly Albania has not been included in this analysis of the relations between state and society in the European communist states. Albania still deliberately shuts herself off and refuses to enter into normal diplomatic or cultural relations with the Western states. As a result, the state of information about the politics of this communist state is considerably less advanced and offers at present insufficient material for serious studies. Moreover, from the special point of view of the present analysis, Albania is much less relevant. Because of its delayed development, Albanian society is still in a much more rudimentary phase than that of the other seven states. Indeed, in order to study the basic pluralism of Albanian society, one would have to start with a study of its powerful and well-entrenched clans, a feature now unique in Europe. On the other hand, and partly as a consequence of this, the Albanian Communist Party and state have been able to adopt, and indeed brandish, a policy and ideology of revised and fervent Stalinism, and are accusing the other European communist states, at present involved in the problem of how to adapt themselves to modern circumstances, of revisionism.

Communist apparat-states

It will be remembered that within a classification of contemporary states, as proposed in the first part of this introduction, the communist states could be described more fully as oppositionless communist apparat states. There are two reasons why this new classification was considered necessary (although this author sympathizes with those who believe that to add more such classifications to the too numerous ones already recorded confuses more than it clarifies). The first is that none of the three broad descriptions which are given to them in the political theories of today fully suits and explains them. They are, as will be seen, too narrow and at the same time not fully relevant. The second is that by finding a common denominator for these states in the *Apparat*, of which more will be said shortly, it is easier to understand the kind of political life and conflict within these regimes, described above as the relation between state and society.

The Marxist-Leninist political school, which divides existing states into capitalist and non-capitalist, sub-divides the latter into four categories, or rather stages, in their evolution towards the ultimate, inevitable, classless society.

The first category/stage is the 'national democracies', mainly the under-developed countries of Africa and Asia, emerging from their struggle for decolonization. They are described as societies in transition from pre- or half-capitalist structures to socialism. The leadership, in social-political terms, is taken by a 'national front', embracing all social classes, but with an increasing bias towards the working classes.

The next category/stage is that of the 'people's democracies', four of which exist in Eastern Europe: Poland, Hungary, Bulgaria and Albania, and two in Asia: North Korea and North Vietnam.

These in turn must go through two internal phases. The first is the transition from capitalist to socialist relations and is characterized politically by 'the democratic dictatorship of the workers and peasants'; the second is the transition to the building of socialism, and is characterized politically by the dictatorship of the proletariat.

The third category/stage is formed by the 'socialist republics'; the Soviet Union, the Yugoslav Federation, the German Democratic Republic, the Czechoslovak and the Rumanian Socialist Republics. This stage is also divided into two internal transition phases: the phase of the establishment of socialist economic structures, during which the dictatorship of the proletariat is still necessary; and the phase of the 'building of communism' during which the internal dictatorship withers away and the stage of the state of the whole people is reached.

Finally, the fourth stage is that of the classless societies – or society, since it can be more adequately conceived on a world scale – with a communist economy and spontaneous and uncontrolled political self-administration.

Leaving aside the intrinsic merits or demerits of the Marxist-Leninist social-economic theories, it is clear that from a political point of view their definitions of the communist states obstruct, more than they enlarge, the study of the subject matter. They are prone to ignore, when they deal with communist societies, the perennial mechanisms of conflict (of interests as much as of values) upon which they base their political interpretation of the capitalist societies. Assuming, as they do, that an implicit reduction of political struggle follows the inevitable dissolution of the social classes, the Marxist-Leninist theories ignore, and the Marxist-Leninist regimes actually abolish the functioning of opposition. The Marxist-Leninist theories, and the present communist political systems, distort and try to hide under irrelevant formulae the obvious survival of the political process. It is one thing to argue that organs and forms of self-administration and local self-management might in classless societies replace representative political institutions; it is another to maintain that, however distant the withering away of the state may be now, the rule of one 'vanguard' party can and must bring to an immediate end the permanent political conflicts and activities.

Liberal political theorists, opposed almost instinctively to any autocratic theories, found so many common features between the fascist and communist systems in the thirties, when the two systems co-existed, that a word was coined for both of them: totalitarian. The six main common features of the systems thus lumped together are: the compulsory ideology, the monolithic party, the terrorist political police, the monopoly of communication, the monopoly of all means of armed combat and the centrally directed economy.[8] These features could all be found in the Hitlerite and Stalinist systems of the thirties. The concept of totalitarianism was therefore of real use during the period when political science was studying, from the outside, two systems of government which had more features in common, and opposed to those of parliamentary regimes, than they had outstanding differences. But it gradually became less useful after the main fascist systems collapsed. Also the communist regimes, more monolithic and monopolistic[9] than the fascist ones, showed a gradual internal pluralization as against the rigid features of the Stalinist monolithic patterns. Totalitarianism, used indiscriminately, became confusing when the communist autocracies had to share the stage with the 'new', post-colonial, autocracies. To be sure, they had in common with these new regimes many non- and anti-liberal features, but, from a logical point of view, they could not be put together in one single classification. Thus it is impossible to call contemporary Spain or Yugoslavia 'totalitarian' in the same way as Nazi Germany and Stalinist Russia; and can one say that the UAR, Pakistan and Paraguay are 'totalitarian' like Albania, or East Germany, or China? Where does 'totalitarianism' end, and how far does it still stretch nowadays?

Most contemporary schools of political science and sociology prefer, and rightly so, to define these contemporary autocracies as

[8] The basic book on this subject remains C. J. Friedrich and Z. Brzezinski: *Totalitarian Dictatorship and Autocracy*, New York, London, 1960, second edition 1965. See an important reconsideration of this book in Hugh Seton-Watson's review in *Government and Opposition*, vol. 2, no. 1, 1966. Good discussions of the usefulness of the concept of totalitarianism for present-day states and autocratic states can be found in: Martin Dracht, preface to H. Richer, *Macht ohne Mandat*, Köln, 1965; B. Ludz, preface to *Soziologie der DSR*, Köln, 1965; and Boris Meissner's study in *Sowjetgesellschaft im Wandel*, 1966, W. Kohlhammer Verlag, Stuttgart.

[9] To use Raymond Aron's useful, but not sufficiently used, expression in which he blends the idea of monolithic political power with that of the monopoly of all means of production obtaining in communist states.

one-party states. This name expresses the implicit and explicit differences between the multi- and the single-party systems. (What is more it includes also such no-party states as Saudi Arabia or Ethiopia – which in the present classification belong to the first category of oppositionless states.) While this is an elastic and indeed very comprehensive analytical framework, it leaves out two important groups of states.

The first of these groups is formed by those communist and non-communist states which are in reality one-party states, but which, on paper, allow more parties to function in form. China, East Germany, Bulgaria and almost all 'People's Democracies' have maintained in constitutional existence, though empty of political substance, former parties which serve the present purpose of the regimes as 'front organizations'. But in Poland, where the main school of political interpretation is centred on the theory of the 'dominant' or 'hegemonic' party, there exists in addition to former parties, which are now merely front organizations, an independent political *group* called *Znak*. Znak,[10] while it agrees to collaborate openly with the 'hegemonic' party, is not controlled from within and directly manipulated by it. For formal and substantive reasons these states can not easily be called one-party states.

The second group which now also drops out of the general definition of one-party states includes all the African, Asian, and even Latin-American states which were formerly one-party states. Here the parties had been the leading political force in the struggle for liberation and decolonization and had afterwards carried on the new mandate of the mobilization of all national resources for the rapid development of the country. But in the last three years they have been successively and rapidly replaced in power by the army, or by some form of military Junta based on the direct support of the armed forces. While it is true to say that in the great majority of these cases the new governments set up by the army only super-impose military control on the structures, ideology and definitions of the former one-party regimes, one must inevitably recognize that the number of one-party states has been thus reduced.

The expression, oppositionless states, thus coined, sums up the theory that the safest criterion for distinguishing between contemporary autocracies – or, to use Georges Burdeau's ingenious

[10] See *infra*, p. 250.

expression, monocracies[11] – and contemporary pluralistic-constitutional regimes generally called *democracies*, is the existence or non-existence, within their political and constitutional structures, of a political opposition – that is of institutionalized organisms and procedures for the open competition for power. In all these states, from China to Yugoslavia, and from Tanzania to the USSR, the one permanent, political common denominator is that all of them ban political opposition.

But, as was previously noted, the states which undertake mobilization for the transformation of the social and economic foundations of society, be it for limited national purposes or for universal purposes in the future, need to build up an Apparat, which becomes the backbone of the new state, which in turn becomes an apparat state.

The expression Apparat is used in political language mostly in connection with the Communist Party apparat, and it describes, in the narrow sense, the internal organization, leadership and cadres of the party, through which the decisions taken by the leadership are implemented by the cadres who drive the groups and individuals in society to carry them out. More will be said of the Communist Party apparat in the chapter on 'The Network'. But here let it be said only that the expressions Apparat, or apparats, apparatus or apparatuses, carry in the communist political language greater weight than is given them in non-communist political semantics. In the latter the expression, used mostly in connection with the apparat of the Central Committee of the Party, has otherwise a vague connotation – and a slightly pejorative one, since it is associated with the derived '*apparatchiks*', by now an ugly word. From Lenin to Khrushchev political leaders of the Communist Party, in moments of particularly profound reflection, have referred to the problem of the apparat or apparatuses as the central one. Thus in a note scribbled in 1921, the crucial year for the future of the Soviet state, Lenin exclaimed: 'We would all have perished long ago but for the apparat.'[12] And in one of his most important speeches at the crucial 22nd Party Congress on 19 October 1961, Khrushchev was heard to observe that one day

---

[11] In his *Traité de Science Politique*, vol. VII, Paris, 1957, which contains also an interesting discussion of the effect of socio-economic pluralism on political life in *monocracies*.

[12] Lenin, *Complete Works*, vol. 32, p. 341, London, 1965.

'the peoples will administer society without any special apparatuses', thus referring, unlike Lenin, to the fact that there are other apparats, apart from that of the party. But like Lenin, Khrushchev showed, after more than forty years, that for the man in the seat of power, the apparat or apparats remain the central feature. It is thus proposed to use *Apparat* here in a broader sense and to conceptualize it. In other words not only are there more and wider apparats than the party-apparat, and therefore the notion could be broadened to contain all of them; but *Apparat* as a concept applies to a wider sphere of the characteristics of non-opposition states than the party. Indeed whereas there is an Apparat in the structure of all oppositionless states, there is not necessarily a party, or, for that matter, a single party. Moreover recently in many of the non-communist one-party states (from Algeria to Nigeria) the party has been replaced in power by the army, and what can be called the army-apparat has superimposed itself on, and taken over, the former exclusive party-apparat.

An apparat or apparatus, can be defined as any centralistic organization, which, in an oppositionless state holds, in proportion with its share of responsibility in the running of the state, a smaller or a larger part of the coercive power of the state; and which together with other secondary apparats, and under the aegis of the main apparat, forms together the all-embracing state-apparat or as it will be called here Apparat. There are usually eight apparats. The party, the army, the state administration, the political police, the bureaucracy, the youth-organization, the planning commission and the trade unions are all apparats. The apparats show, from a structural-functional viewpoint the same organization and direction, going upwards from the council to the inner council up to the leader and downwards from the council to the executives, through the cadres to the administration. But all secondary apparats are united, under the command of one, *main* apparat and form the Apparat, as a whole.

The main apparat is not always the same. In the USSR it is the party-apparat. In Egypt it is the army-apparat. In Portugal the government-apparat. The main apparat can also be changed, as in Ghana or in Algeria, where the army-apparat came to the fore, displacing the party-apparat into a secondary position. In some cases, and for shorter periods, there exists also a duality of apparats: army and party, state administration and party, etc. The main apparat exercises its authority over the secondary apparats by the fact that it provides the leader, by the fact that it is the most central and developed, and by the fact that at each level, the organs of the other apparats are under the supervision of those of the main apparat.

The eight apparats, which cut across all the mechanisms of the state, form, when brought together under the command of one main apparat, the all-embracing Apparat (spelt, for clarity, with a capital), which in turn ensures the running of the communist state.

But with this we come to the question of how the new state is formed under the command of the Apparat, when the transformation of society is at stake. The problem of this transformation is posed when a society is found to be backward and inefficient by comparison with other societies; when by its own internal activities it creates disorder and hampers its own output and progress; and when one of its internal groups produces a vision or programme which could be of benefit to the society as a whole, and would urge it forward, relatively, by comparison with other societies, and in its own absolute terms. Then solutions will have to be found through consultation or, more often than not, through revolution. It is the shapelessness of the organizations of such a society which is then being denounced – and, where a state is already functioning, its inadequacy for the tasks of organization. It is claimed then, by the doctrinaires of such states, that what is needed is a new mobilization, economic, social and political. A new skeleton and scaffolding for the state is thus proposed, according to the doctrinaires – modelled on a different structure. In other words this means that an external, para-administrative, apparat can take over and mould the state on its own pattern and structures, and become the backbone of the new state. The Apparat-state is thus born. The relations between state and society, which are the stuff of politics, are in the case of the Apparat-state rendered more difficult for three reasons. The Apparat-state must be dictatorial, centralistic and monopolistic. The Apparat itself must tend to be monolithic and vulnerable to any forms of pluralism. Yet precisely because it attempts to conduct, control and co-ordinate all the activities of the society, the Apparat-state must, sooner or later, accept the *checks* of the other forces in society which deliver the goods and services required by its functioning, and without which the entire state life would come to a standstill. And because it aspires to guide and indeed stimulate the energies and minds of the population, it fosters a greater potentiality of dissent.

In proposing to study the politics of the seven European communist states listed at the beginning, this book disagrees with the theory that the party, and its apparat, is in *full* control of the society and that it imposes on the society its *unchanged* plans and aims. The spreading of this belief is, to be sure, deliberately sought by the party and its apparat in order to project an image of infallibility. On the other hand, it is also the innocent result of the fact that for too long now studies of communist politics have been focused more on how power is produced and administered by the state, than on how power can be and is encroached upon, limited and ultimately deflected by the necessary checks and dissent of the other forces of society. It is this permanent, although unrehearsed, and inevitable, although hidden, relation of conflict between these particularly ambitious states and these particularly resilient societies which will be studied here.

PART ONE

THE FRAMEWORK AND THE
NETWORK OF POWER

This chapter will contain a brief general theory of power in the European communist states. As politics is the subject of this study, it is natural to begin with a description of how power is actually held and exercised.

Current Western political science expresses the general view that a communist state is a totalitarian dictatorship. This dictatorship conducts the entire economic, social, political and cultural life of the people over which it rules. It is exercised directly and exclusively by the Communist Party, which has at the top a rarified leadership (Politburo or Praesidium), and a leader (First or General Secretary). After periods of transition a personal leader must ultimately take sole control and responsibility. This is so in all dictatorships but especially in a totalitarian one, where the leadership can even less be shared. Lower organs of authority with functions roughly based on those of the main sectors of the Politburo/ Praesidium and the more numerous ones of the Central Committee control the life and activities of the state. Each of these branches of the party hierarchy enjoys and can rely on the help of the similarly ramified organs of the political police, the army, the trade unions, and the state administration, all subordinate to the party.

This is, very broadly, how Western political science views the mechanics of real power in communist states. It contrasts these real aspects with the description of the functioning of states as expounded in Marxist-Leninist political theories. According to these theories the communist states are working-class states intended to install the classless and a-political communist society, after which both state and party will wither away. During the period of the dictatorship of the proletariat the representative organs of the working-class state are gradually replaced by the organs of direct democracy necessary after the abolition of private ownership of the means of production. The basic units of this kind of society and state are the communes. Their assemblies are the expression of the will of the people, and their councils, under different names, are the basic organs of administration, or rather self-administration, in all communist states. This structure repeats itself at every higher level (district, region) until it reaches the Supreme Soviet or Assembly which is described as the supreme seat of power and of sovereignty. It can be divided into more than one chamber. The chambers elect the Praesidium, which in turn appoints the Council of Ministers, the supreme executive organ. Ultimate power is thus concentrated in the hands of the same few persons who combine the top functions of both the party and the state. It should also be noted that Western political science generally assumes that the main structures of power of all communist states, including the European communist states, are more or less approximate copies of those of the USSR.

The official communist political theory differs from the Western interpretation in that it emphasizes the social-economic structure of the new state and explains it in these terms. The socialist ownership of the means of production generates a different system altogether: the system of self-administration. The more advanced the evolution towards the final establishment of common owner-ship, the further will spontaneous self-administration be pushed. The theory of the communist state, is founded, like that of other states, on the component theories of society, of sovereignty, of representation, of the constitution, of the party, etc. These theories form the doctrinal framework of the European communist states. They deserve to be, even if summarily, re-examined in order to try to grasp how this theoretical structure is made to contain the actual network of real power.

I. THE FRAMEWORK

The theory of the society

Marxist-Leninist theories can be described as anti-political, for two main reasons. First they assert that, conditioned as they are by technical advance, the economic and social activities of men deter-mine all their other activities. Secondly, they assert that political activities are aspects of the *alienation* of the *homo economicus*, the man who cannot appear in societies based on exploitation.

But the fact that Marxism-Leninism is an anti-political philosophy does not mean that it does not contain a political theory of its own. It gives a great importance to the political action of the revolutionary classes and parties. But these are, one may say, the politics to finish all politics. They are the expression of the *voluntaristic* philosophy of Marx, Lenin, Stalin and Mao. With a clear realization of the tasks confronting each one of them in what they visualized as the continuous fight in history for the victory of world communism, these four political and ideological leaders have urged the revolutionary forces to use politics in direct, ruthless and efficient ways. All four of them have stressed that the revolutionary parties should try by all possible means to come to power so as to be able afterwards to demolish the structures of the old class-ridden political state and establish the structures of the classless, a-political, economic society. There is no doubt that the contemporary conceptions of many Marxist-Leninists, as individuals or even groups or schools of thought, differ in many respects from those of their predecessors. Stronger doubts have been cast, in the last two decades, on the speed and feasibility of the withering away of the state. (This incidentally leads the contemporary leaders of communist states to emphasize the new importance of the revolutionary classes and parties. They are now not only the ultimate destroyers of the old state, but also the devoted caretakers of the new state which replaces it.) But all genuine Marxist-Leninist schools of thought assume once and for all that as money is necessary only in the economic and commercial capitalist exchanges, so politics as an activity is necessary only in the social exchanges of the class-societies of the exploited men, and will therefore happily disappear when the future integration of free men in the future economic societies will be achieved.

On this, indeed, all the political theories of all communist states, and parties, agree. Moreover, in the case of the European communist states it is worth noting that on the one hand, the Yugoslav school of thought, which has by far the most pragmatic approach towards the contradictory realities of the economic, social and political life of the community, is also the most utopian one. The Yugoslav theorists claim that Yugoslav society is nearest to the final goal of de-politization. On the other hand, the Polish school of political thought, which goes further than any other in accepting that forms of social and political pluralism exist in society, has also produced to date the most searching inquiries into the problem of *alienation* and into the difficulty of integrating men in any kind of state, whether capitalist or not.

But torn as contemporary communist political doctrines may be between the utopia of the depolitized societies and the dire realities of the coercive state, this utopia still remains the strongest counter-attraction of Marxism-Leninism, especially in the new continents, to liberal and otherwise pluralistic doctrines. The rival claims of equality and liberty; the question of which conditions the other; the priority of economic or political freedom – all these are still considered by the vast majority of the population in developed or under-developed liberal pluralistic states as the crucial questions to be answered in the social-political realm. The intermediary presence, and influence, of the owner or purveyor of the means of production is seen to affect the production and well-being of the entire society. It is believed that the liberal state protects and encourages the apparently selfish and shortsighted profit-making activities of private and what is worse, very often, foreign owners. This is compared unfavourably with the long, objective, perspectives which seem to inspire the disinterested planners of the future national development. They are thought to have no private strings attached to their visions, and to be able to start their reforms by an over-all and overdue nationalization.

It is therefore natural that the socialist – or common – ownership of the means of production, which is a social-economic factor, is described in the constitutions of the USSR and of the European communist states as the principal foundation of these states. In the first constitutions and programmes of the Communist Party of the Soviet Union, and the first constitutions of the People's Democracies, the common ownership of means of production on which the entire communist state life is based was described as leading directly to self-administration and self-management. In their view, in a society in which there are no differences between owners and non-owners, and between those who sell and those who buy labour, communal life, at all levels, could not but be based upon the spontaneous participation of all in the decision-making processes. The 'general will' here assumes a new and higher form: genuine and direct participation in decision-making without questionable representative procedures. The Soviet or local council, initially a political organ, becomes through the transformation of society, a social institution. But this result will be obtained only when the state, and the other coercive organizations, will have withered away. 'We are moving towards communism, in which the people themselves will administer society, without any special apparatuses' said Khrushchev at the Twenty-Second Congress of the CPSU.

Another, apparently contradictory, link between socialist ownership and the need to maintain the state in existence was stressed at this same party congress. The role and importance of the state as the guardian of the common weal, and of the party 'as the leading and guiding force of Soviet Society' were according to the programme, enhanced during the period 'of full-scale communist construction'. And the same programme proclaimed that this period had now been reached in the evolution of Soviet society.

But, here already, the CPSU programme and the Soviet constitution lag behind those of other communist states, as for instance the 1963 Yugoslav constitution. This constitution is based on the contention that Yugoslav society has already entered a new stage in the development of social ownership. The administrative organization of the country is already centred on the activities of social self-management.[1] The system of popular power brings with it, implicitly and explicitly, the form of 'government by assembly' – from the communal assemblies at the bottom to the Federal Chambers at the top. This form of government alters and cannot but limit in theory the rights of the state and curtails even more the shrinking prerogatives of the state administration. It also defines differently the role of the party ('League') which according to point VI of the preamble is 'to strengthen the socialist and democratic consciousness of the citizens'. The role of the party is being changed from 'the ruling organization of political society into a socio-political organization which will become part and parcel of this same society and of its constitutional system, and will become its internal force, subordinated to it' – to use the formulae of a Yugoslav political scientist, Jovan Djordjević.[2] Indeed, Yugoslav

---

[1] 'Self-management by the citizens of the commune is the political basis of the social-political system' (Art. 73 of the 1963 Constitution).
[2] Jovan Djordjević: *The anatomy of political institutions in a society in transition*, Futuribles, Paris, 1965.

political scientists and politicians express the suspicion that Stalin in the past used the theory of the party and the state as guardians of the new emerging society merely as a cover for the totalitarianism of the 'dictatorship of the proletariat'.

Aspects of communist legitimacy

Every assertion of sovereignty has to develop a theory of legitimacy.[3] The specific aspects of the theory of legitimacy of the communist state are: the class struggle, the mandate of history and the ideology.

The social foundation of the legitimacy of the communist state is the notion of class. Like any other state, the revolutionary state is also described as the instrument of rule of a social class. Social classes were, according to this theory, a feature of the history of mankind, stretching from the very origins of social life up to capitalist society. It is true that during the historical span of this society, technical and ideological revolutions will bring about the abolition of social classes and the emergence of a new, final, society. Nevertheless, during the phase of the final struggle between the classes, between those fighting for the abolition of the class society and those resisting them in the hope of maintaining it forever, the state remains the political instrument of the different classes which control different states. The working-class first achieved power in one state, Russia, in 1917. Since then, continues the theory, contemporary states fall into two main categories and an intermediary group.

There are class states of the bourgeoisie. There are class states of the working classes. And there are the class states of a mixture of classes: the national democracies of the third world.

Almost everything that can be said about the communist state as a class instrument has been said in the main works of Marx, Lenin, Stalin and Mao Tse Tung – and in the vast non-communist literature on the subject. This is indeed the point on which both views converge. The Marxist-Leninists express as clearly and

[3] Probably the most searching recent, if contradictory, works on the problem of legitimacy in communist political philosophy are: M. Merleau-Ponty: *Humanisme et terreur*, Paris, 1951; Leonard Schapiro: *The Origin of the Communist Autocracy*, London, 1954; Friedrich and Brzezinski: *Totalitarian Dictatorship and Autocracy*, Harvard, 1965; Raymond Aron: *Democratie et totalitarisme*, Paris, 1965, and Dolf Sternberger: *Grund und Abgrund der Macht*, Frankfurt, 1962.

uninhibitedly as their non-communist critics the idea that the state of the revolutionary classes should be used by them as a ruthless instrument for the 'liquidation' of the exploiting classes and the basis of their power of exploitation: the private ownership of the means of production. Non-communist literature and philosophy, on the other hand, do not fail to single out this fundamental aspect of the communist doctrine of the state. They show that in theory, as much as in practice, the dictatorship of the proletariat is bound to remain forever not only a dictatorship of the party, said to represent the proletariat, but also the dictatorship within that party of a few men or even of one man.

The same is true also of the problem of ideology. Here too the classical works of Marx and Engels themselves, and of Lenin, Bukharin, Max Adler, George Lukacs and Adam Schaff have each defined the fundamental relation between the socialist state and the ideology. (The same problem was discussed also by non-Marxist authors like Karl Mannheim and Max Weber before the Second World War; while some relatively recent works have cast new light on the discussion.[4]) A study of Marxist literature shows how much the meaning of ideology has changed in Marxist-Leninist terminology. Marx used it in a critical sense, as the naive expression of the belief of non-materialistic philosophies and theories that ideas and faiths can alter the history of mankind. Lenin, however, insisted on the necessity of the 'theoretical struggle' and of a militant doctrine, binding for the revolutionary classes and parties. The meaning given in Marxist-Leninist political terminology to the word 'ideology' is now generally understood as the reasons or faiths which lead the members of a 'conscious' group, class or society, to see how their 'praxis', i.e. their own 'creative' action becomes the cause of change in their own surroundings and circumstances.[5] Projected upon the background of legitimacy in a communist state[6] ideology (or in this case using David Easton's

[4] Raymond Aron's works: Jeanne Hersch: *Ideologie et realité*, Paris, 1955; M. Merleau Ponty: *Les aventures de la dialectique*, Paris, 1953; Daniel Bell: *The End of Ideology*, Glencoe 1960; Donald MacRae: *Ideology and Society*, London, 1961; R. Lane: *Political Ideology*, New York, 1962; Irving Fetscher: *Der Marxismus*, Frankfurt, 1966, are among the most notable contributions to the subject of the relation between ideology and politics with which we are here concerned.

[5] Or to use Dan Bell's more striking formula: 'ideology is the conversion of ideas into social levers' in *The End of Ideology*, loc. cit.

[6] Which Georges Burdeau, loc. cit., calls 'The ideological state'.

precise expression: 'The legitimating ideology')[7] can be defined as the link of allegiance of the population to the professed motives and values of the regime. The population is considered to endorse these motives and values implicitly through its participation in activities sponsored or undertaken by the regime, and explicitly through the catechistic rites of indoctrination.

It is precisely this link of allegiance (which in any case was always weaker in the post-Second World War European communist states than in post-First World War Russia) which is constantly growing weaker – thus weakening also the legitimacy of the communist states. Revolutionary fervour is being gradually replaced by respect for efficiency and good administration. The firm catechisms of the early period are being watered down by the exceptions and deviations imposed by daily realities. As routine overtakes the revolutionary charisma, ideology is gradually being replaced by pragmatism. Moreover with the growing pluralization of functions and attributions in the new social life, the formerly unique 'class-ideology' is fragmented into the separate – even opposing – opinions, interpretations and beliefs of different groups, layers and sections. The right to dissent is openly advocated. Thus, rather than submit to frontal attacks and direct confrontations, it is the former 'monolithic' ideology which withers away. In all communist states it becomes more and more amorphous, and more like a set of not so controversial principles, acceptable to as many as possible of the people expected to take a share in the self-administration and self-management. Of these principles the one which provides the broadest basis of allegiance to the state is still the common ownership of the means of production. But this is where the 'ideology' of the workers of the under-developed and non-industrialized societies differs from that of the majority of the members of a fully industrialized society. Even among the communist states there is a growing difference of general ideology from this point of view. Whereas, for instance, the Chinese ideologists suspect the Communist Party of the Soviet Union of becoming the mouthpiece of the ideology of the industrialized towns of communist Europe, rather than that of the revolutionary classes of the agrarian states in other continents, the ideologists of the Soviet bloc suspect the Yugoslavs and the Czechoslovaks of going too far on the

[7] In *The Systems Analysis of Political Life*, loc. cit.

questions of economic incentives and private property. But of this more will be said later in this chapter.

Finally, legitimacy in such states, like all legitimacies, is founded on the association of the power-holders with historical circumstances, continuity and tradition. Dynastic continuity, for instance, is the basis of the legitimacy of monarchies, that of any nation state is the continuity of national sovereignty over long periods upon the same territory. The communist states add to this two kinds of historical association; one is the association with the revolution: governments are legitimated by a great act of revolution. The other is the association with the history of mankind as a whole. These vaster links are projected upon the past and upon the future. The links with the past stretch back to the entire evolution of the human race seen as a struggle for emancipation from the exploitation of men by men, through the recurrent institutions of the social classes. Here the appearance of the communist state marks the end of the proto-history and the beginning of the future history of free men. But while the association with the past is deterministic, and to some degree mythological, it is from the association with the future of human history that the communist states and parties draw a different legitimacy, active and voluntaristic. The future society ought to be made and shaped by the transitional instrument of the state through the dictatorship of the proletariat.

But the mandate of the dictatorship of the proletariat (which conditions the mandate of the state, which conditions that of the party) is closely limited to one single historic operation: the abolition of the state. Marx used the metaphor of revolutions as the steam engines of history – and the implication was that the party was the steam-engine of the revolution. The metaphor is particularly telling because steam-engines are very conditioned vehicles: they must always follow the rails, and their itineraries are laid down in advance, as is their final destination. This conditional mandate, and legitimacy, has a direct bearing on the political psychology of the citizens of a dictatorship of the proletariat, in contrast with that of the citizens of a democracy. To carry the previous metaphor a little further, it can be said that whereas the citizens of a non-revolutionary state, or polity, are dwellers, those of revolutionary dictatorships are travellers. The former dwell in their dwellings, are expected to live and die in them and to bequeath them, improved, to their heirs.

The travellers of the communist states, invited to pass quickly and at great sacrifice through the phase which separates them from the ultimate destination, develop a sense of fervour, of impatience and (soon after) of lassitude, when the journey seems too long and the destination out of reach. The dictatorship of the proletariat, its state and its party have now lasted half a century in Soviet Russia. Yet Lenin gave fifty years as its maximum duration.[8] In Russia this is now often questioned and the 22nd Congress Programme was a confused and cumbersome attempt to proclaim the end of the dictatorship. But in the European communist states this particular aspect of legitimacy has been questioned even more, and there the point is made with greater insistence and impatience. In Yugoslavia the advent of the new society has already been proclaimed.

This historicism also has a direct effect on the attitude towards opposition of all communist states, including the European ones. The irreversibility of the historical process once assumed, it could not be voluntarily interrupted by the alternation of governments and phases of policy. Political opposition is equated with treason, treason to the revolution. What is more, as politics itself, in this theory, is bound to dissolve in the total dissolution of the class-society, political actions, expressions of the class-struggle, are doomed for ever. Of all oppositionless states, the stand taken by the communist states against opposition is the most fundamental and rigid. Their legitimacy is, from this point of view, more aggressive and more *total* than that of any other state, since it cannot allow institutional channels for the competition for power to carry out alternative policies. Insofar as these states represent the revolution, all opposition directed against them is, as for the Jacobins, counter-revolution. Indeed, precisely because of their identification with the march and majority of History, their relations with their adversaries can, according to their classic doctrine, be solved only by the most extreme means of political combat. Here again, although on this point the logical impasse is as

[8] 'At the end of 1920 Lenin told the Spanish socialist Fernando de los Ríos that a very long time "perhaps forty or fifty years" would be necessary in Russia for the transitional period of dictatorship.' Leonard Schapiro: *The Origin of the Communist Autocracy*, loc. cit., p. 189.

agonizing for the progressive Yugoslavs as for the conservative Russians, one can detect a more pragmatic and conciliatory attitude in the doctrines of the European communist states. The Polish doctrine of the hegemonic party among other parties, is a case in point.

Sovereignty, representation and responsibility

In communist political doctrine there is little to distinguish between legitimacy and sovereignty, a more formal notion. But sovereignty includes of necessity the elements of representation and responsibility. In pluralistic-constitutional states the former is obtained through the mechanism of free elections, and through the organization of political parties and of interests and groups. The latter is achieved by the institutions of constitutional control which, generally speaking, amount to the separation of the legislative, executive and judiciary powers. In communist political philosophy the meanings of both representation and responsibility are explicitly different because communist states are said to be *direct* and not *representative* democracies. According to this concept the true sovereignty of the people, that is the true embodiment of the eighteenth century fiction of the sovereign or general will, comes into being only when the people take possession of the state-power and of the means of production of the nation. Separation of powers becomes thus unnecessary and indeed incompatible because, in theory, the 'people' legislates, governs and gives judgement together. It is, to use the Marxist expression, a 'corporation in action'.

But in practice it has not worked out at all like that. At this point the crisis of the communist states, and of their theory of power, has come to a head. It has not worked, first because the communist state and its direct democracy or self-administration have not yet appeared: after more than a half-century the 'transition' is still not finished. And, secondly, it has not worked, because although the communist leaders and theoreticians have now recognized that any present or future political society must be based on some forms of representation and responsibility, the mechanisms and institutions by which it was hoped, or pretended, that they could be adapted to the communist, or communizing, political societies have failed.

This question is now being discussed in all the European

communist states and, even if less widely, in the Soviet Union. There is actually a double debate to be followed. One is the debate within each of these states between the authorities proposing new institutions and theories and, as it were, the 'people'. In some of these countries, as in Yugoslavia and Poland, the 'people' prefer the old institutions and procedures, either directly by supporting the critics of the proposals or indirectly by scepticism and indifference. Each new set of reforms is therefore as ineffectual as the last. The other debate is carried on between the different national schools of thought, and especially between the Soviet, Polish and Yugoslav doctrines of the state.[9]

The Soviet doctrine is, on the one hand, the most dogmatic insofar as it clings to the theory that, to quote Professor V. Kotok, 'in the socialist countries, popular representation reflects the sovereignty of the people in all the fields of social life, no longer only in the field of politics' ... 'As "corporations in action", endowed with both legislative and executive powers the representative bodies do not see their competence limited.' On the other hand, it produces a most interesting modulation, based on the principle that Soviet Russia, as a great state, has a different system from that of the smaller states. To quote the same author: 'The greatest part of the work is done by the representative organs and their executive apparatus. In the great socialist states, called upon to direct daily an extremely involved social production it is impossible to replace these organs by the self-management of the people.' Faced with this permanent and fundamental contradiction the Soviet doctrine only recommends the improvement of the representative mechanisms, forever needed and yet forever repressed.

In the Polish doctrine the Sejm (the Polish Parliament) and the people's councils have general competence to direct economic, social and cultural life. The influence of these representative bodies is felt on the policy and activities of state authorities, although only one per cent of the population (in the USSR two per cent) takes part in their work. But the party, which in Poland

---

[9] See in this connection: *The deadend of the monolithic parties*, a special issue of *Government and Opposition*, vol. 2, no. 6, January 1967, dedicated to the comparative study of the different communist theories of power, as well as the papers by V. Kotok (Moscow), Witold Zakuzewski (Cracow) and Miodrag Jovicić (Belgrade) presented at the International Political Science Association round-table held in Warsaw on 23–24 September 1966.

is a 'hegemonic' party, is openly acknowledged as the fundamental means of influence on state activity.

The Yugoslav constitutional organizations are claimed by their doctrinaires to represent the establishment of popular self-management and self-administration, and within it the attempt to limit the influence of the executive. The executive's norm-making powers must be gradually reduced. The differentiation between the political-executive and the administrative functions must be accentuated. Above all the main influence of the party (League) must be transferred from the executive organs to the Legislative Assembly.

But although the differences between the communist schools of thought themselves on such important points as self-management, the rule of the party, and the separation of powers still are very deep, the differences between all these schools and the pluralistic-constitutional doctrines remain even deeper. The fundamental distinction lies in the fact that whereas communist political systems are anti-political and want to discourage and abolish politics – the pluralistic-constitutional systems are based on the idea of the continuation and improvement of political activities and of representation and responsibility.

Some contemporary Western political scientists and especially sociologists, try very honourably to find the common features of *all* systems. This leads to a growing assimilation of representative and non-representative democracies. They are said to 'converge' in the sense that whereas the former seem to attach less and less impor-tance to politics, in the area of consensus, the latter, emerging from sheer totalitarianism, develop some forms of representation and responsibility. Yet one might as well remember some self-evident but essential differences before making further analogies. Take for instance only those which are entailed in the behaviour of the individual voter in representative and in non-representative states. In the former the voter knows that a few individual votes can in close contests 'sway' a result; in the latter the majorities are always overwhelming. In the former full political information is almost pressed on him by the contradictory media; in the latter he receives indoctrinated, scant and restricted information. In the former he is encouraged to express his views and to join any political forces or associations; in the latter when individuals take attitudes contrary to those of the authorities, they are still persecuted by them, even if by subtler means than the primitive Stalinist ones.

Or take for instance the basic differences in the accountability of the government. If the body to which the government is accountable – be it Parliament, Supreme Soviet, National Assembly – is not truly and fully representative, it lacks the mandate, and authority, to require the government to account to it. Nor does the government fear it. Indeed the members of these Parliaments, Soviets or Assemblies are in more than one sense appointed by the government, which controls the lists of candidates and the election results. In these conditions it is these bodies which fear the government; and they do not fear the 'people' whose power to revoke their mandates is purely theoretical. In pluralistic-constitutional states, on the other hand, such a revocation can happen and happens often at the periodical electoral consultations.

Sovereignty and 'socialist internationalism'

The second meaning of the concept of sovereignty is that described in international law as the independence of one state in its relations with other states. Accordingly, some peculiarities in the relations between the European communist states themselves and especially between them and the communist great power, the USSR, should be noted.

The relations between the Soviet Union, as a federation, and the component Federal Republics have changed very much. In the constitution of 1923 the Union republics were described as totally sovereign.[10] But the trend since 1923 has been towards a progressive unification of the constituent republics in the main body of the state. In the constitution of 1936 and in the ideological statements of the new Programme of the CPSU, as for instance that 'the

[10] There are in the USSR fifteen Union republics and within them twenty autonomous Soviet Socialist Republics subordinated to the respective Union Republics. The Supreme Soviet of each of the Union Republics was the legal holder of full sovereignty. They each had their own constitution, and more important than anything else, the right to secession. The Autonomous Republics differed in that they did not have this latter, essential right. The sovereignty of the Union Republics and, altogether, the definition of the USSR as a federal state, is of some importance from a national, but even more so from an international point of view. It should be remembered for instance that the USSR has three seats and three votes in the United Nations and in all kindred organizations – one for itself and two for the Ukrainian and Byelo Russian Union Republics which were already in existence when the 1923 constitution was drafted).

boundaries between the union republics are losing their significance', the independence of the Union Republics was openly underplayed. The trend is significant in practice as well as theory: for the centralizing and unifying actions of the Economic Plan carried through the party and state-administration have blurred a great deal of the alleged separate sovereignty of the Republics. As for the autonomous republics they have become simply sub-administrative units.

The same unifying trend was observed also in Yugoslavia. The constitution of 1946 unambiguously defined the Republics as sovereign (although they did not have, as in the 1923 Soviet constitution, the right to secede). But the Fundamental Law of 1953 failed to repeat the formula. On the contrary, whereas the 1946 constitution delegated some federal powers to the Republics, the Fundamental Law of 1953 and the 1963 constitution stress the exclusive sovereignty of the Federation.[11]

The relations between the European communist states and the communist power were bound, sooner or later, to hinge upon the concept of sovereignty. On its definition and importance, even 'within the family of communist states', passionately opposed views were bound to clash. They will continue to do so as long as a communist power has enough strength to attempt to 'control and guide' the entire family and to curb or even abolish their national sovereignty under the pretext of ideological internationalism or economic supernationalism.

The USSR now has three different types of relationship with the European states considered to belong to her zone of influence. The sovereignty of each state is affected by its particular relationship to the great power. There is first the *status of neutrality* granted to Finland and Austria, and acknowledged by the Soviet Union and by the Western powers. The sovereignty of both states is protected against the possible demands of the USSR to do some things, give some pledges and assume some special responsibilities on the grounds of a co-ordination of policy or common defence with her. But, on the other hand, under their respective peace treaties they are pledged *not* to undertake some actions which a sovereign state without a neutral status could undertake: such as

---

[11] This particular aspect of Yugoslav politics will be discussed at greater length in Part Two, *The party and the local administration*, pp. 121–7.

to join military alliances or permit the establishment of bases on their territories, etc.

The second kind of relationship was that imposed by the USSR after the war upon the former enemy-states liberated by her army: Rumania, Bulgaria, Hungary and the zone of Germany which was later to become the German Democratic Republic -- (GDR) or East Germany. They had to pay reparations. They had to provide for the subsistence of the Soviet armed forces on their territory. They had to accept intensive bilateral economic exchanges with the USSR, including also the creation on their territories of joint companies with the USSR as an extra-territorial share-holder. This clear situation of Soviet suzerainty faded gradually away not, as could have been expected, after the signature of the peace treaties in 1947, which on the contrary, coincided with the worst period of Stalinist rule, but after the beginning of the post-Stalin policy of co-existence. The main changes occurred especially after the resumption of relations between the USSR and Yugoslavia which had broken down in 1948 precisely because the latter defended her sovereign rights against the great power and bene-factor.

The third kind of relationship was established later with the European communist states, excepting Yugoslavia which remained totally independent, through the signature of the Warsaw Treaty Organization pact on 14 May 1955 (a day before the signing of the Austrian peace-treaty). By this, on the one hand, the sovereign states of Poland, Rumania, Hungary, Czechoslovakia, Bulgaria, the GDR and Albania (since then lapsed) and, on the other hand, the USSR, undertook to place their armed forces under a single command. The supreme commander has been ever since a Soviet Marshal. This is one of the points being raised now by the other member-states when discussing the reorganization of the Warsaw Treaty. It is not only a matter of prestige. In reality this amounted to allowing the USSR to command the military organiza-tion of the entire region. This was linked with intensified economic integration under the auspices of the *Council for Mutual Economic Assistance*, or COMECON, an inter-regional economic organization set up in 1949 with almost the same membership and the same hierarchy. Similarly, bilateral treaties of friendship, co-operation and mutual assistance were signed between the USSR and each of the Soviet bloc states. By this network of agreements the USSR exercised a direct control on some essentially sovereign rights of these sovereign states. In spite of the stiffening reaction against such control by the majority of the governments of these states, it still exercises them.

It is interesting to notice here how, during the main phases of this reaction, the arguments between the governments and parties of the respective European communist states and those of the USSR came to turn more and more on the definition of sovereignty and sovereign rights. First came the open clash between Yugoslavia and the USSR in March–June 1948. The arguments then made public set the pattern for the discussion of interference and non-interference in internal affairs in relations between the USSR and the CPSU, on one side, and the other states and parties of the European communist world. In the Soviet–Yugoslav dispute, since it was more a quarrel between parties than between states, and since the communist mentality at the time was still more concerned with ideological problems than with simply national ones, the word sovereignty was not employed too often and too specifically in the documents exchanged. But the questions whether communist Yugoslavia owed a debt to Soviet Russia for her liberation and formation; whether the diplomatic, economic and intelligence representatives of Soviet Russia should have different rights from those of any other friendly state representation in Yugoslavia; and whether economic co-operation between the two states should entail special rights for the USSR in the Yugoslav economy, all these directly involved the main issue of sovereignty.

The second phase, inspired immediately by the Yugoslav example, was the almost simultaneous reactions of the new Polish and Hungarian governments in September–October 1956. Both these revolutionary governments tried to modify in different ways and with different results, the relationship of their states with the USSR, by making them hinge on the issue of sovereignty.[12]

The third phase, in which the use of the word sovereignty becomes crucial, originated with the quarrel between Rumania and the Council of Mutual Economic Assistance on the question of whether a socialist country should submit to socialist supernational

[12] Thus Gomulka on 21 October 1956 said that the first main question under consideration was the problem of Poland's sovereignty, and Imre Nagy on 31 October 1956: 'We are living through the first days of our sovereignty and independence.'

planning. The Rumanian party stated categorically in its crucial declaration of 23 April 1964, that: 'the sovereignty of a socialist state presupposes that it alone should have full and effective control in directing the economy'. It subsequently stretched this doctrine to all other fields and relations.[13]

This attitude, once adopted, could not but lead slowly – or precipitately as during the 1956 Hungarian rising – to its logical end, namely to question the curbing of the sovereignty of the European communist states because they belong somewhat forcibly to two organizations through which the USSR 'co-ordinates' the region: COMECON and the Warsaw Treaty Organization. In the spring of 1966 it was rumoured that Rumania, who had already blocked the supernationalization of COMECON as part of her campaign of rehabilitating her sovereignty, had asked for a reconsideration of the conditions of her participation and that of the other member states in the WTO. She had particularly stressed that the USSR should not use nuclear weapons without first consulting her allies in the Organization – she allegedly asked that the head of the organization should be elected from among all member states by rotation and should not be always and exclusively a Russian officer.

The changes in the concept of sovereignty were the result of a change in the definition of the nation, and consequently of the basic law of 'socialist internationalism'. This change was and is noticeable in most communist parties, not only the European ones in this case. It is a reaction against the frustrations imposed upon them first by the COMINTERN before the war, and then after the war by the Communist Party of the Soviet Union acting, under Stalin, as one of the main agencies of Russia's open 'great power chauvinism'. But among the East European communist parties it was particularly noticeable in the Yugoslav, Polish and Hungarian parties, and above all now in the Rumanian party.

There are two aspects to this change. The first is, as it were, the rehabilitation of the concept of nation, and its inclusion among the fundamental elements of a communist society. The second is the

[13] It should be noted here that in the meantime in the triangular polemic between the USSR, China and Albania, China, the other communist power, had taken an offensive stand against the USSR's way of forcing the other communist states to execute her orders. Before the Rumanian-COMECON conflict came into the open China had already accused the USSR of 'great power chauvinism', an expression which is now in the communist states the slogan opposed to the USSR's previous imperialistic methods.

impact which this re-orientation has on the relations between the communist power-holders and society. It forms, in some of these states, a new point of congruence. The concept of nation had to be rehabilitated against the old Engelsian theory that the 'non-historic' nations will be swept away forever by the big socialist internationalist revolution; and it had to be rehabilitated against Stalin's systematic persecution, first through the COMINTERN and then through the COMINFORM of 'nationalistic tendencies' in any communist party of the Soviet bloc. A theory was first put forward showing that Lenin had always recognized the political and social importance of the nation. To be sure, this question was at the centre of the Soviet–Yugoslav polemic of 1948–53. The Yugoslavs, however, were not too eager to choose it as their main battleground. But after the Polish and Hungarian modulations of 1956, it is the Rumanian party which, since 1964, has gone beyond anything Marx or Lenin might have said or not said on the subject, and has transformed this rehabilitated concept of *nation* into the main foundation of a communist, or at least of Rumanian communist, society.

This, as will be seen later in this book, formed a new bridge between this very isolated party and Rumanian society. The new nationalism, constantly and uninhibitedly fanned by the party leadership, is in communist countries like Rumania the most successful means of contact between the state and some layers of society. It is in terms of nationalism that whatever dialogue exists between the power holders and public opinion is conducted. At the same time, such an attitude is very contagious and spreads to other parties.

Constitution and constitutionalism

Etymologically, from the Roman constitution to the constitutions of Clarendon, the word 'constitution' was used to describe the collection of laws or decrees made by the Emperor or by the king. There were in history all kinds of constitutions, just and unjust, harsh or tolerant, conservative or progressive, reactionary or democratic. Thus it is not the existence of a written text which is the *conditio sine qua non* of the internal liberty of a country – the best example of the contrary being Britain where the fairest *functioning* of a political system is based on an unwritten constitution. Moreover a constitution, as a text, can have many other purposes.

The modern constitutions which at the end of the eighteenth century laid the foundations of parliamentary democracy in America and Europe had, apart from their value as charters and as sets of rules and procedures for democratic government, a clear value and purpose for propaganda exhortation. They, or at least their preambles, were meant to be as much a manifesto as a code. The former purpose is undoubtedly present in communist constitutions, and especially in the two early Soviet ones and in the present Yugoslav and Chinese constitutions. Both the Yugoslavs and the Chinese now believe, for opposite reasons, that they are projecting a theory of society which might exercise a greater appeal than the Soviet Constitution of 1936 to the peoples of the world: to the peoples of Europe in the case of Yugoslavia, to the Afro-Asian peoples in the case of China.

The communist constitutions[14] fulfil this mission by defining their own conception of the state. Thus, they all define what the 'sovereign will' or 'the will of the people' is in their conception, which differs from that of the 'sovereign will' or the 'volonté générale' of the American and French constitutions of the eighteenth century. From the first declaration of November 1917 of the Second All-Russian Congress of Soviets, up to the Castroist Cuban constitution of 1959 one definition and explanation of the socialist state was most important and most unusual: once private ownership of the means of production is abolished, the socialist state of workers and peasants appears as a transition to the future classless society. It follows that such political organs as exist in the period of transition, during which all political organs have not yet been replaced by exclusively social organisms, will be organs of integration – of a double integration: that of the state in society, and that of the individual in the state and in society. The first Russian Soviets – those of 1905, as well as those of 1917 – were described for all intents and purposes as the 'government of the people by the people', and they were believed to be the reincarnation on a different ground of the French *commune* of 1870. The soviets, or, since it will be easier to call them henceforwards by a generic name, the *councils* at the various levels at which they are formed – village, district, region (republic in the case of Federal Russia and

---

[14] See a complete and up-to-date discussion of the East European communist constitutions in H. Gordon Skilling: *The Governments of Communist East Europe*, Cromwell comparative government series, New York, 1966.

Yugoslavia) and Supreme (All-Union or Federal) councils – are the broad open organs of direct government by the people, combining administration and legislation. Indeed one of the main principles of the communist political philosophy is the abolition of the separation of powers between the executive and the legislative.

It is here, on the question of the existence or non-existence of the separation of powers, that the word constitution (and especially *constitutionalism*) takes a different sense. A constitution is above all the set of regulations through which the functioning of the independent powers of the state (the judiciary, the executive and and legislative) are brought to a clearly defined, and impartial, order. The contradiction between constitutionalism and communist integrationism can be retraced easily in the constitutional history of Soviet Russia in its two different phases. The two early Soviet constitutions, of 1917 and 1923-4, were both, genuinely or hypocritically, documents of transition. National sovereignty was certainly defined – but it was expected apparently to dissolve in the truly international world of communism. The state of the dictatorship of the proletariat was also described – but it too was expected to wither away in the warmth of the economic society. (It is significant from this point of view, and more on this subject will be said in subsequent chapters, that the one institution added to the system of 1917 by the constitution of 1924 was not the Party, still unrecognized, but the *Unified State Political Directorate*, the political police, to be known afterwards as the OGPU, later the NKVD, now the KGB. For this was the phase in which the state was still seen as an instrument for the destruction of the previous state, of its adherents, and of the notion of state itself – to be replaced by the free notion of society.)

It was in 1936, with Stalin's constitution (ironically granted in the years of one of the worst periods of his terror and purges) that the fundamental contradiction was created in the philosophy of state of the communist doctrine. In 1936 Stalin had to express openly, through his political doctrine and through his constitution what had rapidly become under his leadership the obvious double reality of the structure of the USSR. The first such reality was that socialism was to be built in one state alone, a great power at that, and therefore sovereignty had to be acknowledged, defined. The national sovereignty of the USSR was enhanced and projected in the national and international communist ideology, without fear or inhibition that it could lead to national chauvinism and imperialism. The other reality was Stalin's clear realization that the state would *not* wither away, but on the contrary would be maintained and strengthened, in view of the unprecedented tasks ahead of it: internally to run the process of social mobilization and thus the life of the society, and externally to prepare for the possibility of war. Some institutionalization was therefore required whereby the dictatorship would receive a broader mandate, and the participation of individuals and groups in its functioning could be furthered by some means of representation. But this would come nowhere near the true political representation (obtained through free, multi-party, elections) which could bring down the dictatorship if the electorate so decided.

The dichotomic doctrine of 'direct-democracy-cum-representation' was then created. The fundamental contradiction between *constitutionalism* and *dictatorship* which is now the main bone of political contention in all communist states was aggravated with the passing of time and with the articulation of the debate around it. Moreover, what happened in reality was that the contradiction was intensified in both directions: legislative as well as executive. In the first case, preparation and elaboration of laws remained in the hands of the top group of power holders who, after their own internally organized processes of consultation, alone decide on the main laws, decrees and plans. The executive, on the other hand, divided into the political top-echelon and the lower frightened petty bureaucracy, soon showed and continues to show its gravest and most dangerous defect: lack of efficiency. The activities of the new state were threatened with congestion and paralysis. Economic disorganization and deadlocks of all kinds were the immediate aftermath of an indifferent, if not hostile, bureaucratic administration. It is at this vital juncture of communist state-life that the party and its apparat play their part.

The Party

The party was not at first recognized by the communist constitutions. Its role was defined in the 1936 Soviet constitution as 'the leading core of all organizations of the working people, both public and state'. This formula with understandable variations, is to be found now in all contemporary European communist constitutions, with the exception of the Rumanian constitution of 1965, in which the role of the party is more strongly emphasized than in any other. In the 1963 Yugoslav constitution, perhaps in order to help people forget the dark memories of the first decade of omnipotence of the party, its role is defined as an 'animator of the conscience of the masses'. And contemporary Yugoslav political philosophy claims that it will dissolve and is dissolving gradually into broader forms of organization, such as the 'Socialist Alliance'.[15] This shows that the Communist Parties themselves are divided in their minds about how best to project, or to conceal, their public image.

Indeed, it is characteristic that even the first constitutional definition of the role of the party was accepted in Soviet Russia only after some two decades of party rule: in the constitution of 1936. This was certainly due in part to the fact that no new constitution had been produced there between 1924 and 1936. This was the moment, mentioned earlier, when Stalin was ready to recognize publicly the fact that the state and its main components were going to remain in existence for a more or less unlimited time. But it was due very much also to the fact that in 1917, and in 1923–4, Lenin and the early revolutionaries had grave misgivings about the wisdom of acknowledging constitutionally the existence and importance of the party. The most striking proof of this is that in 1924, when the party and its dictatorship were struggling for dear life, for the very survival of the regime, Lenin and his colleagues showed their readiness to institutionalize the political police, but still kept the party in the non-constitutional shadow. In constitutional terms therefore it was the state political police (to be known first in 1922 as the State Political Directorate, and since 1923, and in the text of the Constitution, as the 'Unified State Political Administration') which was presented as the defensive organ of the revolutionary state against its enemies 'in the purely political sphere'.[16] It was for Lenin, as for Robespierre, one of the arms of the revolution, or of the revolutionary state.

But the party, which still carried with it under Lenin some of the psychology of a clandestine *Berufs-revolutionäre* organization working from the shadow, could not be so easily institutionalized

---

[15] See on the Socialist Alliance *infra*, p. 243–8,

[16] Lenin's expression in 1921, quoted in L. B. Schapiro: *The Communist Party of the Soviet Union*, London, 1964, p. 264.

by the constitution. There were probably two main reasons for this. First, there was no room for political parties in any past constitution to which the Russian communists could look with sympathy. If political parties were the expression of class-struggle why should their existence be confirmed in the constitution of a state set up only to abolish the class-struggle?

Secondly, there was and is an essential contradiction in the very concept of a 'single party' as an instrument of power. Much has been said in contemporary political science and political sociology about the concept of the one – or single – party.[17] And a lot will have to be said in this book on this central subject. But two points should be made here. The first is that on strictly etymological grounds the expression one-party, or single-party, forms a contradiction in adjecto because the word originates from the old French verb *partir*, to share or to divide, and cannot therefore describe anything which is either the whole or unique. A party is a group, or a body, united in some specific views and in support of some interests and characteristic causes, which it believes to be beneficial for the community of which, however, it remains only one segment.[18] But then, and this is at the core of Lenin's reluctance in the twenties and of Tito's in the fifties, to overstress the *constitutional* role of the party, it implies that there might or indeed should be more than one party (or parts). Parties have appeared in political history as often in the form of groups supporting certain causes or opinions as in the form of groups opposing an existing or potential grouping, or groupings, centred on contrary causes or opinions. Parties were originally factions and were born of the opposition between factions. It is in the very logic of parties that they should be plural and dialectic. For someone who, like Lenin in the twenties, had just banned parties, or who like Tito in the fifties, could not allow parties to re-form, to stress the *constitutional* role of the party as such was to lay himself open to the awkward demand for the same treatment for other parties.

But when, in 1936, Stalin needed to institutionalize the permanent dictatorship of the proletariat, he had no choice but to accept the contradictory notion of a constitutional single party.

[17] See for instance Raymond Aron's analysis in the discussion 'Can the party alone run a one-party state?' in *Government and Opposition*, January 1967.
[18] Even Stalin recognized this when he said: 'As to freedom for various political parties, on this we have our own views. A party is a part of a class, its most advanced part', in *Bolshevik*, July 1950.

In this his own inclinations and judgements had been strengthened by the formidable confirmation of the success, in theory and in practice, of the single parties of Italy and Germany. Moreover, for Stalin's ultimate realities even the party was a fiction. For the party itself, under him, was only one instrument of personal rule, and he infiltrated, undermined and supervised it by means of his other, more flexible instrument, the political police.

The party is given three qualifications in the constitutional realm of communist political theory: it is the ideological vanguard; it is the hard core of the state and public organizations; and it is the main organism allowed to present candidates in elections.[19] As the hard core of the state and public organization, the party can be better defined as the backbone of the Apparat, or the main apparat. Of this more will be said in the next section of this chapter which deals with the interior organization of the Apparat itself. But it is essential to note here that the statutes of all European communist states contain, as does the original CPSU statute, on the one hand articles which empower the central committees of the parties to control and direct the activities of the National Assembly, the government and the superior organs of the social organizations; and, on the other, articles which empower the party-organs at all levels to control and direct at their respective levels, the functioning of the main state organs and social organizations.[20] This text supplies the original explanation of the mechanism through which the party becomes the main-apparat. But it is also the text which explodes the constitutional fiction of the supreme power of the Supreme Assemblies and councils of the people, as well as the fiction of the power vested in the peoples' assemblies and councils at all levels.

Finally, it is useful, and particularly relevant to the argument of this book at this juncture, to note that whereas the statutes describe 'democratic centralism' as 'the rights of all members in any of the organs or organizations to discuss openly the instructions or proposals of the leadership', they expressly forbid the formation

---

[19] The complete definition of the 'role of the party in the proletarian revolution' is contained in the resolution of the Second Congress of the Communist International, under this heading.

[20] This particular text is a paraphrase of the formulation in the Czechoslovak party statute, chosen here because it represents a middle way between the more extreme statutes like the Rumanian, and the more evasive, like that of the Hungarian party.

of 'factions' within the party. Such factions are considered to be, by their very existence, anti-party.

As for the role of the party as the principal, if not sole, source of candidates for elections to the constitutional assemblies, the procedure by which this is achieved takes three main different forms, according to the respective communist states. In the Soviet Union there can be party candidates and non-party candidates; the party organization, in consultation with the workers and peasant meetings of the soviets, puts forward only one candidate agreed upon by all those concerned, in the single lists approved by the party (although in principle there could be more candidates). In most of the European communist states the main electoral organization is not the party but some broader 'front' which draws up the lists of candidates. In the lists the candidates of the party concerned are openly in a majority. Finally, in states with more than one party, the parties sometimes unite in electoral fronts and agree among themselves, as in East Germany, on a division of seats based on a percentage basis. In Poland, on the other hand, they go to elections on separate lists but with an agreed margin of 66 per cent to 50 per cent by which the number of listed candidates exceed the available seats and with the permanent agreement that the Polish Workers Party as the 'dominant' or 'hegemonic' party will have an absolute majority in the Sejm and will rely on the collaboration rather than the competition, of the other parties in its legislative and executive dominance.[21]

The party is therefore both monolithic and monopolistic. Monolithic is the expression coined by Marxist-Leninist terminology itself for the interior discipline and unity of this exceptionally centralized political organism. The compulsive ideology; the individual dedication and sacrifice of the members; and the prohibition of any interior groupings by attitudes or orientations make of a communist party, in power or not, one of the strongest and hardest organizations known in political history. Together with the Fascist parties (whose discipline produced the same results but was based also on some charismatic and mystical elements) they are as monolithic as any organization has ever been. Moreover, the party leadership everywhere is bound to attempt to make the parties even more monolithic, especially now that they have to

[21] See the section on 'Parliaments', pp. 253–68.

fight against new fissiparous tendencies. Indeed, whereas some party leaderships might be reconciled to the idea of some kind of gradual dissolution of all institutionalized organs of the dictatorship of the proletariat, no party leadership, not even Tito as late as October 1966, accepted the idea that the party itself should lose its internal cohesion or its leading role in society. The appeals of all party leaderships for firmer discipline through 'democratic centralism' are proof of their concern to safeguard the party's essential monolithism.

However, while the party can thus be described as monolithic, the state which it runs cannot be so described even if this is taken to mean a state run by a monolithic party. From this point of view it is more correct to call the party *monopolistic*, a term coined by Raymond Aron which has not been sufficiently followed by others. *Monopolistic* describes more adequately the aim and purpose of the party, which is to acquire the monopoly, that is the exclusive control or exercise of the activities of the state which is in reality, and as long as it does not dissolve, the monopolistic proprietor of the means of production and employer of the resources of society. This definition leads to the main question which this study endeavours to answer: How monopolistic can a monopolistic party be, or as Raymond Aron himself phrased the question, how non-monopolistic can a monopolistic party be?[22]

Finally there is the constitutional leadership, which is embodied in the persons of the head of state, the prime minister and in the case of war and defence of the commander of the armed forces. The duality between the constitutional and the non-constitutional establishments is solved in two ways. The first is the cumulation, in the persons of the party-leaders or leader, of the top-state functions and representative posts. Then there is the subordination of inferior party officials, holding the top-state functions, to the top party leader or leaders: the First Secretary of the Politburo. Within the general scheme of the collaboration between the main apparat (in the case of our states the party apparat) and the constitutional organs of integration, the main apparat retains, as a condition *sine qua non* the main political responsibilities.

[22] *Government and Opposition*, January 1967, loc. cit.

2. THE NETWORK

'We should have perished long ago but for the "apparatus".' Lenin.
Plan of the pamphlet *The Tax in Kind*, 1921.

What can be called the general theory of industrialization has an exceptionally wide application – and permeates a large number of far-ranging contemporary theories and *Weltanschauungen*. In sociological philosophy, and thus in philosophy, Ernest Gellner recently tried to replace the vague and by now out-worn concept of 'progress', by the more sinewy 'industrialization'. In economics and political sociology, and thus in political science, industrialization cannot but be the solar plexus of the expanding theories of development. The contemporary Marxist-Leninist theories use industrialization as a corollary of their main political justification and as an alternative argument for their relevance in countries and regions of the world in which the economic background and the social conditions of the twentieth century do not correspond to those described by Marx in the Europe of the nineteenth century. Voluntaristic industrialization, carried out through political and economic mobilization by a far-seeing 'vanguard' party, according to a plan drafted by national – or international – groups of politicians and experts, is put forward as the only solution for the needs of an under-developed, under-capitalized and absolutely or relatively backward country. Examples such as India, undergoing industrialization in conditions of full constitutionalization, do not move the adherents of this theory.

On the other hand, the same theory has been used, since Schumpeter, Colin Clark and W. Rostow made their main contributions to the subject, to state the contrary view which might run as follows: the communist political system can attract and be of temporary use mainly, if not only, to under-developed, under-capitalized countries, going through a rapid process of economic development – from Soviet Russia in the 1930s to China in 1950, to Eastern Europe in the 1940s, and to the African, Asian and Latin-American countries in the 1960s.

These two points of view are in reality the two sides of a coin. They are both justified according to the side from which the question is looked at. Historically, Marxism as a doctrine was the first attempt to express in a set of 'scientific laws' the axiom of the primacy of economic and social conditions – which since the twentieth century at least has become the commonplace and panacea of the art of government everywhere and may still continue to be so for a long time. Historically, too, it cannot be denied that it was in a state constructed on the Marxist-Leninist premises that the first economic plans were launched, and led to such a great success in industry that many societies everywhere have wanted to copy them. This attraction was and is still felt in spite of the fact that, on the one hand, the success in industry was darkened by the failure in agriculture; and on the other hand, that the methods used to run the economy entailed, in Stalinist Russia and in Hitlerite Germany which carried the former's methods to the worst extremes, an immolation of all political rights and freedoms of individuals and of the community.

But, seen from the other side, the fact is that history is not a copyright office. It is, rather, to change the metaphor, a distiller of co-existing doctrinal and political mixtures, retaining from them what is ultimately authentic. In our time Marx and Engels' works have been made to repay the debt of inspiration which they owed to the economists and great economic doctrines which preceded them, and from whose works they had borrowed freely, as all doctrines do. But in their case, as they had carefully wrapped everything in their own terminology, their successors and exponents wanted to make people believe that everything had already been discovered by the masters. By now too, Marx and Engels' theories have been found to be wrong and wanting (in for instance two of their main economic tenets: the theory of the concentration of capital and the theory of the impossibility of the rise of real wages). They were not only proved false but turned upside down exactly as Marx claimed Hegel was treated by Feuerbach and made to prove the contrary and to serve contrary purposes by Keynes and by the modern economic schools. Mutatis mutandis, the same thing happened to the first Soviet Five Year Plans. Once they had been put into effect in Russia, the essential mechanisms on which they were based were afterwards reproduced, adapted and adjusted in many different forms. Different plans have appeared in several communist or non-communist countries in the last quarter of a century. But they were made to fit into the general scheme of development and, generally speaking, used more harmonious and less totalitarian methods than the Soviet prototype.

Whichever way one looks at the plan, either as a strictly economic programme or as the general guide of a country through the stages of its evolution, one sees that it is the backbone of development. The plan is the main time-table for economic growth by industrialization, organization of agriculture, and direction of trade. These economic operations carry with them the social aim of urbanization and absorption of rural manpower and especially agricultural over-population; the cultural programme of widespread education, abolition of illiteracy and improvement of communications and of the flow of information; and above all, and as it were as a final result of these efforts, the technical advance: the main transformation of the economic and social structures of the country as a whole.

From the narrower point of view of this analysis the plan can be divided into three main stages, or phases, in which the main *actors* are different or called by different names although the three successive groups more often than not overlap. The first stage is that of the vision, projection and drafting of the plan. In this stage the *Intelligentsia* are the main actors. The second stage is the transformation of the plan into a policy and indeed into a set of laws or decrees – and during this phase the main actor is *the Party*. And the third phase is that of fulfilment and of implementation, and here it can be said, somewhat over-simplifying, that both the Party and the Intelligentsia converge into, and become something else, namely the *Apparat*.

The relations between the party and the Apparat form, from many points of view, one of the principal themes of this book. Here, some general aspects of the influence of the plan of industrialization on relations between the state and society, the new state and the new society, will be touched on. One important aspect is the changes brought into the 'intelligentsia' itself (which is one of the main links between the state and society) before and after the setting-up of the Apparat for industrialization. Another is the setting-up within the state of the nucleus of what is called here the Apparat, after the operation of industrialization and general economic mobilization has been decided upon. The nucleus is usually formed by the Economic Council and, especially, by the State Planning Commission. The practice and institution of the Nomenklatura, less well studied in the West, are highly characteristic of this phase.

Intelligentsia and Party

'Intelligentsia', which even nowadays is defined in the OED as 'the part of a nation that aspires to independent thinking' and which is rightly assumed to mean the reforming idealistic group of intellectuals of a society, can be given when projected on the background of the process of development a supplementary interpretation. This interpretation strikes especially those authors who have observed the intelligentsia as it appeared in the nineteenth and twentieth century in Russia *and* in the countries of Central and Eastern Europe. (In the twenties the Polish author Machajski-Wolski produced the most illuminating analysis of this specific phenomenon. In the forties and fifties the British historian Hugh Seton-Watson has successfully projected his findings on Eastern Europe upon the newer Afro-Asian intelligentsias.)[23] According to this interpretation intelligentsia can be described in somewhat over-simplified terms as the coalescence of the intellectuals of a nation when faced with problems of its economic and social future, into an interest-group militating for active development and into an ideological group militating for a populist ideology.

This occurs mostly in under-developed and under-capitalized countries. Historically speaking these are the countries where industrialization has not been effected slowly and gradually, as in Britain, in the eighteenth and nineteenth centuries, or at least as in the rest of Western Europe and, more rapidly in America in the nineteenth century. In such countries and societies, only the efforts of the state as such could replace the otherwise absent private initiative and resources. It is in such societies that the technicians, the professionals, scientists, scholars, writers, artists

[23] See especially his *Pattern of Communist Revolution*, Methuen, London, 1955, where he asserts that revolutionary parties are almost everywhere led by the intelligentsia. He bases his theory on his findings on Russia and Eastern Europe, where 'at the turn of the nineteenth and twentieth centuries intellectuals enjoyed in the countries of agrarian economy a prestige and influence out of proportion to their numbers, and *relatively much greater* than those of their more numerous and more cultured counterparts in northern and western Europe'. Here, too, 'the phenomenon of the *frustrated intelligentsia* (was) the central problem in the revolutionary movements of the twentieth century' (p. 5 and p. 8 respectively).

and students coalesce into a militating group. It demands on behalf of the people that the state or at least some public corporations take over the main means of production, mobilize the national manpower, and place them under its command, and their leadership, in order to achieve immediately full employment and rapid growth in production, and ultimately the modernization of the economic and social bases of the society. This is equally true of the intelligentsias of Russia and Central and Eastern Europe which coalesced during the nineteenth and twentieth centuries; of the Latin-American, Iberian and Afro-Asian countries which coalesced during our own decades; of the intermittent coalescences of intelligentsias in Italy in the twenties and in Germany in the twenties and thirties; in the USA in the thirties, before Roosevelt's New Deal; and, in a more limited and discriminating way, in Britain and France in the sixties.

Perhaps this use of the term intelligentsia could be made clearer by a comparison between *intellectuals* and *intelligentsia*. Three main differences are relevant from this point of view. First, the intellectuals are individuals in certain professional groups; whereas the intelligentsia is itself an interest group with a basic populist ideology, which might lead the whole or parts of it to association with a political party or movement, whether left- or right-wing. Secondly, individual intellectuals depend on public recognition of their status. This recognition may be accorded by the public as direct consumers, purchasers of works or services, or customers for advice and counsel; and even where intellectuals are retained by private employers or other intermediaries, it is still public recognition which determines the value of their work or services. By contrast, the status of the intelligentsia as an entire group is not fully recognized without the intervention of the state or of magnified corporations. Finally, whereas individual intellectuals share in and indeed might guide the public-opinion-forming activities of society, the intelligentsia as an interest group participates in the decision-making processes of the *dirigiste* state.

Thus the intelligentsia, an expression first coined in Russia in the first half of the nineteenth century,[24] becomes the leading

---

[24] The intelligentsia in Russia was, in the penetrating definition of Vladimir Weidle, 'the new elite, sharply distinct from the governing class'. This was the elite formed by the young *raznochintsy*, who 'went to the people' (*v narod*), from the Zemstvos, the Universities and indeed the prisons, as opposed to the

revolutionary group[25] of the under-developed countries, united by a *national* and *socialist* ideology. The twin national and socialist interacting trends of thought of any intelligentsia are in a sense most accentuated in the case of the Eastern and Central European intelligentsias which, unlike the Russian one, had to fight on two opposite fronts: against their own obsolete and selfish governing classes and against the aggression of foreign powers. This duality of purpose was afterwards to be reflected in the specific East European brand of communism in power: *national communism.* (In this sense Soviet Russia's own communism was and is, for the intrinsic reason that it is the policy and ideology of an Empire, an *imperial communism.*)

Be that as it may and coming back to the functional part played by the intelligentsia in the first phase, and as it were the phase of opposition against the old regime, it can be said that it is incumbent upon this group to outline the programme of development and to assess the priorities of the needs and the possibilities of the countries concerned. Thus while the party, more often than not revolutionary, is engaged in political action agitating for a programme of political reform, the intelligentsia, behind it, thinks in terms of the national, social, and economic mobilization of resources needed by this reform. More often than not too, during the final struggle for power between the revolutionary party and the old order, the intelligentsia, as the counter-elite opposed to the conservative elite, is an integral part of the opposition

administrative elite, the *chinovniks* whose services were dedicated to the legitimate government of the Russian Empire. But this relation between an elite and a counter-elite has also an etymological relationship. In Russian the opposed words *raznochintsy* and *chinovniki* are axed around the root 'chin', which itself means rank. On the other hand, Ortega y Gasset argued that, in Latin, *intelligentsia* descends from the gerundival adjective *intelligens*, which in its turn derives from the verb 'intelligo' or 'intellego', which derives from 'lego' ('inter lego') which also forms 'eligo' ('ex-lego') which gives 'electus-elite'.

[25] When in 1885 Plekhanov wrote in the first pamphlet on 'Social Democracy in Russia' that 'the working men will join our revolutionary intelligentsia in its struggle with absolutism' he was merely stating the fact that the intelligentsia was the most influential group. Under Struve's influence, and in the light of the rapid growth of the working class during Stolypin's industrialization, the doctrine of the social democratic party postulated the need for the leadership of the workers in the future society. But already in 1902 Lenin in *What is to be done?* was arguing that the party would be the leading force because it was animated by an active and voluntaristic consciousness as opposed to the narrow and sleepy 'trade-union consciousness'.

party or parties. Finally, more often than not, immediately after the successful seizure of power by the party the intelligentsia is integrated by the party in the new Apparat. The relations between this group and the party, within the Apparat, will be analysed at length in subsequent sections of this book. But here we are still at the phase when, precisely, the Apparat is set up and formed initially by the merging of the party, the intelligentsia, part of the old administration and the newly emerging, and hastily educated, cadres.

The setting-up of the Apparat

The party having come to power, the economic part of the programme outlined in opposition is transformed into a plan. This operation took almost identical forms in the USSR in the thirties and in the European communist states in the forties.

The plan in itself is a law, or indeed the Super-Law. Article 11 of the Soviet constitution, and Article 15 of the 1946 Yugoslav constitution, give it full constitutional endorsement by stating that the state directs the economic life and development of the country 'in order to carry on the general economic plan and to exercise control over the economy'. The Law-Plan is, after the constitution, the source of the legal power of the state's monopolistic ownership, control and direction of the economic and social resources and activities of the community. It is the second charter of a developing state. The Law-Plan divides the territory of the country into economic units or regions, which it binds together, even more closely, through its general co-ordination and organization. It also divides, and this is a more important and more general feature of all Plans, the operations which it directs, organizes and controls. These are roughly speaking the following: Industrial growth: industrialization, technology, efficiency. Agricultural growth: the promotion of collectives or co-operatives, mechanization, modernization. Communications: extension, intensification of transport. Mobilization of labour: recruitment of agricultural and industrial manpower, technical education, absorption of agricultural manpower in industry, creation of administrative personnel. Welfare: social organization, cultural life and education, communal institutions. Financing: national income and budget, wages, expenses. Investment: raising of funds for capital expenditure, distribution of investments, reinvestments and capital accumulation. Political and ideological background: information and communication, activism, mass-education.

By now, of course, there are many differences in the ways in which planning is effected in various countries and even between communist countries. Probably the most interesting is the difference between Yugoslav planning since 1952, and the planning in all the other East European countries – from the USSR who started her first plan in the late twenties, to Rumania who launched her first plan in the fifties. In the plans of the USSR and in those of most of the other communist states, as well as in the first (1946) Yugoslav[26] plans, the entire operation was and is centred on and indeed conducted by the state. In the Yugoslav plans since 1952, however, the accent has been made to fall on the self-managed enterprises, and the plans are now said to be the concerted operation of the enterprises, the social community and the state.

Planning, says the 1963 Yugoslav constitution, is done by the workers from the working-organizations, as leaders of production and of social work, and by the socio-political communities in fulfilment of their socio-economic functions. The Yugoslav doctrine openly criticizes the old system whereby the state is given full and special powers to carry out the plan. Thus Djordjević :[27] 'the general characteristic of this method of planning reflected the conception of "socialist planning" as developed in the Soviet Union and in other countries. But this led to the tightening of the economic and political administrative monopoly of the state. Due to this monopoly the economy was placed in a framework designed to give it a uniform evolution, but this centralizing state-mechanism replaced natural economic activity by decrees, regulations and orders issued by the centre and by the offices of administration, by a clutter of orders and counter-orders, written and unwritten. . . .

[26] In Yugoslavia (see especially an important study by Jovan Djordjević: *Le système de planification en Yougoslavie*, in *Revue de Science Financière*, Paris 1966) planning went through two different phases. The first (1946–50 (–2), was the phase of state-planning, or of the administrative guidance of the economy. The second phase (1950–62) was that of social planning which was the reflection of the fact that workers' self-management had been introduced as the main social-economic system. The monopoly of the state is then, allegedly, diminished and the economic-legal autonomy of the enterprises is strengthened. It is the enterprises which, in theory at least, become responsible for the launching and the carrying out of the plan.

[27] loc. cit.

Like all acts of total power in the economy this method of planning . . . was, in reality, neither efficient nor economically or administratively rational.' Between 1951 and 1957 Yugoslavia adopted only one-year plans, which tried to find the links and the transitions between state-planning and communal or social planning. Since 1957, new five-year 'social' plans were produced; to be complemented by one-year 'social' plans. Their mechanism was not based any longer on state-orders and decrees but on 'optional' proposals put forward initially by the Federal Office for Economic Planning and adopted by the Executive Councils of ten assemblies in a final 'Resolution' of the Federal Council and of the Economic Council of the Federal Assembly, who have the constitutional prerogative to issue the five-year social plans.

There is, of course, as great a difference, in theory, between the Yugoslav social plans and the Soviet-inspired economic plans, as there is between the Yugoslav vision of the state melting-away under the effect of social ownership and the Soviet and Soviet-inspired conception of the maintenance of the state as guardian of the 'common weal'. But in practice this boils down ultimately to the difference between a rigid, centralistic and intensive state-monopolistic way of planning -- and an increasingly decentralized, more 'optional' and especially less generalized and altogether less embracing area of planning. The part of the state in the plan, which is not denied even now in the Yugoslav conception, is undoubtedly shrinking since the self-managed enterprises and the self-administered local units have acquired and are acquiring an increasingly determining influence in the preparation and discussion of the plan. But the shrinking of the part of the state is inevitably accompanied by a dilution of planning, and in any case by a curbing of the controls set up for the implementation of the plan. Flexibility and diversity are the other sides of the coin of decentralization and of the enlargement of the sphere of macro-economics. The new Yugoslav experiments in planning, followed by the Czechoslovak and the Hungarian, must be logically linked with the spreading pluralization of social, economic and political life in these countries; as such they must be considered as *attempts* to give greater flexibility to the rigid communist economy. But planning in fact remains essentially a centralizing operation carried out by the state, however much in the background.

The three main stages of the plan are: *nationalization*, whereby the central organ takes possession of the means of production and of the resources of the country; *articulation*, whereby the central organ creates and mans the framework of the entire organization for the eight separate sectors; and, *implementation*, whereby the central organ, with its ramified network, begins the supremely responsible task of directing and supervising the work, and output, of innumerable units. Together, these should form the gigantic beehive replacing, to continue the metaphor, the swarming life of the society as it was before the advent of the plan.

Nationalization is the simplest operation of all. A revolutionary government expropriates all 'means of production' or indeed private property. The articulation is effected initially by setting-up at all levels and in all areas the units proposed by the plans, and by calculating the number of jobs necessary in each unit for the working of the plan.

The size of the Apparat-personnel

The jobs are in reality key-posts, or what is called in the original language of the communist planners the 'responsible posts' or 'posts of responsibility'. They form the basis at higher levels of the nomenklatura-lists. Here is a diagrammatic list of these posts, as found in all communist plans, and which were first known in the Russian administrative and legal terminology as *dolzhnostnoye litso*:[28]

(a) Heads of institutions and of state and co-operative economic organizations and enterprises.

(b) Directors-general, and heads of independent departments of ministries, institutions and enterprises, or co-operative and public organizations and functions similar to them.

(c) Technical managers and chief engineers.

(d) Chief and principal accountants, if they head the respective accounting departments.

(e) Chiefs of working sites or production sections.

(f) Judges, prosecutors and state arbiters.

[28] The actual list used here is reproduced from decision No. 139 of 17 January 1953 of the Rumanian Peoples' Republic, detailing the 'posts of responsibility', announced in and provided by the Communist Rumanian Labour Code of 8 June 1950. See my book: *Communism in Rumania*, London, 1964, p. 167. For more information on the Russian *dolzhnostnoye litso* see especially: J. Barrington Moore, Jr.: *Soviet Politics. The Dilemma of Power*, Harvard University Press, 1950. As for *Nomenklatura* see *infra*.

(*g*) Leaders and responsible heads of administration in scientific, educational, literary and artistic institutions.

(*h*) Inspectors of republic-wide and regional competence attached to the units specified under para. (*a*) above.

(*i*) Regional delegates of the State Committee for the Collection of Agricultural Products.

(*j*) Heads of departments attached to the executive committees of regional, city and *raion* peoples' councils.

(*k*) Legal advisers of ministries and other central agencies of the state administration, and heads of legal departments.

(*l*) Chief editors, deputy chief editors and chief departmental editors.

(*m*) Secretaries general of newspaper offices.

(*n*) Heads of health units.

(*o*) Administrators of pharmacies.

(*p*) Elected employees paid by the organizations which elected them.

(*q*) Secretaries of the office of ministers and deputy ministers.

(*r*) Station-masters of the principal railway stations.

(*s*) Commandants of vessels in the merchant navy.

(*t*) Heads, administrators, and leaders of economic sections, departments, and similar units of canteens, workshops, and all other sub-units organized on the principle of independent management, even if they are not actually corporate bodies.

(*u*) Heads of state stores and of co-operative commercial enterprises.

(*v*) Heads of security and fire brigade sections.

(*w*) Deputies or legal alternates of the functions listed above in the present decision.

But, roughly speaking, this list, crystallized in the *nomenklatura*[29] lists and multiplied by the number of units which might exist in any communist state, according to its territorial size and demographic numbers, forms the network of the planning society, or the Apparat.

The personnel of the Apparat, or the cadres, can be divided in two categories, the top echelon, or the nomenklatura-personnel, and the low category, or the petty bureaucracy. The nomenklatura-personnel is formed by all the responsible posts of the individual apparats, filled according to the required conditions. How vast the Apparat is in terms of cadres, and in terms of total numbers of posts to be occupied by specially trained and competent persons,

---

[29] See *infra* the section dealing exclusively with this institution.

can be broadly assessed in two ways. First by looking in Russia (with some useful indications of the same categories in Poland) at the numbers of what Soviet statisticians call the intellectuals and white-collar workers, and then by looking at the numbers of the intelligentsia, which after the establishment of the new state becomes, as noted before, the social and professional categories of those who man the apparats. Here, first, is the composition and numbers of the intellectuals and white-collar workers.

NUMBERS OF INTELLECTUALS AND WHITE-COLLAR WORKERS
1959 CENSUS[30]

Type of worker	Number
1. Workers in state administration and public organizations including:	2,389,000
(a) heads of state administrative bodies and social organizations and their subdivisions	392,000
(b) heads of enterprises and their subdivisions	955,000
(c) government employees (juridical personnel, inspectors, and so on)	1,042,000
2. Technical-economic intelligentsia including:	4,991,000
(a) engineers and technicians (excluding engineers occupying positions as heads of enterprises)	4,206,000
(b) agrotechnicians	477,000
(c) planning engineers and statisticians	308,000

[30] Reproduced from V. S. Semyonov: *Soviet Intellectual and White-collar Workers* in G. V. Osipov (ed.): *Industry and Labour in the USSR*, London, 1966. The author explains that 'The stratum of intelligentsia and white-collared workers has a heterogeneous composition. The concepts intelligentsia and white-collar workers have different meanings. Neither is a clearcut social category because they characterise working people from the point of view of the nature of their work, which is intellectual. The concept "employees", white-collar workers implies that the given category of people are employed by state or public organizations and carry out specific work, functions and duties, for a specific salary. Under Socialism the vast majority of the intelligentsia are employees. However not all employees can be classed in the category of intellectual workers. In the conditions obtaining under socialism, the categories engaged in what can be described as genuinely intellectual work include the technical-economic and scientific-cultural intelligentsia, many workers in the State, Party and ideological apparatus, a considerable number of state employees and of the military intelligentsia, and a part of the militia. The work of certain categories of office employees, communications employees, retail trade and catering workers . . ., employees of communal and service establishments . . ., many State employees . . . and a certain section of military personnel and the militia cannot be classed as brain workers.'

3. Scientific and cultural workers including: 5,294,000

    (a) teachers, educators, scientific workers   2,836,000
    (b) medical workers   1,702,000
    (c) cultural administrators   462,000
    (d) artistic administrators   190,000
    (e) professional writers and journalists   104,000

4. Office employees including: 2,912,000

    (a) bookkeepers, accountants   1,817,000
    (b) cashiers   413,000
    (c) clerical personnel   536,000
    (d) agents and filing clerks   146,000

5. Transport employees (conductors)   334,000

6. Communications employees (radio-telegraph, telegraph, telephone operators)   476,000

7. Retail trade and catering workers, including: 2,452,000

    (a) shop assistants, kiosk and snack-counter managers, etc.   1,166,000
    (b) waiters   184,000

8. Workers in communal and public service establishments including: 2,307,000

    (a) janitors, watchmen   2,030,000

Out of the twenty-three million odd people forming this category, and according to the definitions given in Soviet statistics (see previous footnote) the intelligentsia proper would amount to some fifteen million. This is confirmed by the following detailed statistical breakdown.

THE COMPOSITION OF THE SOVIET INTELLIGENTSIA[31]

	1926	1956
All intelligentsia (in thousands)	2,725	15,460
Heads of enterprises, constructions, sovkhozes, kolkhozes, machine tractor stations, establishments and organizations	365	2,240
Mechanical personnel (engineers including chief and senior engineers, architects, technicians, foremen, dispatchers, norm-controllers, station-masters, etc.)	225	2,570
Agronomical, veterinary and agricultural personnel	45	376

[31] From *Narodnoye Khozyaystvo SSSR v 1958 Godu*, pp. 656, 672, as quoted by L. Labedz: 'The Soviet Intelligentsia' in Richard Pipes (Ed.): *The Russian Intelligentsia*, New York, 1961.

Scientific workers (professors, lecturers in higher educational establishments, research workers) excluding heads of scientific institutions and of higher educational establishments	14	231
Teachers, lecturers and educators	381	2,080
Cultural-educational workers (including those in charge of clubs, libraries, publishing enterprises) and art workers	90	572
Physicians (excluding dentists), heads of medical and curative institutions	57	239
Intermediate medical personnel (dentists, *feldshers*, midwives, nurses, laboratory workers, pharmacists)	128	1,047
Planning and accountancy personnel	650	2,161
Judiciary staff	27	67
Students of higher educational establishments	108	1,178
Other groups of intelligentsia	571	2,609

If, however, one excludes the students, and includes the foremen (who have in the meantime acquired the status of intelligentsia and who, as will often be seen in this study, are now a pivotal category both in the social stratification of the communist states, and in the structural framework of their industrial administration), and if one also includes the members of the personnel of the party and the political police, who are most probably not included in the statistics (and who in 1937 amounted to yet another 1,751,000,[32] though a great number do overlap with some of the internal categories of the intelligentsia) one obtains a rough, but safe, estimate of the numbers of the Soviet Apparat-personnel. What is also important to note, at this juncture, is that it is the moment of the launching of the plan which increases extraordinarily the size of the intelligentsia in the state (in Russia from 2,751,000,000 in 1926 to 9,591,000,000 in 1937) together with its status and importance.

In Poland,[33] in 1939 the number of 'white-collar workers' was 700,000 and rose to 2,100,000 in 1963. This, according to Szczepanski, was due in particular to the rapid growth in numbers of the administrative employees. 'The number of persons in the leading (what is called here *responsible*) posts of the state and industrial administration and in enterprises of various kinds also increased rapidly' Szczepanski adds illuminatingly. He also draws the attention of students of these phenomena to the following three processes: (1) a new wave of people in the thirty age group is by now

[32] Labedz, loc. cit.
[33] Jan Szczepanski: 'The Social Structure of Polish Society', in *Kultura*, 29 December 1963.

occupying the top and responsible posts in administration; (2) there is an equally fast growth in the numbers and categories of managers in the various branches of the national economy; (3) there is a similar growth in the numbers of the non-decision making, and therefore non-responsible administrative-office employees (what is rightly called the petty bureaucracy or even bureaucracy) which Szczepanski describes as 'amorphous' and as 'not constituting a social-political force'. This coincides roughly with the Russian data and findings, and generally speaking, forms a reliable pattern in all European communist states. The only difference is the ultimate respective percentages of the intelligentsia, or the responsible posts, or the Apparat, and within them of the internal subcategories of upper and lower intelligentsia and leading and non-leading cadres, or nomenklatura or non-nomenklatura posts. These changes are partly due to the numbers of technical cadres available in each of these countries at a given moment – and to the extent of their respective national talent or tradition for administration, East Germany and Czechoslovakia, being the most advanced from this point of view.

The selection of the Apparat-personnel: the Nomenklatura
But who are these millions of people who form the ruling network of a communist state? How, on which criterion, and by whom are they recruited, selected, appointed and kept under control? The institution of the Nomenklatura goes a long way toward explaining how the personnel comes to fill the categories – and how a central organization, in the case of the communist states, the party, can control the entire operation from within and therefore, by means of what can be described as white terror, exercise its power over the vast machine. The importance of the control of appointments was revealed in the conflict between the 'Workers' Opposition' and the party in 1921. Lenin exclaimed: 'Why have a party, if industrial management is to be appointed ("mandatory nomination") by the trade-unions, nine-tenths of whose members are non-party workers?'[34]

For some reason, among which is the not surprising fact that Soviet and other communist sources do not openly describe what the nomenklatura is, this institution is given very indifferent

[34] In 'The Party Crisis', *Pravda*, 21 January 1921.

treatment in the many works on the Soviet system.[35] But from some more detailed studies[36] one can get a clearer idea of its functioning, and it is only by putting together its different and apparently contradictory aspects that this elusive system reveals its coherence and importance. The nomenklatura is first of all a series of lists of posts which cannot be filled without the special scrutiny and approval of some special organs. But they vary, in their definitions and applications, according to the level, size and specific characteristics of the respective organ of the Apparat (party and state-administration alike). Each of these organs have therefore a category and a number of posts to watch, which are under their jurisdiction (and this is where Fainsod's use of the word fully applies). The lists of the posts to be specially scrutinized by the respective organs range from the limited number of special jobs which might be of interest to subordinate organs, to those which might be of interest to the Central Committee of the party on a wide national plane. The three categories of the party-nomenklatura are by far the most important. They contain in their jurisdiction all the main 'responsible posts', which are manned by the intelligentsia, and which form the top-echelon of the Apparat.

The following is the nomenklatura in use in Soviet Russia until 1963, according to data published by A. Lebed:[37]

Nomenklatura of the 1st category (Plenum of the CC of the CPSU)

1. Members and candidate members of the Praesidium of the CC of the CPSU.
2. Secretaries of the CC, including the First Secretary.
3. The President of the Committee of Party State Control.
4. The President of the Party Commission.

    Appointment to and movement within these cadres is dealt with exclusively by the Plenum of the CC of the CPSU

[35] It is surprising to find, for instance, in Merle Fainsod's important study *How Russia is Ruled*, Harvard, 1965, that the institution is given no special treatment and that in the few incidental references to it it is freely translated by *jurisdiction*, which is neither exact, nor illuminating.

[36] For instance T. H. H. Rigby's unpublished thesis on *Selection of Leading Personnel in Soviet Russia*, University of London, LSE, 1958, F. Barghoorn: *The Politics of the USSR*, loc. cit., and A. Lebed: *Podgotovka i raspredeleniye rukovodyashchikh kadrov SSSR*, Institute for the Study of the USSR, Munich, 1965 (roneotyped).

[37] Lebed, *Podgotovka*, etc., loc. cit.

Nomenklatura of the 2nd category (*Secretariat of the CC of the CPSU*)

1. Heads of the departments of the CC, their deputies, heads of sectors, their deputies, instructors of the CC.

2. Editors of the central party and government press organs.

3. Ministers, their deputies, members of the colleges of ministries, heads of the main state agencies, their deputies, leaders, their deputies and members of state committees, heads of departments of the central bureaux and their deputies.

4. The entire apparat of responsible workers in the ministry of foreign affairs: ambassadors, attachés, secretaries, trade representatives.

5. Secretaries of okruzhkoms, obkoms, kraykoms and the CCs of the CPs of the Union Republics, those in charge of departments of these committees, secretaries of Gorkoms in the state capitals, the chief editors of their press, presidents of the Soviets of Ministers and of Praesidiums of the Supreme Soviets of the Union Republics.

6. Presidents, and their deputies, and members, of the Supreme Court of the USSR, the Procurator General of the USSR, his deputies and assistants, the procurators of republics and oblasts, the heads of the KGB down to and including the heads of oblast level administrations.

7. The composition of the Praesidium of the Supreme Soviet of the USSR (excluding the president who comes under the nomenklatura reserved to the Plenum of the CC); presidents and deputies of the Union Soviet and of the Soviet of Nationalities of the Supreme Soviet of the USSR, presidents of the commissions of the Supreme Soviet of the USSR, heads of departments and their deputies in the apparat (secretariat and chancellery) of the Praesidium of the Supreme Soviet of the USSR.

8. Military personnel down to commanders of divisions and heads of the political departments of divisions.

9. Presidents of sovnarkhozes, their deputies and heads of administrations.

10. Leaders and their assistants of the VTsSPS, VLKSM, sporting organizations, social organizations.

11. Leaders of creative organizations (Union of Soviet Writers, Composers, etc.) and the directors of their printed organs.

12. Leaders of the central scientific institutions, the Institute of Marxism Leninism, the High Party Schools (the Academy of

Social Sciences under the CC of the CPSU, and the high party schools under the CCs of the Union Republics.)

Appointment and movement within these cadres is dealt with by the Secretariat of the CC of the CPSU.

Nomenklatura of the 3rd category (*Departments of the CC*)

1. Secretaries of the raykoms in the capital cities, responsible workers in the central scientific and research institutions.
2. Leaders of enterprises of All-Union significance, directors of trusts, etc. (if they do not fall within the nomenklatura of the Secretariat of the CC).
3. Responsible workers in central government institutions, to the rank of inspectors, controllers, 'revizors', etc.

Appointment to, and movement within these cadres is dealt with by the corresponding branch of the CC of the CPSU.

There are also nomenklaturas in the competence of the CCs of the Union Republics, kraykoms, obkoms and raykoms. Whether in the field of economic or administrative activity, any appointment must be confirmed or agreed to by the corresponding organization of the CPSU in whose nomenklatura the post falls, even if the candidate is not a member of the party.

The importance of the nomenklatura seems to have decreased and to continue to decrease, and again more rapidly in the European communist states than in the USSR. This might be so for two reasons. First, it is obvious that its controls and its procedures are of greater importance when the Apparat is being set up than when it has been functioning for decades. And then, again, the fact that the party is losing its omnipotence and is forced to accept further collaboration with other organs and institutions might bring things to greater normalcy. If in the new appointment boards, there were members representing other institutions than the party and the political police, the procedures would become less awe-inspiring than they were in the Stalinist years. But the fact is that in a communist apparat-state the nomenklatura is still the ultimate symptom of public recognition or subsequent disgrace of any individual employed in the state-machine. The approval or disapproval of the candidates for any nomenklatura-post, combined with the 'files' of the cadres department, keep the individual within the layers of the 'responsible' or 'leading' persons – or throw him out into the cold of the un-(Apparat)-persons. To be in a nomenklatura is a status. The nomenklatura jobs are responsible and carry privileges and prerogatives. To be rejected from a nomenklatura is a stigma. It is in this terrible difference and contrast that lies the subtle terror, exercised upon people within the machine, as opposed to the sheer direct terror suffered by 'the enemies of the regime'.

The command economy

Once the network of the all-embracing plan is established, or at least its needs ultimately assessed, the branches of the old state-organization, army, police, administration, trade unions, etc., are refurbished and re-organized so as to correspond to the new needs of the future economic system: the planning- or command-economy. Other new administrative organs and centres appear only after the centralistic economic structure has been decided upon. Indeed their creation is made necessary by the demands and the functions of supplementary centralization. Some of these institutions deserve to be mentioned at this point, for they are essential nexuses in the co-ordinating and supervising operations.

The first to strike the eye is the State Planning Commission, which under this name or with slight variations is to be found in all the constitutional structures of the communist states, from the extremely centralistic one of the Soviet Union to the very decentralized one of Yugoslavia where it now shares its attributions with the Economic Council and with the Economic Chamber.[38] In Russia, the State Planning Commission was, under Stalin, after Stalin and is still now, the centralistic organiser and controller of the Economic Plan. Only between 1957 and 1962 was the Gosplan somewhat eclipsed during Khrushchev's economic reform when he tried to revive the Republican Councils of National Economy or Sovnarkhozes. The intention of the reform was to blend, through these Councils or Sovnarkhozes, the local decentralizing administration with the state central planning and to help

[38] See *infra*, pp. 260-4.

the party to inject its own dynamism into the Stalinist state-machine crippled by bureaucratic complexity. But in 1962 a new reform again strengthened the hand of the central organs, and especially of the State Planning Commission, against the local ones.

At the other, decentralized, extreme, in Yugoslavia the Economic Council is described now as a specialized consultative organ of the Federal Executive Council, composed primarily of professional economists and scholars. However, even in Yugoslavia the final adoption of the revised and discussed plan or plans is made on behalf of the Federal Council by the Economic Council. The Economic Council is therefore the supreme organ of co-ordination and has a direct supervision of the entire economic life, in collaboration with other apparats and institutions directly or indirectly linked with it. It is a permanent feature of the planning operation.

The State-Planning Commission is the specific new apparat of any country undertaking active development, and is to be found in communist countries as well as in India or in other non-communist countries. It spreads over the entire structure and territory of the state, with its own ramified hierarchy, and is given a fair share of authority and power over all other state-authorities. It is the originator and guardian of the plan, the charter of development. The State-Planning Commission is irreplaceable. It might, as in Soviet Russia, and especially in the Khrushchev and post-Khrushchev eras, be made to overlap with some other organisms, such as the Economic Councils of which the last two were the State Scientific-Economic Council, created in 1959, and the All-Union Economic Council created in 1962. It can and has been put under the tutelage of some other Supreme Councils, or controlled by ad hoc committees – but it has never lost and never will lose its specific raison d'etre in the mechanics of a developing state. Even in Yugoslavia, where centralistic organs have been diluted and seem to be gradually absorbed into consultative organs, it remains in existence as the Federal Office of Economic Planning. It is this office which prepares the initial version of the plan, and after the wide ranging discussions now required, it is still this office which prepares the final document.

In the State Planning Commission the intelligentsia have the last say. This explains why the State Planning Commission, is not an intrinsically reactionary institution. For instance in Czechoslovakia in the sixties, the main initiative and the appeals for economic reorganization and decentralization came from the influential group of the state-planners. They were afterwards entrusted with the implementation of the reform and with the power necessary to carry it out. But much more will be said about the role of the State Planning Commission in the European communist states in further chapters.

Two other institutions, and apparats, specific only to communist states, are the *Prokuratura* and the State-Arbitrator (*Gosarbitrazh*). These are mixed legal-administrative organs needed in states where constitutional separation of powers was abolished as a result of the adoption of a centralistic political-economic system. The *Prokuratura* has a vertical, self-contained and widely ramified hierarchy and specialized personnel and its head is vested by the constitution with 'supreme supervisory power over the strict execution of the law by all ministries and institutions subordinated to them, as well as by public servants and citizens of the USSR'. This organism, which is to be found exclusively still but ubiquitously – though it is losing influence in Yugoslavia – in communist countries has been interpreted in Western legal and political studies in two different ways. It has been considered either as the example of the total subordination of the judiciary to the party (the Procurator General must be a member of the party, and is responsible only to the Praesidium of the Supreme Soviet). Or it has been considered, optimistically, as a sort of Conseil d'État, a judicial offshoot of the administration, taking the place of the judicial courts as the sole legal check, from within, on the power of the rulers. (This is perhaps the more widespread view and it is, naturally, disappointing, for those who share it, to realize that the Procuracy does not after all do much to protect the citizens against the state.) But the Procuracy and the *Gosarbitrazh*, are the special judicial organs of a state which has itself become a huge and intricate closed administration within a new constitutional framework.[39] The *Prokuratura* is not concerned with the relationship between the citizens and the state but with that between the administrative units themselves of the mechanism

[39] One of the few Western authors to clarify this aspect is Julian Towster, who in his *Political Power in the USSR*, OUP, 1948, said (p. 310): 'The search after insurance of accord between action in the numerous localities over the vast domain of the land and the will of the ruling summits of both pyramids expressed in Party directives and Soviet norms is chiefly responsible for the peculiar position occupied by the judiciary and the Procurator General in the Soviet hierarchy.'

of the state. The *Prokuratura* has existed since 1922, as one of the vague new institutions of the revolutionary state. But its practical importance secured recognition after 1933 (and was confirmed in the 1936 constitution), that is *after* the moment when successful industrialization and full collectivization had transformed the Soviet state into a large monopolistic system.

The Procuracy and the *Gosarbitrazh* check the functioning of the machine in motion. It is this aspect which is stressed also in the new constitutions of most European communist countries, and especially in the Rumanian and Czechoslovakian. A special law[40] in the latter state lays the accent on the fact that the Procuracy should protect the social order and the state machinery of the republic and should educate the citizens in observance of the laws and other rules of socialist common life and in fulfilment of civic obligations. Thus the importance of the *Prokuratura*-Apparat increases when centralization increases, and decreases when new conditions of pluralism can re-emerge. Or, in other words, when the Constitutional Court goes down the Procuracy raises its head, and the *Prokuratura* retreats into the shade when the court shines forth again. This is, again, the typical evolution in Yugoslavia where the *Prokuratura* had of late to give back to the Courts many of the functions and attributions it had taken away from them, and where its own competence and purpose shrinks accordingly.

Thus in all communist states, from the very centralistic to the more decentralized ones, there exists from the very moment the plan is put into execution, a new centralistic complex, formed by the supreme economic authority, the state-planning apparat, the *Prokuratura* and the Arbitrator, and the system of nomenklatura. The party animates the new and old organs from within in order to make them respond to the new task of mobilization for and execution of the planned development. The armed forces, the police (militia and security), the trade unions, the youth-organization and especially the state-administration, to quote only the most important ones, are supposed to be turned into dynamic organizations, which will fulfil their administrative tasks only by adapting them to the new dynamic goals. Together they form the all-embracing and propulsive Apparat, shaped as a hierarchical pyramid. But the fact that the Apparat, thus formed by all other apparats, is self-contained does not mean that it is always totalita-

[40] Of 30 October 1952.

rian. For, whereas the plan can contain the totality of the activities of the state in its vision and programme of the future, the methods by which the plan can be fulfilled could have, in principle at least, a consultative character, with a system of checks and balances so built in that it would broaden the decision-making processes until, though centralistic, they could not be described as totalitarian.

All institutions, and especially administrative institutions, are what the different political systems make of them. Thus the administrative apparats, which exist in a state-structure can have their power increased or reduced. Their impact upon the political life as a whole can be intensified or attenuated by the amount of responsibility and initiative they are entrusted with.

In the last resort, it is the relation with the supreme political authority which determines the attitude and values of any administration.

The mobilization of society by the party, or by the army or by a combination of both

In this somewhat summary attempt to retrace the stages in the formation of a communist-apparat state, we have reached the stage when the state, taken over by the Apparat, is about to mobilize society. The preceding stages were the coming to power of the party; the proclamation and definition of the new constitutional framework; the setting up of the network of the Apparat to fulfil the tasks of administration, of running the command economy, and of political and social mobilization; the banning of opposition and the installation of the party as the sole political force. The next step is the political and economic mobilization of society; and when this has been achieved, and the command economy has been established, the choice will have to be made between the continuation of coercion, which ensures political safety but leads ultimately to social and economic inertia, or the adoption of the methods of stimulation and of free participation. These latter favour economic vitality, but they lead to the increased pressures of the plural forces of society which challenge the party's self-granted political monopoly.

There are, by and large, three ways in which the creation by the Bolshevik Party of a new communist Apparat-state in 1917 is extrapolated for the purpose of theoretical generalizations. One is that of communist philosophy itself. It sees this creation as the voluntaristic fulfilment of the historically and economically determined process of the change from the capitalistic class-society to the communist classless one. The proliferation of the Russian example in the world at large is, according to this philosophy, a matter of historical inevitability, though greatly accelerated by the revolutionary action inspired by the Soviet party in all parts of the world.

A second approach emphasizes the 'totalitarian' aspects of 1917. It singles out the fact that Fascist Italy, and especially Nazi Germany adopted, continued and aggravated the methods and techniques of Bolshevik Russia. This interpretation is therefore inclined to lay stress on the new possibilities offered to dictatorial regimes by the advent in the twentieth century of mass-societies, of the command economy and of *étatism*. The old type of authoritarian dictatorship is transformed by these phenomena into the new, monopolistic and totalitarian type of dictatorship, which confiscates all private property, assumes all controls and directs all private lives for one single, nationalist or internationalist purpose. The totalitarian interpretation fears the extension, in this century which has seen great concentration of economic, social and cultural means and resources, of those political doctrines which advocate an ever increasing concentration of political responsibility into one single organism.

But there is a third way of looking at this event and of projecting it onto a wider canvas for the sake of extrapolation. This approach directs our attention to the fact that the most profound and specific reason why such an otherwise detestable political regime can gain and keep power and is still being imitated in the world is precisely its capacity to mobilize a laggard society for the purpose of speeding up its development. Of course, as the totalitarian theories rightly stress, the Bolshevik regime provided this justification to the Fascist, Nazi, and any other monopolistic dictatorships of this century. But if the main object of setting up an Apparat state is the mobilization of society, then, on the one hand, one should be able to find in history examples of the take-over of the state by an apparat and of its transformation into an apparat state before totalitarian parties existed. And on the other hand, one can observe that even now, when totalitarian parties and dictatorships have existed for over half a century, other apparat-states exist simultaneously with them, in which the operation of taking over the state and mobilizing society has been undertaken by other political organisms and their apparat, and not by a totalitarian party and its apparat. It is specifically contended here that the mobilization of a society can be carried out either by the party, or by the army, or by a combination of both.

Two comparative analyses will be attempted here in order to illustrate two cases where a party has not been the prime agent. The first is a comparison between the Russian Leninist-Stalinist Party-Apparat state of the twentieth century and the Hohenzollern Army-Apparat state of the seventeenth and eighteenth centuries. To illustrate the second case, a comparison will be drawn, also very sketchily, between the birth of the Russian communist state and the Yugoslav, Chinese, and for that matter Cuban communist states. Whereas the Russian Apparat state owed its existence to the party, the other three (which, incidentally, are the only communist states born after the Russian revolution, which do not owe their existence to the presence of the Red Army on their territories) were engendered by an inextricably involved Party/Army or Army/Party combination.

The Army-Apparat state and the Party-Apparat state. To turn to the first illustration, it is obvious that a comparison between two such utterly different regimes as the Hohenzollern Army state and the Russian Party state must remain irrelevant for any other purpose than the comparison of the techniques of social and political mobilization. It is also obvious that the differences in epoch, mentality and position between the Hohenzollern rulers and the Russian revolutionaries are unbridgeable. The former attempted, by means of the efficient army they had built up, to make Prussian society into a coherent and well-organized polity, and the Prussian state into a formidable and feared great power. The latter tried to transform, by means of the efficient party they had built up, the backward Russian society into a dynamic and egalitarian polity, and the new Russian state into a revolutionary great power. Finally, neither explicitly, nor implicitly, does this outlining of similarities suggest that the Hohenzollerns were the actual forerunners and inspirers of the Bolsheviks, or that Lenin studied Prussian doctrines directly. (Indirectly he did, of course, through Engels and Clausewitz, and the use of some expressions such as 'professional revolutionaries' and 'People's Commissars' are oddly reminiscent of the Prussian *Berufsmensch*, *Berufsstände*, and *Kommissare* in, for instance, *Steuerkommissare*, *Kriegskommissare*, *Oberkriegskommissare*, through to *Generalkriegskommissar* in Berlin.)

But when it comes to the intrinsic techniques of the take-over of the state by the apparat, and the mobilization which it carries through, similarities appear not only in the situations. They appear, odd as it may seem, even in the written language of the founders and doctrinaires of these otherwise so different historical experiences. The method of juxtaposing some of the basic texts has been used here to illustrate the point.

Frederick William, the Great Elector, at least since 1640, and Lenin, at least since 1902, declared, in similar situations, but in entirely different circumstances, that what was needed was to create at least one internal, para-administrative force, well-tempered and properly organized and disciplined: for the former this was to be the new dynastic army to be welded together over and above the separate armed forces of the Hohenzollern lands, for the latter the new party to be formed out of the disorganized and undisciplined revolutionary Russian parties, and especially the untidy and cumbersome Social-Democratic Party.

'Alliances,' Frederick William wrote, 'to be sure, are good, but forces of one's own still better. Upon them one can rely with more security and a lord is of no consideration if he does not have means and troops of his own.'[41] Lenin wrote: 'To govern you need an army of steeled revolutionary communists. We have it, and it is called the party.'[42] Frederick William, the Elector, purged the army ruthlessly and reduced it in the first years of his reign to 2,500 perfectly reliable men. (Under Frederick William I it grew to 83,000 men.) In January 1917 the Bolshevik Party, emerging from illegality, numbered 23,000 men (in 1918 it had 200,000 members), and Lenin's idea of the revolutionary party was of 'a small, compact core, consisting of the most reliable, experienced and hardened workers with responsible agents'.

[41] In his political testament of 1667, quoted in Craig, op. cit., p. 2: 'Frederick William I welded into a single hierarchical system the older offices, concerned with the administration of the dynastic states and traditional regalian rights, and the new military-fiscal agencies of the absolute state. He reorganized the whole machinery of executive royal power on the central, provincial and local level.' Hans Rosenberg: *Bureaucracy, Aristocracy and Autocracy. The Prussian Experience 1660–1815*, Harvard, 1958, p. 39. See also with different contexts: Otto Hintze, *Staat und Verfassung*, Leipzig, 1943, Gordon A. Craig: *The Politics of the Prussian Army, 1640–1945*, OUP, 1956, S. E. Finer: *The Man on Horseback, The Role of the Military in Politics*, London, 1962, and, to some extent, Stanislaw Andrzejewski: *Military Organization and Society*, London, 1954.

[42] In Lenin, *Collected Works*, vol. 32, p. 62.

Frederick William created within the army a new commanding body, the *General Quartermeister*, which was the first model of the general staffs to be found in all modern armies. Lenin created at the Congress of 1906, in Stockholm, within the Social Democratic Party, and without its knowledge, an illegal bolshevik Central Committee, as the central organization designed to prepare and lead an insurrection.

One of Frederick II's historians, Marwitz, describing the officer corps of the Prussian Army thus established, said that their main characteristics were 'renunciation of all personal advantages, of all gains, of all comfort – yes, of all desire if only honour remains! On the other hand every sacrifice for this, for their King, for their Fatherland, for the very honour of Prussian weapons! In their hearts duty and loyalty, for their own lives no concern! What other classes and how many people, above all, in our present age, can pride themselves on such convictions ?'[43] This is almost identical with descriptions of dedicated party-members given in all communist statutes and catechisms, starting with Lenin's original one in *What is to be done?* Party-members must 'devote to the revolution not only their spare evenings, but the whole of their lives'.

The Prussian army had an 'esprit de corps' and even an 'esprit de parti'; the party its 'partiinost'. Frederick William offered to the officers a full professional occupation, education and training – and within the army there was complete equality of status, the King himself, the leader of the army, wearing the same coat as his officers. Lenin insisted that 'such an organization should consist above all of people professionally engaged in revolutionary activity and animated by a spirit of complete centralistic democracy'.

The army was to be an organism with the dual purpose of keeping order at home by giving to the country organization and discipline, and winning battles outside against enemy states and powers. The party was to come to power, establish and run the new state and lead the revolutionary movement in the world. Both had an ideology. Both had power as their goal, the one in the present by remodelling the dynastic state on the new type of organization, the other in the future, by seizing power in order to remodel the state.

The army and the state it could create were to be the 'rocher de bronze' of Frederick William's description – who in his words was

[46] *Aus den Nachlasse Friedrich August Ludwigs von der Marwitz*, Berlin, 1852 quoted in Craig, op. cit., p. 16.

prepared 'to leave to the Junkers the hot air of the Landtag'.[44] Lenin knew that the party, emerging from the revolutionary struggle, would set up a new state and new institutions, and he left to the other opposition parties 'the parliamentary comedy'.

With this we come to the mobilization itself. Both the Prussian King, and the Russian revolutionaries, believed that if the state could be organized differently it could be revitalized so as to attain high results at home, and prestige and leading influence in the world. The main method proposed to achieve this aim was that of 'mobilization', for great national and international aims and for economic development. (The Hohenzollerns themselves had in view the *Industrialisierung* of Prussia.) This involved mobilization of all resources and energies, of incomes, labour and output as well as mobilization of the moral and spiritual energies of the nation and of the society.

This mobilization should be carried out by the most advanced classes of the society: under the Hohenzollerns, the Prussian nobility, in Lenin's Russia the proletariat, led, respectively, in Prussia by the military professional estate as 'the foremost and the most brilliant estate'[45] – and in Russia by the professional party. As Lenin put it, 'The party is the leader, the vanguard of the proletariat, which rules directly'. The Army-apparat and the Party-apparat will govern by dictatorship. They will set up the new institutions on which the new social-political organization will be moulded. 'Thus, out of the war commissariats of the Great Elector grew the formidable administrative apparatus of Frederick the Great's time . . . which made possible the organization of the resources of the state – for national purposes and provided the machinery for executing the policy.'[46] In Lenin's conception, on the other hand, the seizure of power by insurrectional means by the party was 'the only way of making the party take over the Soviets, the new organs of the will of the people', and the framework of the new structure of the state.

Frederick II wanted the new political system to be 'as coherent as a system of philosophy, so that finance, police and the army are co-ordinated to the same end; namely, the consolidation of

[44] Craig, op. cit., p. 11.

[45] Both Frederick William I and Frederick II used this expression, as quoted in Rosenberg, op. cit., p. 152.

[46] Craig, op. cit., p. 15.

the state and the increase of its power'.[47] Lenin (in *The State and Revolution*) wanted 'Communism to make the state all-comprehensive, so that "nobody" could oppose it'.

Thus the conception of the organization of what can be called the Army-apparat inspired also the organization of the Prussian Apparat state; and the conception and organization of the Party-apparat did the same for the communist Apparat state. In both, and other similar cases, the transfer of power and the formation of the new state were the result of the establishment and of the success respectively of each of these Apparats. In both cases the Apparat preceded the new state, formed it and ran it. In the international range of the states of today both apparats, the army and the party, form and run Apparat states, and indeed sometimes change over. Whereas in Europe the Party-Apparat states have predominated, in Africa and Asia it is the army which, of late, seems to be more successful in establishing or taking-over from the party, the Apparat states of these countries.

The party and the army, as political forces. The similarities found above between the army and the party as the two main apparats which in history[48] have been able to set up and sometimes continue to run, states of their own conception and style, have practical origins. One, historical, is that an insurrectional party, and therefore especially modern monolithic parties, have to mould their organization and functions on those of an army. One is reminded of Stalin's exclamation: 'In our Party, if we have in mind its leading strata, there are about 3,000 to 4,000 first rank leaders; our Party's generals; 30,000 to 40,000 middle rank: our Party's officers; and about 100,000 to 150,000 lower rank Party command staff: our Party's NCOs'.[49] The integral discipline, the *esprit de corps*, the self-dedication and the main function of the party as an institution come originally from the army, as an institution.[49]

Lenin, through Clausewitz and through his earlier studies in strategy, was convinced from the beginning that the revolutionary

[47] C. P. Gooch, *Frederick the Great*, London, 1947.

[48] In his *Roman Revolution*, Ronald Syme argues that even Julius Caesar had a party, the Caesarean Party, or party of the liberators, which survived him, and the initial nucleus of which was formed by 'the generals of the Gallic and Civil wars, rewarded already for service or designated to high office' (p. 59, Oxford paperbacks, London, 1960).

[49] In 'Mastering Bolshevism', in *Foundations of Leninism*.

party should be formed and should behave as an army; and that it should impose upon the new state its spirit of discipline, hierarchical organization and ruthless energy. There is a well-known passage in his text on 'The Breakdown of the Second International' (1915) where he says: 'Let's take the modern army. This is an organization which we can take as a model. And this organization is particularly good for that because it is elastic and through it millions of people can be handled by a few strong-willed men.' The text then develops the metaphor at great length, showing how the party should be a new army.

Thus, the party itself being, in many ways, the projected image of an army, it follows that the states which each of these institutions bring into existence, and run for longer or shorter periods, should have many common features and similar orientations. (But the obvious difference is that whereas the army creates a state, and runs it, in theory, for the period during which the state's organs and institutions are not strong and independent enough – the party is a political machine which not only wants to create the state but also to run it indefinitely. Even here, however, as will be seen, there are especially in the modern world amphibious bodies, party-army, army-party, which make these distinctions more difficult.)

Another obvious characteristic which the army and the party have in common, and which enables them both to set up and run a state is that they are both, in Finer's[50] phrase in the case of the army, *'purposive instruments* . . . rationally conceived to fulfil certain objects'. They have five main features: centralized command, hierarchy, discipline, intercommunication, *esprit de corps*, and a corresponding isolation and self-sufficiency. These features make of such organizations effective apparats and potential main apparats, that is backbones of the entire structures of new states. But, to paraphrase de Jouvenel when he said that 'power is potentiality'[51] potentiality is power, and what the army has more than the party is the direct power. To quote Finer again: 'The military possesses vastly superior organization. And they possess *arms.*' This is the power of intervention, occupation and ultimately coercion which

[50] S. E. Finer: *The Man on Horseback*, London, 1962.
[51] Bertrand de Jouvenel: 'The Means of Contestation' in *Government and Opposition*, No. 2, January 1966.

the party cannot acquire if it does not use the army for this purpose, or if it does not create, from within its own organization, armed forces of an insurrectional-terroristic character. Indeed more often than not, contemporary revolutionary parties do create their own armed organizations. But the fact that the army remains in any state the apparat with force and with arms puts it in the position of being the likeliest potential alternative to any government and the arbiter of the situation in times of crises.[52]

But the main feature party and army have in common, when one looks at them as potential state-founders and main-apparats in the contemporary political world, is that both organizations can and must carry out the operation of mobilization. By this, as already noted, is not meant only the 'call-up' or 'recruitment' of conscripts or forces, in military terms, or of labour-forces, in social-economic terms, for the execution of the general plan. What is meant by mobilization is the whole action of persuading and forcing an entire local, regional, national and foreseeably international community, to engage its population in a planned and co-ordinated general activity. What is also meant is the maintaining of the community thus mobilized in a spirit of permanent dedication to a definite, visible or still invisible, goal which demands that the effort continue unabated until that goal is reached. The goals of mobilization may be limited as in the case of a national development plan (usually proposed and carried out by an army-dictatorship) such as the 'guided', 'basic', 'presidential', organic', 'selective' or 'neo'-democracies of the military regimes of Africa, Asia and Latin-America; or unlimited, as in the world-historical phases of the communist states and movements. There are to be sure, other apparats which can become the main-apparat in an apparat-state. For instance, the political police, which is a military-civilian ramified organization, can, if unchecked, exercise the greatest coercive power. But in modern times it is the army and the party, the former becoming ideological-political, and the latter becoming insurrectional-military, which have, more frequently, created new states or transformed old states into modern Apparat-states.

The Communist Party states and the Communist Army-Party states. The only communist states which have *genuinely* emerged in the world since the emergence of the USSR – and by genuinely is meant those communist states which were not created directly by

[52] See *infra* 'The army's check on the party'.

the Soviet Union acting as a dominant power and whose 'revolutions' were not caused by the passage of the Soviet Army through their territories – are Yugoslavia and China, and in a sense also Albania and Cuba. But then it should also be noted that in both Yugoslavia and China, the new states were the product of a slow building up carried out by an amphibious organism, the party-army; or, in other words, the Communist Party transformed for a while into an army of liberation.

In the case of Yugoslavia this transformation[53] was carried out by the Partisan Army led, like the Yugoslav Communist Party, by Tito. The army worked through the People's Liberation Committees, political-administrative-military organizations, the first of which was set up in July 1941. In February 1942 the supreme staff of the People's Liberation Army, stationed at Foča in Bosnia, issued the so-called 'Foča regulations' which were in fact a new administrative charter. According to these regulations the People's Liberation Committees were representative bodies of government composed of members elected by free and universal suffrage, provided the candidates were fighting in the national war. The People's Liberation Committees had the task of supplying the partisan units and citizens, of maintaining order in liberated territories, of ensuring the functioning of the economy, cultural activities and medical services 'as well as to exercise all administrative functions except those which belonged to the authorities of the People's Liberation Army'.[54] These were, seen in retrospect, soviets set up by an army which was formed and controlled by a party. From the new kind of Soviets the new state of People's Democracy was going to emerge. Indeed 'as a matter of fact', says Vratuša, 'the entire organizational structure of the new state emerged as a system of People's Liberation Committees, ranging from the lowest to the highest level – the Antifascist Council of the National Liberation of Yugoslavia, which was the supreme political and legislative body of New Yugoslavia'.[55] At the historical second session of this body, held on 29 November 1943, in the Bosnian town of Jajce, which marked the establishment of the new people's state based on a federal system, it was stated that 'the People's Liberation Committees

---

[53] See especially a very lucid description of the administrative revolution in Anton Vratuša: *The Commune in Yugoslavia*, loc. cit.

[54] Ibid.

[55] Ibid.

were the basic organs of the people's authority'. The *ad hoc* People's Liberation Committees became afterwards the basic People's Committees, which were in the 1946 Yugoslav constitution 'the highest organs of government on their territory'.

In China (where recent events showed how closely linked together in political leadership the party and army still are) the entire story stretches over almost a quarter of a century. It goes from the late twenties to the fifties, and across World War II, which did not have in China's case the same fundamental importance as in the case of Titoist Yugoslavia. But the operation of setting up a framework of administrative areas of self-government began under the control of the network of the dual party-army apparat, united under Mao's leadership; and was inaugurated in China in earnest in November 1931 after the collapse of the Canton commune in 1927, with the establishment of the Soviet Republic of China in Juichin, Kiangsi. Immediately afterwards the nationalists started their military campaign to destroy the Soviet Republic and forced them out into the long march to Yenan. During the Sino-Japanese war the communists in 1937 voluntarily abolished their own Republic, and again put the stress of their military-political-administrative command on the military aspect, describing it as the Eighth Route Army. In a speech of 6 November 1938 Mao Tse Tung made it clear that 'As a national war of resistance is going on, we must further contend for military power for the nation . . . Our principle is that the party commands the gun and the gun will never be allowed to command the party. But it is also true that with guns at our disposal we can really build up the party organization, and the Eighth Route Army has built up a powerful party organization in North China. We can also rear cadres and create schools, culture and mass movements.'[56]

But as the Eighth Route Army, later known as the Eighteenth Group Army, went forward on its march to victory, the new state organs and the new state were emerging. 'As the Communists expanded their military power they established border region governments operating on a number of different administrative levels . . . According to the Laws and Regulations of the Shensi-Kansu-Ningsia Border Region, for example, the basic system was composed of a pyramid of people's councils elected by direct, universal and secret vote. The structure was held together by

[56] Quoted in George Paloczi-Horvath: *Mao Tse Tung*, London, 1962, p. 176.

"democratic centralism": starting from the *hsiang* (town) government at the bottom and proceeding through the *Hsieu* (country) and on up . . . Another central feature of the border region government was the three-to-one system whereby the Communist membership of any given administrative organ was limited to one-third of the total.'[57] But at the same time the Communists were 'three-in-one' : they were carrying out a threefold task – political as party-members, military as soldiers, and administrative, as the holders of the responsible administrative posts.

From this brief analysis of the similar ways in which the Yugoslav and the Chinese communist states were built up, one can see the difference between them and the other communist states. To be sure all communist states, with Cuba's exception, were helped to birth by a war which destroyed the frail structure of the previous states: the First World War in the case of Russia: the Second World War in the case of Yugoslavia (and of Albania); the Sino-Japanese war, and, partly, the Second World War, in the case of China, and the quasi-occupation of their territories by the Soviet Army in the case of the other European communist states. In Russia's case the party, by revolutionary insurrectional means, seized the capital and administrative centres of political power, and won, as an apparat, the control over the entire administration of the state including also that over the armed forces (which were afterwards reorganized and remodelled). In the case of the European communist states the extraneous, but determining factor of the fall of the states in the zone of operation of the Soviet Army and in the zone of influence of Soviet Russia as a great power, produced, politically speaking a comparable situation. Here the local party, as an apparat, was given the possibility, in different conditions of sovereignty, to take over the centre of political power and from it the entire administration, including the subordinated armed forces.

But in the case of Yugoslavia and China, the Party, used to the full the opportunity offered by foreign occupation. Each organized a new army and turned itself into a dual apparat-Party-Army, becoming respectively the Partisan Army and the Eighth-Route-Army for immediate practical as well as political purposes. Each new state was thus established progressively from the periphery to the centre. (This latter aspect is to be found also in the

[57] Robert P. North: *Chinese Communism*, London, 1966, pp. 148–9.

case of Castro's Cuba.) This is as different from the central *coup d'état* of the Communist Party in the other cases, as it is from the Army's central *coup d'état* in Ataturk's Turkey, Nasser's Egypt or Ayub Khan's Pakistan. A twofold operation carried out through two functionally different apparats by the same leadership is a special form of the birth of a state.

But whereas the birth of a state through the action of a dual apparat (Army–Party) occurs infrequently, the cases in which the state is run by a duality of apparats (combining indistinctly to form the main apparat) are much easier to observe. Thus, Stalin's Russia under the party and the political police apparats, Salazar's Portugal under the army and state administration, Franco's Spain, at the beginning under the army and the party, and Peron's Argentina under the army-apparat and the trade unions apparat are only the best-known examples of such cases.

Finally there are the numerous cases of the substitution of one apparat by another in the position of main Apparat: the army instead of the party in most of the African 'one-party-states'; the party eliminating the political police from the dual main apparat in Khrushchev's Soviet Russia, and, in different circumstances of sovereignty, in many European communist states; and the tendency of the state or regional administration to replace the party in some of the communist states, of which more will be said later.

But at this point the conclusion which can be drawn is that in the apparat states, the main apparat, which runs and sometimes has formed the state, can be one or another of the apparats contained within the Apparat as a whole; it is not always the same one, and it can even share, for a shorter or longer while, the main controls with another apparat.

Coercion versus efficiency

The Apparat being for all intents and purposes a centralistic organism, and the Apparat-state being by definition also a non-opposition state, it goes almost without saying that the Apparat-state is a state using in its relations with society the means of coercion, more than those of consultation. It can degenerate into the different forms of terroristic state.

The analysis made in the preceding pages concentrated, for obvious reasons, on the political and social aspects of the Apparat-states. The more massive economic aspects were neglected, and little was said about the difference, with all the political consequences it carries with it, between the industrialization and the running of such states. However gigantic a task, it is actually easier to industrialize and collectivize the state than it is to undertake the permanent running of the economic and social complex of this new state.

In the first phase success can be measured in terms of mass-mobilization, building up of new plants and productive units, industrial and agricultural and, especially, in terms of absolute growth in production, obtained at any cost. The success of the plans for overall industrialization in most communist states in the first phase was undeniable – and was and is responsible in great part for the attraction the communist example exercised upon the under-developed countries. But in the second phase, the much longer and slower one of actually running the machine thus constructed, the breakdowns appear much more quickly and more evidently. The magic criterion of *growth* is replaced by the subtler and in any case much more elusive criterion of *efficiency*. While growth is absolute production, efficiency is production measured in the relative terms of productivity, not only the economic productivity, but the ultimate productivity of society forced to bear the burden of production and its growth. In economic terms efficiency is calculated in costs of production, labour, capital accumulation and investments. In general social terms efficiency might be abstractly evaluated in the amount of participation in the common work, of interest shown in it by those engaged in it, and in the value, however assessed, of the effort thus obtained.

Economic growth can be obtained by means of coercion, or what is called 'command economy'. The natural tendency of an Apparat, and of the Apparat-state, operating from a very tight centre of decision-making, through very diversified and ramified organs of implementation and execution, is to use the method of coercing the individuals and groups concerned. As a result of the repression of opposition and the principle that the society must unconditionally obey the state, the groups and individuals in the Apparat-states have no recourse against the decisions involving them taken by the remote centres of power. On the contrary the apparats, and the Apparat, are so organized as to constrain every group or individual to contribute in the ways open to them to the general schemes of operation. Such an operation, aiming only at total and somewhat immediate results, can best be achieved, in the opinion of communist doctrinaires, by total discipline and therefore total coercion. This is fully confirmed by Lenin when he said: 'The state is a sphere of coercion. It would be madness to renounce coercion, especially in the epoch of the dictatorship of the proletariat so that the administrative approach and "steerage" are indispensable.'[58]

Coercion takes in times of crisis the extreme form of terror. In movements or phases of crisis such as revolutions, war, internal or external crises or economic crises (whether produced by the new demands of the Apparat-state or by the deadlocks its functioning produces) terror is the main method of keeping order – and that applies to all dictatorships in the world at all times. This amounts to the truism that in any dictatorship those who refuse to obey orders will be forced to do so. Moreover, since everyone is practically under permanent orders in Apparat-states because the command economy is completely controlled, those who refuse to submit to the general means of coercion will be made to obey through more special means of terror. Here fear of authority is complemented by fear for one's life and for one's family. But though rapid and effective, these means are only primitive, and cannot last indefinitely in more articulated societies.

Lenin and Stalin, like the Jacobins, acknowledged terror and state terrorism as a necessary means of achieving the revolution. The literature on this well studied and in a sense inexhaustible subject is so vast, ranging from the explicit justifications by Trotsky, Lenin, Stalin and Vishinsky (and especially Trotsky) to the writings of Koestler, Hannah Ahrendt, David Rousset, Merleau Ponty, Erich Fromm, C. J. Friedrich and Brzezinski and Merle Fainsod[59] that the present work will make no attempt to enlarge on it. But two distinctions should perhaps be made when one looks at the subject of terror as an acknowledged instrument of government and a style of policy in the communist Apparat-states.

The first is that, as pointed out already, these states use two kinds of terror in two separate spheres. One is the terror the Apparat-state exercises, as an oppositionless state, against anything which it

---

[58] In 'Once again on the Trade Unions', January 1921, loc. cit., vol. 32, p. 98.
[59] Who has an excellent chapter on 'Terror as a System of Power' in his *How Russia is ruled*, loc. cit.

regards as opposition. This includes all the sins, of commission or omission, against the regulations of all kinds to which the individuals and the groups in the society should submit. The suspicion of opposition covers not only acts perpetrated or unfulfilled obligations but even intentions and thoughts. The range of persecution is universal; and the ever increasing severity and brutality of sanctions endless. Terrorists and terrorized are locked in a permanent duel of accusations and recriminations, of attacks and counter-attacks. These can easily lead either to some kinds of mass extermination by the exasperated government, or to some attempt by the exasperated population to put an end to the rule by terror by some kind of revolution. This terrorism of the state against the so-called opposition which allegedly wants to destroy the system from without (usually the accusation of 'treason' is linked with allegations of plotting with external enemies) takes institutional forms and becomes one of the basic elements of the doctrine of the 'defence of the state' of such regimes.

But this is a different terror from that exercised by the Apparat-state within the sphere of the state, that is within the large spheres of the society in which individuals and groups are coerced to collaborate with the overall efforts of the state to fulfil its goals and achieve its purposes. Here a subtler terror of social pressure is enforced. Its instruments are education and indoctrination; the according of recognized status to the employee, and in particular the status of Apparat or Intelligentsia or Nomenklatura. It also uses secondary means of pressure and of persuasion: promotion, money-lending, privileges – or their negative alternatives: demotion, loss of advantages and loss of status. The pressure thus exercised by the Apparat on the people within the Apparat is more efficient although much more silent.

The second distinction to be made within the general theory of terror in a communist state (when seen as an Apparat-state) is that the degree of terrorism it exercises against 'opposition' and 'apparat-employees' alike, corresponds to the increase of influence within the Apparat of one of two apparats. One is the political police, which, in operations and phases described as 'critical', carries with it and under it the militia, part of the armed forces and the bulk of the administration. The other is the more special, but essential, apparat of the Prokuratura. The rapid coagulation in time of crises, or alleged crises, within the Apparat of the apparats of security police, Prokuratura and state administration, pushes the political police into the place of the main apparat. Coercion is as we have seen the natural tendency of the Apparat of a communist state, normally led by the party. But when terror is carried to the extreme this also has the effect of turning the security police into the main apparat. It is in such times that the obvious symptoms of forced labour, concentration camps and mass deportations appear. And they appear not only, and not principally, as means of collective punishment, but as the means by which the primitive main apparat (this time the political police) attempts to undertake in terrible caricature the functions of social and economic mobilization of the Apparat as a whole.

But, on the other hand, coercion is not sufficient for the running of the economic and social tasks of the Apparat-state, if an attempt is made to run it on the basis of *efficiency*. Efficiency cannot be produced merely by coercion. Efficiency can be obtained only by *participation*: the skill of mobilization is to combine forcible recruitment with a kind of commitment. This, in its turn, cannot be obtained without enlarging the process of decision-making, and ultimately changes its one-way orientation from the Stalinist image of the *transmission-belts*, to a two-way, or multi-way, consultation. Efficiency can be attained only as a result of the interest shown by the agent in the successful result of the operation to which he is committed. This interest can be stimulated by incentives, but primarily it must be aroused and sustained by participation in the decision-making process, or processes.[60] For, indeed, decision-making itself is only a series of concentric circles in which the participation of an individual or group leads from one of the spheres to another, until it reaches the general sphere of information and deliberation.

It is at this point that the study of the *politics* of an Apparat-state actually begins. Having reached the stage of the inevitable and permanent test of efficiency, the European communist states must

[60] 'Yet a man who wants to narrow down the new system of management to a mere system of incentives or market relations, while at the same time preserving the old administrative nature and methods proves that he has not progressed further than the point where we were in 1958, and he would fail just as much as we did then . . . The introduction of the new system of economic management implies the democratisation of our society . . . of the entire political and managerial sphere.' Speech by Ota Sik, at the Thirteenth Congress of the Czechoslovak Communist Party, 4 June 1966.

improve and consolidate their processes of decision-making. They have, therefore, to face the inevitable realities of the *checks* which those called upon to participate in the decision-making will exercise upon them, and of the *dissent* which they feel entitled to express against the methods and the aims of the power-holders.

PART TWO

THE PLURAL CHECKS

The founders of the communist state believed that once political opposition was banned, opposition itself would disappear. 'Either you are on this side, or on the other, but then your weapon must be a gun and not an opposition. This follows from the objective situation and you must not blame us for it', Lenin asserted categorically in the principal speech he delivered on the problem of recurring opposition *after* the party's coming to power. On the same occasion he made his famous remark: 'I think the Party Congress will have to draw the conclusion that the opposition's time has run out and that the lid is on it. We want no more opposition!'[1] Are these assertions made in the twenties still valid in the sixties?

The communist leaders also believed that in the oppositionless states thus established the Apparat, which in their case was the party-apparat, could run the new state alone, and be, as it were, the central organ from which all orders and directives emanated and towards which all information converged. Stalin, who knew this second phase better than Lenin said: 'Not a single important political or organizational question is decided by our Soviet and other mass organizations without guiding direction from the Party'. He also described, in a famous formula, these organizations as 'transmission belts which rally the labouring masses under the leadership of the party'.[2] He was sure, then, that this was how it would work. This, in fact, is how it actually worked under him, and we can now see and analyse all its effects. Does this Stalinist conception remain a common assumption for all communist power holders ?

Part Three of this book will discuss 'the manifestation of

---

[1] In the speech at the Tenth Congress of the RCP (B) in 1921, Lenin, *Collected Works*, 32, p. 200.

[2] Both quotations from Stalin: 'On the problems of Leninism', in *Problems of Leninism.*

dissent' in the European communist states, that is how the recurrent oppositional attitudes and activities can be and are expressed in an oppositionless state. In the present part, dealing with the plural checks, it is the Stalinist assumption that the Apparat alone can conduct all the principal activities of the state, which is questioned. The problems here are, first, whether indeed such a state of affairs can really exist in any kind of Apparat-state, communist or otherwise. Secondly, whether in the periods of political stability coinciding with the periods of economic efficiency the power holders do not have to institutionalize the necessary 'bargains' which they have to make with those who, in society, deliver the goods and the services? In other words, this part will deal with the checks and pressures exercised by the plural groups of the Eastern European communist societies on the party. But here, once more, a few preliminary explanations may be needed.

When one speaks of plural checks, one speaks of pluralism. But pluralism is not only, or exclusively a political concept (in the sense of pluralistic-constitutional). Any society is to a certain degree pluralistic, and therefore cannot be monolithic, but the less amorphous and more developed a society, the greater the degree of pluralism. This is a truism in sociology. But from a political point of view, the relations between the power holders and those who can provide or withhold contributions indispensable to the functioning of society, or what Montesquieu described as the relationship between 'le pouvoir' and 'les contre-pouvoirs', leads to the demand for political pluralism.

The 'feudal' political system is an outstanding example of pluralism. Power was divided amongst a multitude of barons, provinces and 'estates'; not even the vassals themselves could *belong* monolithically, bound as they were to pay what Marc Bloch called 'the plurality of homage'. Moreover it is only with the theory of the divine and absolute monarchy, which was clearly formulated only when the barons, provinces and estates demanded further controls over the rulers, who in turn, as the nation-state took shape, began to require more revenues for the defence of the entire territory, that the unity of power, sovereignty, was openly spoken of. In fact it preceded only by very little the appearance in history of the state itself; and it evolved from the concept of dynastic sovereignty to national and then popular sovereignty. In the modern pluralistic-constitutional state the interest groups are fully articulated and developed in social classes and economic and professional categories – as well as in their political, religious, or ideological allegiances. The liberal constitutions are, in fact, the description of the 'checks and balances' required in this constant inter-play. But even if and when these constitutions are abolished, the inter-play cannot be abolished with them. The pluralistic 'bargains' continue, thus affecting and curbing the main decision-making processes.

On the other hand, to speak of 'groups' and 'interest groups' in the context of the communist societies, seems to be a novel and still controversial matter. Many authors have indeed simultaneously started to include the concept of interest groups in sovietological research but with different meanings and approaches. One must sympathize with the attempt made by H.G.Skilling,[3] who himself, as previously noted, uses for these studies the modern tools of political sociology, to bring some methodological order into this problem. The attempt however has not fully succeeded. On the Western side authors like T.H.H.Rigby, John Armstrong, N.Ehrmann, F.Barghoorn, R.Pethybridge, Z. Brzezinski, V.Aspaturian and R.Conquest,[4] and on the Eastern side authors like the Yugoslav J.Djordjević and the Czech M.Lakatos are given the credit for having pioneered this new approach. But as in homoeopathic treatments, in these analyses the dosage and use of the approach can lead to three different results: it can either heal, or be inconclusive, or do harm. Among those who try to define, and therefore to analyse in depth, the different categories of interest groups we can distinguish the following: Rigby's main division between sectors of the bureaucracy, informal groupings of officials, areas and occupational groups, etc.; Huntington and Brzezinski's categories of social forces (peasants,

---

[3] 'Interest groups and communist politics' in *World Politics*, April 1966.

[4] John Armstrong: *The Soviet Bureaucratic Élite*, New York, 1959; N. Ehrmann (ed): *Interest Groups on Four Continents*; V.Aspaturian in Macridis (ed): *Foreign Policy in World Politics*; R.Conquest: *Power and Policy in the USSR*; T.H.H.Rigby: loc. cit. and article in *Problems of Communism*, XII, 1963; Brzezinski and Huntington: *Political Power USA/USSR*, New York, 1963, and Brzezinski: article in *Problems of Communism*, I, 1966; R.Pethybridge: *A Key to Soviet Politics*, London, 1962, and F.Barghoorn in Pye and Verba (eds): *Political Culture and Political Development*, Princeton, 1965.

workers, etc.), specific interest groups (intellectuals, scientists or minorities), and policy groups (the military, heavy and light-industry managers, agricultural managers and state bureaucrats); Pethybridge's two major groups (the party apparatus and the government bureaucracy), and two minor (the economic élites and the army); J. Djordjević's distinction between those who (*a*) participate directly in the process of governing, (*b*) hold 'strategic' positions in the political system, and (*c*) represent the special interests of citizens.

Another classification of the pluralistic forces in the communist states of Eastern Europe will be useful for this work in particular and for political theory in general. This classification has three main categories, according to the extent to which these forces can 'check' the party (the main apparat):

(*a*) the other apparats
(*b*) the social-economic classes and groups, and
(*c*) the legislative and judiciary organs, the media of information, and the cultural organizations.

(*a*) In communist countries the party apparat succeeds in obtaining and maintaining more or less constantly the upper hand over the other apparats and becomes thus the main apparat. But the other apparats, which can exercise a direct power of coercion (and in some cases deliver a proportionate amount of striking power), are animated by their own *esprit de corps*. They are, to some extent, the administrative rivals of the main apparat. Besides, in the realm of the apparats, the controls over the party are institutionalised and encouraged by the communist constitutions and statutes. (The setting-up in the USSR in 1962 of the Committee of Party and State Control was a further proof of the need for the institutionalization of checks within the Apparat itself.)

The following apparats, with which the party has to maintain a close collaboration check on some aspects of its activity: *the Army, the Security Police, the Trade Unions*, and *the State* and *Local administration*.

(*b*) With more diffuse means and without, in most cases, a direct power of coercion or striking power, but with massive means of 'bargaining' as producers, the social-economic classes and interest groups also exercise strong checks on the decision-making power of the party. Thus *the peasants*, especially in the more backward countries can, when pushed to the extreme, refuse to deliver the goods and strike or indeed sabotage collectively. They can thus endanger the functioning of the state and the cohesion of the society. The two most advanced communist parties in Eastern Europe, the Yugoslav and the Polish, gave up on this account, their intention to collectivize. The agricultural producers' unions and associations formed now in most countries as 'transmission belts' might work in the direction shown by the party; but they might work also in the opposite direction. The *workers*, here regarded separately from the apparat of the trade unions, can strike spontaneously, or deliberately slow down and harm production. The workers are the privileged political class. This is why they were the first to act as they did in Berlin in 1953 and in Poznan in 1956. On the other hand, their claim for a direct participation in industrial management remains the main bone of contention in the dictatorship of the proletariat and perpetuates over half a century the 'workers opposition'. Finally, in all the European communist states, the 'élites' or the *intelligentsia* formed by all the experts in responsible posts in the apparats or in production, from managers to foremen, control, directly and indirectly, the party's decision-making.

(*c*) The constitutional and cultural bodies are, in a sense, relics of the pre-revolutionary representative regimes. The party believes that it can manoeuvre them from behind. Yet they can and do develop an institutional consciousness of their own, if and when they can begin to act more independently. Thus the *courts* and the entire *judiciary* can, when they succeed, after a shorter or longer time, in emancipating themselves from total obedience to the revolutionary party, recover some of their institutional 'power'. The *Parliaments* or *National Assemblies*, which in Stalinist conditions met seldom and only to approve hurriedly of measures already taken by the party and government, become naturally, as institutionalization progresses, functional centres of debate. This fundamental question will be discussed at greater length in the final section of Part Three, on the 'manifestation of dissent'. The *Federal organs* exert a powerful influence on decentralization, which is a secondary process of pluralization, and maintain natural reservations against the central administration from which they demand a larger participation in the decision-making processes. The *Press* and all other media of information, infiltrated and controlled from within and without as they are, develop at some time their own professional, if not institutional, mentality and strive to exercise a more independent influence. The *Churches*, the *Universities* and other cultural organizations are, as will be seen in the later discussion of 'Dissent', the main centres of articulation of public opinion.

Now, a word about 'checks'. 'Interest groups' are like rocks under the water: less visible under the high tide of terror and in full view at the low tides of calm, they are nevertheless always there. They have to be reckoned with in any circumstances because in any circumstances they exercise a certain amount of pressure and, to continue the metaphor, must be negotiated by the state vessel. The negotiation becomes more lucid and articulate when a regime, losing its initial revolutionary impetus, is faced with the current business of running the state and its enterprises with efficiency. The negotiations are necessary because the interest groups can help or hinder all state activities by their own action. Authors like the American Löwenstein, the French Burdeau, the German Dahrendorf and the Canadian Bergeron[5] do not hesitate to describe this action of the other 'interest groups' exercised upon the power-holders as *controls*. In so far, however as the expression control, both in usual political terminology, and even more so in communist terminology conveys, to most people, the idea of the supervision by the power-holders (by the party and the Apparat) of all other activities, it seems more advisable to use in this work the expression *checks* (in preference also to counter-checks, restraint of power, and many other expressions).

But 'checks' means something quite different from an organized struggle for power between organized bodies within the body politic. Neither the secondary apparats, nor the other 'interest groups' are homogeneous enough to project a completely clear consciousness of their ultimate political potential strength and of their ultimate political aims. This is where the party, in the party-states, and the army, in the army-states, benefit from their acknowledged supremacy and 'mission'. The main apparat, party or army, is strengthened by the legitimate ideology and

[5] Karl Löwenstein: *Political Power and the Governmental Process*, Chicago, 1957; Georges Burdeau: *Traité de Science Politique*, Tome VII, Paris, Soufflot, 1957; Gerard Bergeron: *Fonctionnement de l'État*, Paris, Collins, 1965. This latter work is by far the most important from this point of view, as it elaborates an entire theory of the controls within the functioning of any state (pp. 35–86).

by the constant flow of propaganda and indoctrination which gives to its sometimes fictitious power an almost mystical authority (as for instance, in the case of the Soviet Party under Stalin's personal control and that of the political police). But the other, secondary, apparats have to acknowledge this authority, are imbued with its catechistic articles of faith and loyalty, and are made to feel that their own aggregation around some ideology of their own would be tantamount to factionalism and, ultimately, treason. And the main apparat, because it provides the leaders for the entire Apparat and the state and because it has an effective right to control the others and to appoint persons of its choice to their key-positions, renders their homogeneity and self-reliance even more precarious.

To associate, therefore, as do some sovietologists[6] the names of party leaders with some of these 'interest groups' is to build a too detailed speculation on an initially insecure basis. The struggle at the top, between leaders who favour one or another policy indirectly beneficial to some and harmful to other interest groups, is unknown to the public until it flares up in some stormy drama and unexpected aftermath. In these stormy dramas the leaders of other apparats, but especially of those two apparats able by their own organization and strike-force to make or unmake a coup (the army, the political police and in some cases the trade unions) can and do play a part, and can try to make the balance tip in their favour. But this is still a struggle at the rarefied top, between leaders of the Apparat who at that height are ultimately interchangeable. This struggle is waged without the active participation or indeed encouragement of their 'interest-group' which may or may not be called upon by them to execute the moves required. Again, some of the secondary apparats do indeed sometimes gain a consciousness and *esprit de corps* on behalf of their own rights and the part they play, or should play, in the policy making of the state. But this is usually achieved by small internal groups formed by younger members of the *corps* or organization who are further from the struggles at the top than the institutional leaders of these secondary apparats.[7]

[6] As for instance Brzezinski, in an article in *Problems of Communism*, I, 1966.
[7] See from this point of view a useful distinction between the 'colonels' and the 'generals' made by Hans Daalder in his *The Role of Military in the Emerging Countries*, The Hague, 1962.

To speak of checks means that as long as the party requires goods and services in order to attain greater efficiency in its economy and administration it has to obtain them from the other interest groups by way of 'bargains' and compromises in the decision-making process. After all 'checks', in plain as well as in political language, means the action of control which can be exercised in the course of an operation by those whose influence is implicit in their participation in or withdrawal from it (and for that matter control itself, coming from the French *contre-rolle* meant originally institutionalized audit). To speak of plural checks means therefore to acknowledge this inexorable division of labour, which is usually ignored in the communist studies of society because of the heavy stress laid on the ubiquity and omnipotence of the party.[8]

Finally, on account of the two basic differences between Soviet Russia and the European communist states, which were already alluded to in a previous section, it must be accepted that the resilience of the 'interest groups' was and is stronger in their societies than in Russian society. The fact that she extends over an enormous bi-continental territory, with exceptionally vast resources of raw material and man-power, helps Russia to 'mobilize' them successfully and endlessly for the programmes and plans which happen to be pursued by a communist party. But, for

[8] Perhaps from this point of view Barghoorn's (loc. cit.) formulation comes nearest to the processes envisaged here when he says: 'The party subjects pluralistic structures and aspirations to the organizational and communications pressures for homogeneization, standardization and centralization of which it displays such a formidable array. The problem of pluralism confronted by the party has two main aspects. It must cope with the survivals of attitudes and customs also associated with the largely pre-scientific, and pre-industrial, traditional society upon which the CPSU since it seized power in 1917 has been straining to impose its harsh but dynamic ethos of "progress" . . . Profound changes could result from pressure generated by a combination of the leaders' needs for efficiency and the interests of various functional groups. . . . The party apparatus, headed by Khrushchev, had successfully demonstrated its ability at least for the present, to combine a degree of satisfaction of the professional interests of the managerial and military elites with maintenance of party control over these groups and the co-ordination of their activities with goals and policies formulated by the party leadership.' One should add to this sober and balanced formulation the fact that the party too, in some European communist states more than in others, but in all of them more than in the Soviet Union, has begun to accept that it must delegate more of its power of control and decision-making and shows signs of becoming what Aspaturian describes as 'a conglomeration of interests' and an 'arena', and of changing into a broader, looser and more pragmatic organization.

instance, the existence of virgin lands in Soviet Russia which when brought into cultivation could at once increase the total output of grains had very little to do with the policy of collectivization; and the mobilization of enormous contingents of cheap or unpaid labour under any conditions and in any quantities, which have proved a considerable asset for the success of industrialization, had very little to do with the 'dictatorship of the proletariat'. In both cases the ideological pretences not only were not the cause, but were a positive brake on the advantages offered by the under-developed resources of such a vast country and population. A pragmatic dictatorship, indeed any kind of non-ideological state-capitalism, would perhaps have made better use of them.

Also, on the political plane, the aggregation and articulation of the 'interest groups' were much less advanced in Russia in 1917 than those of their opposite numbers in Eastern Europe in 1944. Moreover, when the communist parties were brought to power in Eastern Europe they had far more limited resources for the endowment of their economic 'plans' in proportion to their territories and populations. As for their political programmes they had to reckon with the fact that in those societies the 'interest groups' could neither be dissolved by terror, nor placated by the replacement by some 'legality' even if socialist, and by some 'democracy' even if non-representative, as was the case in a Russia emerging from the arbitrary imperial regime. They had known better times, better institutions and better organization. The communist parties of Eastern Europe learned therefore much more quickly to recognize the different pluralisms of their societies. Soon, too, and as the history of their twenty odd years of existence shows, the sooner the better for each individual country, they had to alter the Stalinist vision of one-way 'transmission belts' by accepting the reality of some two-way checks.

I. CHECKS BY OTHER APPARATS

The party and the army

The relationship in communist states, or conversely in army-states, between these two organizations is one of the most studied. Practically all the detailed studies of the government and politics of the Soviet Union include a discussion of these relations, often with the avowed object of examining the political rivalries which they show or conceal;[9] and, vice-versa, most treatises on the political role and ambitions of the army include separate examinations of the situation in the USSR or other communist states.[10] As far as this work is concerned, too, some attention has already been given to the 'inherent' relations between the two political-military and military-political organisms. The object of this particular section is to analyse the relations between the party, as the main apparat, and the army, as one of the most important of the secondary ones in, respectively, the USSR, Yugoslavia, and the other European communist states.

The three different regimes have two common characteristics relevant to this point. First, the watch which the Communist Party, as the guardian of the revolution, has kept on the army as its 'inherent' challenger, has proved more successful than in *all* other non-communist one-party states, or indeed in some multi-party states. Secondly, in the more developed of these states the armed forces are part of the 'military-industrial' complex whose influence, as in any other political societies, leans towards conservatism and centralization.

'Praetorianism', 'Bonapartism' or 'Thermidor' were, ever since Engels,[11] denounced by the architects of the communist revolution and state, as the greatest danger to their future and integrity. The new, Russian, revolution saw itself resuming dialectically, and therefore phylogenetically, the interrupted course of the eighteenth-century French Revolution, a century and a continent away. Lenin's generation, especially, was obsessed with the analogy. The communist doctrinaires had their eyes fixed upon that particular branch of the state which handled arms and had as strong an internal discipline and sense of hierarchy as their party itself. The communist political leaders were constantly weighing the possible inroads which could be made into the affairs of the revolutionary state by these internal friend-foes. In all three areas their supervision of and watch over the army is

[9] See for instance the respective chapters in Schapiro (loc. cit), Fainsod (loc. cit.) and Pethybridge (loc. cit.).

[10] See: Finer (loc. cit.), Andrzejewski (loc. cit.) and Huntington (ed.) (loc. cit.).

[11] 'The Armies of Europe' (1855) quoted by David C. Rapaport: 'A comparative theory of military and political types', in Huntington (ed.) *Changing Patterns of Military Politics* (loc. cit.).

one of the operations which they carried out most successfully – each in their different ways.

In the Soviet Union the jealousy between the party and the army had, ever since the beginning, political-ideological undertones. In history it so happened that the Red Army was sooner on its feet as a complete organization, with greater contingents and importance in the state life, than the party itself. The fight for the defence of the Republic against the Germans and the Poles, and afterwards against the White Armies, was for the first four years so imperious that attention was first given by Lenin and by the other political leaders to the raising and organization of the forces needed for defence.

The appointment of Trotsky in March 1918 as the People's Commissar for War set in motion three different trends. In June came the first 'mobilization' ever undertaken by the Soviet government (by 1920 the Red Army counted 5,500,000 men). Then came the recruitment of officers, or in other words of technicians of war, and then the compromise proposed by Trotsky, and accepted by Lenin against the prejudices of most of the leaders of the party, to employ and trust former officers of the Tsarist Army. It was then that Shaposhnikov, Svechin and Tukhachevsky, all of them former Tsarist officers, were appointed to high posts of command. But at the same time some former NCO's like Voroshilov, Budenny and Blücher were appointed, as were also members of the top leadership of the party like Trotsky himself, Frunze, Timoshenko and Stalin. Thus the leadership of the Soviet army was initially formed from these three different groups.

Finally Trotsky's appointment did not start but helped to exacerbate the feud between Stalin and Trotsky which was to be carried to its ultimate and bitter end. As the organization of the Red Army had then a temporary priority and that of the party was somewhat underplayed, Stalin as a party organizer was overshadowed by Trotsky, who made a great impression by his organizational skill in building up the army. Many of Trotsky's short-cuts and impulses were afterwards followed or copied by Stalin when he came to undertake the social-economic 'mobilization'. But during the period in which he served in the army, Stalin was one of the ardent advocates of army control by the party and by the security police, and it was he who installed the *politruks* and *zampolits* in the army. He was always also suspicious that the army might become, under Trotsky, a stronger Apparat than anything else in the state. He saw to it that Trotsky's proposal in 1920 to transform the Red Army into a militia should be rejected, as it was in 1921. Before his open fight with Trotsky he first made sure that Trotsky would be relieved of his army command, that one of his own friends, Voroshilov, would replace him there and that, after Frunze's death in 1924 other Stalinists would get the top jobs; and finally that the Moscow garrison, faithful to Trotsky, could not act in the decisive moments. Later on, in 1936, he began his purges by having Tukhachevsky, who had been initially appointed by Trotsky, executed as a traitor.

The man who, after Lenin's death in 1924, was to start the re-modelling of revolutionary Russia into the great Apparat-state which it is now, had particular reason therefore to fear the army. This fear combined with the general suspicions entertained by the party and the leaders of the revolution against potential Bonapartes, helped to strengthen the Bolshevik Party's resolution to do its utmost to put and keep the army under its control. This it achieved by the institutional, political and security controls in the army at all levels; by the indoctrination and education of the officers and NCO's; and by the fact, that through the nomenklatura, it controlled from above and outside all appointments and changes in the upper ranks. But S. Finer is right in suggesting that the communist 'party control' of the army is not original. If by party control, he argues, is meant 'the authority to whom the military owe allegiance' then why not speak in the case of other armies (as in Persia or in the pre-war Balkan countries) of Royal control? And if by party control is meant the infiltration and purges of the army by a jealous political leadership, that again was and is practised by other parties than the communist and by other dictators, without parties. Perhaps Finer's argument could be better illustrated in the case of the Soviet Union by the fact that the party itself, under Stalin, was controlled by Stalin himself and by the political police; thus its control over the army was to some extent a façade for other controls. Ever since its inception the Soviet Army has been subjected to the controls of both the party and the police, which amounted ever since its formation to a direct and an indirect control by the KGB.

In fact the army suffered more directly from the persecution of the OGPU-KGB than from that of the party (which, in any case, was also victimized under Stalin by the same persecutors). The purges of the army after the end of the civil war, before the Second World War, in 1937, and immediately after it, in 1945, were all carried out, if not at the exclusive instigation, at any rate under the influence of the political police. When the army sided in a more detectable way with Stalin's other successors against Beria, in 1953, it also put forward its demand for the subordination of the entire political police and for the dismantling and absorption of its formidable apparat; and a representative of the army, Zhukov, took Beria's seat. What part the security police played by means of its renewed, though more subtle, influence on the leadership through Brezhnev, in the subsequent demotion of Zhukov and in the new supervision of the army by the party since 1956 is only now beginning to be studied. So too, is the even more interesting crisis of 1963, in which Khrushchev lost his leadership and the military leaders backed his successors.[12]

But when one comes back to the main checks which the army does exercise over the party's decisions in the Soviet Union, its greatest impact on the economic plans appears to be exercised through the influence of what can be described in the communist society as the military-industrial complex, the alliance of interests of the top representatives of heavy industry and of the armed forces (in these cases backed also by those of the security police and of the central state administration). The military-industrial complex stands for the continuation of the priority given to heavy industry for further centralization, for rapid technological advance, and for the orientation of the budgets, and what is more of the plan, to these ends. On the foreign policy plane it stands for the maintenance of bases and the intensification of defence on the Eastern and Western frontiers, in the latter case by means of the Warsaw Pact armies. On the internal political plane it stands for a pragmatic conservatism. These constant attitudes 'check' the ultimate policies, in periods of stability, by means of the influence and pressures brought to bear in the processes of consultation and approval; in periods of crisis these attitudes express themselves in the sudden choice which the representatives of the armed forces have to make between the divided leaders of the

[12] See a penetrating study on this very episode by Roman Kalkowicz in Osteuropa, 10/66: *Die position der Sovjetarmee vor und nach dem Sturz Chruscht-chews.*

Apparat, opposed on some crucial issues. (This is where the 1956 and 1963 crises are so worth study.) The solution of these crises will depend sometimes on the ultimate reaction of the two apparats which can use their inherent striking force one way or another.

The history of the army under the communist regime in Yugoslavia differs from that of the Red Army. As has been mentioned before, the party, transformed into the Partisan-Army, fought a national rather than a civil war (in contrast to the fight in Russia against the White Armies), was then retransformed into the Party-League, and continued in the same close relations with this other embodiment of itself. The head of the party and of the state remained always the head of the army, Marshal Tito. Generally speaking it is more difficult in Yugoslavia to observe the differentiations within the Apparat. This happens because of the common origins and leadership of the party, army and police and because of the almost instinctive orientation of the Yugoslav party toward its own broadening and absorption in wider organisms. Recently (as will be seen in the following section) the Yugoslav government and party acted against the security police, accused of conspiring against and violating the constitutional order. This had profound political undertones because Ranković, the head of the police was also the leader of a powerful faction of the party.

Finally, it must be noted that whereas the Apparat in Yugoslavia was more organically linked together than in any other communist country, the administration of the country itself is more, and more genuinely, decentralized than in any other communist country. Moreover the army has, because of this, one supplementary importance in Yugoslavia. Not only is it, like the police, one of the few nation-wide apparats, cutting across the federal institutions and divisions. (But at the beginning of 1967 the army too was submitted to more regional decentralization.) It is also an organ and a symbol of national unity. In a state where the main, obsessive fear is that of national disintegration (because of the centrifugal tendencies of some of the other national groups, which resent the Serbian rule for ethnic, religious and economic reasons), the army as a central organism assumes also the role of guardian of the national unity and integrity. In its relations with the party, the Yugoslav army has not until now shown any tendency to play an independent role, or to take sides in the involved ideological (social and economic) debate on alternative policies. But it has, and will have an important say in all matters in which the differences of attitudes or the clashes of views, as often happens in Yugoslav politics, touch on the sensitive question of national unity and sovereignty, and thence on the danger of secessions.

In the other communist countries of Eastern Europe the history of the respective armies and their subsequent relations with the party were of yet a third, different nature. In all of them the former national armies were purged almost completely of their former officer corps, and the traditional link between the army and the peasantry through the peasant-recruit was weakened by the fact that conscription was, in the first years, less massive and the national appeal in it underplayed. But this purge was not carried out, as in Yugoslavia, by the new national leadership. There the purge of the former officers of the Royal Army was ruthlessly carried out by the victorious partisans against the Chetniks; but this was a fight between Yugoslavs. In Soviet dominated Eastern Europe, it was carried out by the local communist parties under the direct supervision of the Soviet army and even more of the Soviet KGB.

The heavy hand of these proconsular organizations was felt by all the armies of the states comprised in the military zone of operation and the political orbit of the Soviet Union; but it lay even more heavily on the armies of Rumania, Hungary and Germany (afterwards the GDR), the former 'enemies'. The place of the professional native commanders was taken by what is called the 'political generals', leaders of the party, who like Trotsky and Stalin in 1920-4 were put in charge of the army. But, unlike them, the East European 'generals' were only obeying the instructions of the Soviet army and the KGB. The former asked them to contribute at great speed to the logistic articulation of the Soviet military network in Europe; the latter ruthlessly pursued the infiltration with Soviet agents of the leadership of the new armies of the new states. The conflict and differences were so obvious and the gap between the image of a 'national' army and the reality of the 'subjugated' army so great that in most cases, best exemplified by the appointment of a Soviet Marshal, Rokosovsky, as the head of the Polish army, the positions of leadership were given to men who by their direct allegiance to the Soviet army or police, were most trusted by these two organizations. The function of the respective national army and security police as apparats within the national apparat was, under Stalin, to implement the instructions of the apparats of the foreign power, even in cases in which the main (party) apparat might fail or indeed refuse to execute them.

This unnatural situation could not last for ever, especially in the less terroristic situation which prevailed after Stalin's death. This was seen at once in the cleavages which took place rapidly in the Polish army between 1955–6, dramatically in the Hungarian army in the very weeks of the October–November 1956 upheaval; and more slowly but steadily in the Rumanian army between 1957 and 1958, when, in August of that year the Russian troops left the country. These armies, whose leadership was initially directly controlled by a foreign power, and which were composed of indifferent if not hostile troops, suffered two changes. The first was the appearance of a new generation of officers. They were, to be sure, trained in the special military schools organized and controlled by the party and by Soviet instructors. But they were natives of the respective countries and soon showed a greater spirit of independence and indeed nationalism. The second was the signature, in May 1955, of the Warsaw Pact. With this, some new forms of *regional* organization seemed to replace the formerly direct, *bilateral*, subordination to the Soviet army.

When therefore, after Stalin's death, the political struggle started between the *Muscovites* and the *natives* in some of the East European parties, the pressure put on the army (directly on the officers by the leaders of the nationalist wing, and indirectly on the troops, by the population) produced an inevitable cleavage. Those who were going to remain faithful to their, as it were, vertical and 'internationalist' allegiance to the foreign Apparats, were separated from those who preferred to accept a community of interest with the, as it were, newly self-asserted national Apparats. In Poland, during the long political crisis in which intermediaries from within the still divided party tried to find some compromise between Gomulka, under house arrest, and the CPSU, the internal cleavage in the army was also taking place. So rapidly did it happen that in the week of 18 October 1956 when the Russians wanted Rokosovsky, with Soviet tanks, to occupy Warsaw, the

Russian Marshal found that he had been entirely cut off, and placed in a position where he could not act.

In Hungary the cleavage was even more rapid. There the very officers who were sent to put down the growing rebellion in the first weeks of October, like Pal Maleter,[13] became at the end of the month the spokesmen and leaders of the Hungarian army. On its behalf they supported the demands of the population for the withdrawal of the Soviet army and for the exit of Hungary from the Warsaw Pact. In Rumania the more cautious Gheorghiu-Dej undertook, from within and by shrewder means, the purge of loyal Soviet agents from the army command. He did so by winning over or neutralizing some of the political generals, headed by Bodnaras, who had been the direct agents of the Soviet army and the KGB in the reorganization of the Rumanian army. When in August 1958 the Soviet army withdrew from Rumania and its formal link with the Russian administration was thus severed, the leadership of the Rumanian Workers Party felt confident that they could reckon, to a certain extent, on the new leadership of the army, especially in the crisis when its services would be needed and its national loyalty tested. Further show-downs, on nationalistic grounds, economic or otherwise, were to come in the relations between the Rumanian leadership and that of the Soviet Union.

'To a certain extent' remains however the measure of the trust which the party in any of these countries, and especially in East Germany and Hungary, can have in the leadership of the army. The split within the army did not entirely disappear. Some generals still resent the treatment to which they were submitted; and some others have their doubts about the wisdom of possible further estrangements from collaboration with the Soviet Union. This, combined with the fact that from a political point of view the army leaderships in all these countries are, like that of the Soviet or of the Yugoslav armies, on the side of the conservative 'military-industrial complex', renders it likely that in some situations the leading groups of the military might choose to oppose further internal reforms or loosening of the bloc. On the other hand, the main bulk of the armies, young officers and troops alike, are under the influence of strong nationalist ideas and slogans. They form one of the sizeable groups spreading the new

[13] See an excellent 'memoir': *General Maleter*, by Peter Gozstony, in *Problems of Communism*, March/April 1966.

nationalistic ideology which replaces the former Marxist-Leninist indoctrination in Poland, Hungary and especially Rumania.

The party and the political police

Here, again, the different backgrounds of the USSR, Yugoslavia and the other communist European countries lead to different patterns in the relations between these two apparats. In the USSR and in Yugoslavia, where the security police is not subordinated to foreign controls, it acts in the same way as any such organism in any state. Since its emergence as an administrative organ in modern times (in the Hapsburg Empire and in post-revolutionary and especially Napoleonic France at the threshold of the nineteenth century),[14] the political police has shown a tendency to expand. Its power grows proportionately with the authoritarianism of the regime. It develops three professional, functional malformations. They were, all three of them, lucidly described by two of the first founders of such an apparat, Fouché and Gisquet.

The first is to believe that it has a double mission, namely 'to uncover and to dissolve coalitions and legal opposition to the established authority as well as the murky plots of royalists and foreign agents'. The second is to believe that the police is 'the regulating power which is felt everywhere, without ever being seen and which, at the centre of the state, strikes us by its regulating power although we are unable to divine the cause. Every branch of the administration has a part which subordinates it to the police.'[15] The third characteristic of the evolution of the police appears after it has acquired greater power under a personal dictator, and during a harsher dictatorial period; it then expands beyond the initial sphere of action of political information and projects its own theory of society, and of how society should be ruled. In such a case the police acts on the theory that its first duty is 'to study society, and its state of mind, in order to find out where lies the danger and *in what class* are to be found the enemies'. As Lévy points out, when he quotes these extraordinary remarks of Gisquet, a French Minister of Police in the early nineteenth century, this conception of the persecution of classes and groups of the society on account of their political unreliability, or hostility,

---

[14] See on this subject: Yves Lévy: 'Police and Policy' in *Government and Opposition*, vol. I, no. 4, 1966.
[15] Both these texts by Fouché, quotation from Lévy, loc. cit.

can lead to the extremist twentieth century totalitarian theories of the persecution, or extermination, either of all the Jews or of the entire bourgeoisie, the Kulaks etc.

Thus the political police, which in a pluralistic-constitutional state is subjected to careful public scrutiny, in oppositionless apparat-states finds, like bacilli which become particularly virulent and pernicious in some media, the best conditions for the development of its worst and most deep-seated tendencies. On account of its self-assumed mission to neutralize opposition it pushes the power holders to the systematic banning and persecution of opposition, political first and then social. On account of the need for a strong political-administrative centre it demands that all other branches of the administration should be submitted to its control. It also infiltrates them, from above and at all levels by concealed means and by mercenaries, who, because of their very professional purposes but also because of the traditional contempt with which decent people treat those who are paid to spy on them, prefer to hide their power and even identity. And, finally, because of these two specific functions, the political police, after a time, elaborates its own 'ideology'. This projects a system of government, whereby all individuals, groups or classes in the society are suspected of being 'enemies' of the people (or revolution, republic, state or constitution) and therefore must be kept under organized, permanent and ubiquitous control. The German Gestapo and the Russian KGB were the superlative embodiments of this conception. But they were also the natural outcome of the growth of the political police when and if it is allowed to grow thus far. The origins of the totalitarian state are to be found in the police-states. But whereas a police-state is, since the nineteenth century, any state in which all political opposition is crushed by an organization especially set up to achieve this particular goal, in the totalitarian state this is aggravated by the clumsy attempts of the police personnel, with police conceptions and methods, to run the entire state-machine, thus transforming it into endless labour camps, brigades of inmate-citizens and barracks of mass education.

Of all apparats the one to which the party-apparat is the most vulnerable, and by which it has always been defeated in periods of real terror and personal dictatorship, is the political police apparat. This has been shown both in Hitler's Germany and

Stalin's Russia. Unlike the army, which as has been seen, is constantly suspected of the 'inherent' sin of Bonapartism, the political police fastens like a limpet on to the very body of the 'monolithic' party, from the day it achieves power. Its methods of checking, in other words its actual *checks* on the party, are so perversely moulded on the expanding Apparat and its state, that it is difficult to distinguish between them and to know, at times, which is in command of the other, which *controls*, and which *checks* on, the other. But whenever conditions are advantageous, the political police, as an indispensable apparat of an opposition-less state, will cut out the party and put it under its command. Whereas whenever the party, as a self conscious body and as the acknowledged main apparat, is able to assert its power, one of the first symptoms will be the subordination of the political police and its relegation to the more modest position which it should occupy in a more balanced state. But here again the distinction must be drawn between Apparat-states, such as the USSR and Yugoslavia, where the intricate political controls and checks originate exclusively in internal national developments, and the other European communist states where such developments are conditioned by the external apparats of the suzerain foreign power.[16] Two pairs of cases from each of these two differently situated states will be taken to show how in apparently similar situations the ultimate outcome and meaning comes to be different.

In the USSR, as it is commonly known (and certain aspects of this problem were touched upon in preceding chapters), under Stalin, that is ever since the full-fledged appearance of the Apparat-state, it was impossible to disentangle the façade-party from the real power-holding political police, so mixed were they together under the dominant personality of the dictator himself. But, after his death, and indeed even at the end of his rule, the party was inspired by a clearer idea of its own rights and needs and was prepared, with the backing of leaders of the army, for the show-down with the hidden usurper. Lavrenti Beria had been since 1938 in command of the formidable machine, which had

[16] See a good description in Z. K. Brzezinski: *The Soviet Bloc*, New York, 1961, of the subordination by the Russian MVD of the Polish, Hungarian and East German Security Police which reported only occasionally to their respective Politburos.

reached its apogee of power between 1947 and 1953. It had then transformed the entire Soviet Empire, Russia and her satellites alike, into vast barracks and labour camps. Beria was to be held personally responsible for this, and for the 25 years of humiliation of the party by his own apparat. The struggle between the two Apparats, with the army intervening, reached its climax in 1953, and ended with Beria's execution and the public condemnation and demotion of the police-apparat. (But before that it reverberated in strange ways upon the Apparats of the European communist countries, at the time still under the full guidance and control of the proconsular Soviet apparats.) With the successive deaths of Stalin and Beria the party reached for the first time a real power, equal to its statutory one, without precedent in its history. This was the moment of the granting by Khrushchev of a statute to the party, comparable in Russian history to the moment when the Empress Catherine II granted to the nobility the statutory rank and rights unknown under previous Tsars. So powerful, in reality, were these rights that ten years later the Apparat of the Soviet Union, under the leadership of the party, thus restored and self assertive, succeeded for the first time in sacking its leader. Khrushchev fell in 1963 under the cold verdict of a body he had helped to emancipate.

The crisis in Yugoslavia in June 1966 seemed, for all intents and purposes, to be almost the repetition of the June 1953 Soviet crisis. But the difference was that the personal leader himself, Tito, took the decision to denounce publicly the 'inherent' power-appetite of the political police, to demote its leader, his old comrade-in-arms, Ranković, and to proceed to the razing of its overgrown structures. Indeed, in the debate, made public, some speeches by Tito and by some other leaders, including Ranković himself, spelt out most of the philosophy of the dangers for any society, and especially for a non-opposition communist state, of letting the political police acquire too much control of, and influence in, political life.

Thus Tito: 'We have made the mistake of having left our state security to fend for itself during the past twenty or more years of its existence. . . . Can any organization be left without the control of the party? . . . We must start with the fact that our security service has played an enormous role both during the war and after. . . . But have we the right to forgive what has been happening since, when such an organization becomes deformed and when owing to various malformations a system is created which weighs upon our whole society? The important thing is the recovery of our party by the separation of internal security from the party, instead of as hitherto, the confusion of the two, with the latter straddled by the former.'

Or the report of the special commission of the CC of the YLC: 'state security, created from the struggle against foreign intelligence services and against the activities of the class enemy, has gradually tried to expand its sphere of activities. Certain organs of state security, proceeding from the concept of control of the entire social service by the state security service, have created an extensive network of their collaborators in works, organizations, even in the Yugoslav League of Communists. This network has very frequently infiltrated itself into the entire work of the enterprises, even as far as investments and the cadre policy.' Or Ranković: 'The state security service was really a useful organization, but precisely because of such methods and errors the distortions should be pointed out so that this service will be brought into harmony with our social development and with the needs of this society. The distortions of the service cannot be defended.'[17] Such examples illustrate convincingly the abstract theory of the separation of the apparats and of the supervision of the security police as the perennial power-seeking apparat. Moreover, immediately afterwards there followed a thorough purge of the leadership of the apparat of the security police, giving the impression to the onlooker that, indeed, from top to bottom that entire apparat was being changed and decontaminated.

But in the political circumstances prevailing in Yugoslavia in 1966, of which more will be said in subsequent chapters, the abstract theory of the police-apparat, and of the relations between it and the party, concealed political phenomena more involved than these structural-functional aspects. What was at stake was actually the issue of the future policy to be adopted by Tito, or by Tito's successors. The Serbian centralistic wing of the League, under Ranković, and the decentralizing liberalistic wing under the Slovene, Kardelj and the leaders of the other republics, were in constant opposition. Another set of quotations confirms this deeper theme, which was muffled under the abstract theoretical discussion.

[17] All quotations from *Borba*, 2–3 July 1966.

Thus, characteristically,[18] the main attack on these lines was launched by the leader of the trade unions, Vukmanović, who said bluntly that 'the deformities in the security service were due to factionalist currents within the party itself, and namely the factionalist current which favours the administrative methods of management, and an etatist system of economic activity and management'. Vukmanović also denounced Ranković's double position as 'the organizer of the state security service and the party's organizational secretary'. 'For all intents and purposes,' he exclaimed, 'Ranković has the whole party in his hands.' Ranković himself in his defence played continuously on the same theme, in veiled and enigmatic terms: 'I would not like it to be understood that I have prepared our own programme. What programme could I put forward in our society and the League of Communists? What forces could come out with a political programme for the purpose of mobilizing the people for this programme under our present conditions?' And finally the report itself, overlooking somehow that it was referring to differences between two branches of the state, revealed in clear words the intra-party differences: 'There are forces in the League which openly advocate a policy of a firm hand, which are trying to establish power over the League and to rule through it. Such communists oppose the force of compulsion to the force of the working people organized in the system of self-management.'[19] Thus the clashes of political orientations and political ambitions within the Party League itself (which, as seen in Yugoslavia, forms an unusually broad and strongly welded apparat) were in reality the deeper causes of the crisis. This was shown afterwards by the fact that it was the League which was taken into consideration, and its role in a 'transformed society' re-examined.

In Apparat-states controlled by a foreign power the internal conflicts of views and struggles for power at the top of the foreign Apparat as a whole usually have immediate and contradictory repercussions upon the politics of the dominated countries. For example, the Soviet political police played an independent hand in the politics of East Germany and Hungary.

[18] See *infra*: 'Trade Unions and the Party'.
[19] Document adopted on reorganization and development of the League, as broadcast by Zagreb home service 1 July 1966, quoted in BBC Summary of World Broadcasts, 7 July 1966.

Even before Stalin's death, 'monolithic' Soviet Europe was faced with a drastic choice between alternative policies. The continuation of Stalin's cold, and even hot, Korean war, was wearying the populations, especially in the 'satellite' countries already subjected to great sacrifices and exploitation. On the other hand the possibility of starting a new policy, or 'course', based on external co-existence and internal decompression was fraught with obvious dangers and, in any case, was resisted from within by the Stalinists everywhere. Stalin's timely death rang in the 'new course'. Its philosophy was preached to the CPSU and to the East European parties by the duumvirate Malenkov-Khrushchev. Among the leaders most difficult to convince were the Hungarian Rakosi and the German Ulbricht.

In June 1953 the situation in East Germany deteriorated rapidly. One of the clearest symptoms was the contradiction between the permissiveness of the East German and Russian security police towards the discontented population, who like the workers in the Stalin-Allee had taken to the streets, and the dour inflexibility of the party leadership towards their claims. In reality what was happening was that Wilhelm Zaisser, the Minister of State Security, was challenging Ulbricht's leadership both from without the party, by allowing the public clamour against it to gather momentum, and from within, through his political proxy R. Herrnstadt, the editor of *Neues Deutschland*, with whom he hoped to replace Ulbricht, and who put forward, in these dramatic moments, the policies of the German *Neuen Kurses*. During the first two weeks of June 1953 the agitation, thus fanned, grew unmistakably into a national revolution; all sectors of the population followed the lead of the building-workers of the Stalin-Allee. It was stopped at the last moment by the direct intervention of Soviet tanks which were thus forced for the first time to fire on workers in rebellion outside Russia, while the German security and armed forces proved incapable of resisting the movement. After the revolt was crushed it was learned that Zaisser (and Fechner, the Minister of Justice, a former social democrat, and Herrnstadt) had been dismissed.[20]

Only on 10 July 1953, was it learnt that Beria, in Soviet Russia, had been arrested some two weeks earlier, that is in the week

[20] See a good account of the German crisis, and of its links with the Russian one, in Martin Jänicke: *Der Dritte Weg*, Köln, 1964.

following the events in Berlin. He was afterwards shot, and the mighty apparat which he and Stalin had built, crumbled under the blows of the party. The names of the two leaders of the security police in the two countries were afterwards linked in a formula: 'the Beria-Zaisser experiment'. Whether the attempt by the Russian policy-makers to 'experiment' against the party in power in one of the satellite states, as a means of hitting at the leadership of their own main apparat, the party in Moscow, can be attributed exclusively to the political police and to Beria or whether, as appears more likely it was undertaken also with the approval of at least Malenkov,[21] among the Soviet leaders (who afterwards fell himself from power in the Anti-Party purge of 1957), is a question for historians to investigate further. In any case, the incident provides a typical example of an imperial administration ordering one of the secondary apparats of the provincial administration to act against its main apparat.

Malenkov's name crops up also in the Hungarian crisis, another example of this kind of subordination of the individual East European apparats to the Russian central command. After Malenkov's and Khrushchev's talks with Rakosi in June 1953, when it became obvious that the old Stalinist would never try to apply the new course in Hungary, Imre Nagy was imposed as Prime Minister. Thus in July 1953 the Russian style duumvirate Prime-Minister-First Secretary was initiated in the Rakosi-Nagy combination. As Beria's name was coupled with Zaisser's, so Nagy's can be coupled with that of Malenkov.[22] Nagy was brought to power during Malenkov's premiership. He fell from power in February 1955 after Khrushchev, backed by the 'military-industrial' complex, had reasserted the 'Leninist' policy against the drifting 'new course'. Malenkov's fall almost immediately brought Nagy's downfall. After suffering two years of Rakosi's constant intrigues and sabotage, Nagy was dismissed in April 1955. (He refused to

---

[21] Jänicke, loc. cit., quotes a sentence from Ulbricht's speech at the Twenty-Second Congress of the CPSU in 1961 attacking the 'policy of capitulation of Beria and Malenkov and of the fraction Zaisser-Herrnstadt'.

[22] See for a general description on this very point my: *Breakdown of the Soviet Empire*, loc. cit., p. 70, and for a more detailed one Ferenc A. Vali: *Rift and Revolt in Hungary*, Harvard, 1961, who adds, for instance, the piquant episode of a 1954 meeting in Moscow when Malenkov had to admonish Nagy for the failure in Hungary of a policy for which, in February 1955, he was going to resign his premiership in Russia.

resign in the Malenkov way, as insistently suggested to him by Suslov, who had arrived especially from Moscow.)

Having thus returned to power and the premiership, Rakosi continually wavered between half measures of repression, and half measures of apologetic reform. In the centre of these hesitations there loomed the grave problem of the future of the AVO, formerly AVH, the political police. During Rakosi's first tenure of power, as in Stalin's Russia, the AVH had been the apparat which was in reality stronger than the party. It drew its strength both from the head of the Hungarian regime himself, and from the Soviet pro-consular administration. Indeed so close were its connections with the former that even Rakosi himself was not consulted on all the moves which the AVH made on Soviet orders.[23] The years 1949–53 saw the apogee of the Soviet-sponsored political police: leaders of the party like Kadar, Kallai, Donath were imprisoned and tortured, and Rajk was executed after a typical Soviet-purge trial. But it was precisely Rajk's case which boomeranged so terribly upon Rakosi and upon the AVO. The former was forced to recognize that the sentence against Rajk, and his death, were due to provocations of the police. Rajk's re-inhumation had an electric effect on the mounting revolutionary movement of the autumn of 1956.

After Rakosi's fall, on 18 July, the AVO still maintained its special links with the Soviet command. Soon after the first days of the upheaval, the army and even the Hungarian police collaborated with the insurgents; and the bulk of the party followed Nagy and his 'national line'. The only organization which, as an organization, remained constantly faithful to the Soviet command was the political police. It played a great part in the events sparking off the final revolution. Its provocateurs were planted in the crowds, and then some of its agents, panic-stricken or violently angry, shot at the demonstrators both in the provinces and in Budapest, in the big massacre of Parliament Square. As in East Germany, though, once the movement reached revolutionary dimensions, the local, Hungarian forces were incapable of fighting against it. Soviet tanks once again had to be called upon. The AVO became the principal target of the unleashed fury of the population. A couple of hundred of its agents were lynched, and 3,000 imprisoned. But of these many who were liberated, after the Soviet Army's interven-

[23] Vali, loc. cit., pp. 59–60 gives a good description of this.

tion, became again its most valuable auxiliaries in the ensuing repressions.

The party and the trade unions

If the army was the most carefully watched, and the security police the most pugnacious rival apparat of the party, the trade union apparat proved the easiest for the party to crush and to transform into one of its 'transmission belts'. This happened first in the Soviet Union, and afterwards in all European communist countries. This did not take place, however, without a long-fought struggle. The fight which started in the last decade of the nineteenth century between the workers and the intelligentsia of the socialist movement in opposition took its most acute form in the first years of the Bolshevik government, and reached its climax in the years 1920-1. After the Bolshevik Party had crushed the Workers' Opposition in 1921, it taught the Communist Parties which came to power in Eastern Europe how 'to put the lid', from the beginning, on the demands of the workers for direct participation in industrial management. But here again there were differences between the situation in Russia in 1917 and in Eastern Europe in 1944. The main differences sprang from the fact that in the intervening quarter of a century the working class of the East European countries had had time to build up effective and influential trade unions and thus acquired a strong professional consciousness and militancy. Moreover, in the light of the Bolshevik revolution and of its developments, they sensed that this kind of 'dictatorship of the proletariat' amounted, from their point of view, to state-capitalism. Thus in the most industrialized countries of Eastern Europe, Czechoslovakia, Poland and Hungary – and even in the most industrialized regions of less industrialized countries, Transylvania, Slovenia and Croatia – the trade unions remained mainly associated with the Socialist Parties. The inroads which the Communist Parties made on this association in periods of international crisis, when the patient parliamentary procedures of the Social-Democrats were too slow, did not materially alter the situation. This was so in spite of the fact that the Communist Parties recruited more members from the younger generation of the thirties which felt more directly the effects of the world economic crisis and of the appearance of fascism.

When the Communist Parties in 1944, and after, had therefore to curb these stronger trade unions, they had to carry out two distinct operations. They had to impose on the trade unions themselves a new leadership, controlled and manned by the Communist Party. Instead of acting as the representative organ of the workers in order to obtain fairer conditions from the government for the workers, the leadership would then on the contrary, act as an efficient means of government pressure on the workers for higher productivity. And they also had to neutralize the Social Democrat Party through the usual twin procedures of banning, arresting and persecuting the genuine leadership, and lulling the weaker side into accepting its 'fusion' with, or 'absorption' into a kind of united working class party in which the communists would hold all key-positions.

Here again it has been proved that the banning of opposition does not end it. The basic 'workers' opposition', has not been extinguished after almost another quarter of a century of communist power, in any of the East European countries. In the industrial field itself, that is in the actual enterprises, it is present in the recurrent demands for the setting-up of workers' councils, as organs of self-management. And, on the other hand, the Communist Party fears most and therefore denounces constantly the deep-seated 'social-democratic' attitudes of the workers and trade unions. The workers as a social 'interest group' continue to show a direct interest in participation in industrial management. The trade unions, muzzled as they were, and operating as they have been mainly against the purpose for which they were conceived, continue nevertheless to show signs of resistance and resilience. The cases of Soviet Russia in 1920–1, of East Germany in 1953, to some extent of Poland and Hungary in 1956 and of Yugoslavia in 1965–6 are highlights of the successive phases of this aspect of professional resistance.

There were two waves of 'workers' opposition' in Soviet Russia. The first, that of 1919–20, began under the spontaneous but rather uninspired and uncouth leadership of Shlyapnikov, himself a worker, a Bolshevik of long standing and a former associate of Lenin. Opposition originated in the trade unions but Shlyapnikov voiced it simultaneously in the high organs of the party. Trotsky's intervention in the dispute between the trade unions, themselves under communist leadership, and the Communist Party, sparked-off the reaction of the trade unions. Under Shlyapnikov's and

the much more versed Mme Kollontay's leadership this reaction
now crystallized in public as the 'workers' opposition', publishing
texts of their own and acting as a group, if not a faction, in the
party and outside it. Trotsky had asked for more discipline and
higher productivity in industry. The trade unions reacted to this
demand as a body (and indeed as an apparat in conflict with other
apparats). But at the same time, as Schapiro appositely remarks,
there was also within the party 'a more "liberal" faction',[24] which
included also the two main trade union leaders, Tomsky and
Rudzutak. It was thus agreed, and probably inevitable, that the
entire question should be debated by the following party congress,
the Tenth, to be convened in the spring of 1921.

The Kronstadt mutiny, however, intervened. This was the
military and political climax of the long wave of strikes of that
winter. The mutineers launched the powerful slogan: 'immediate
re-election of the Soviets by free and secret ballot' in view of the
fact that 'the existing Soviets do not express the will of the workers
and peasants'. From this and many other points of view, the
Kronstadt mutiny was a watershed in the history of the workers'
opposition and its possible impact on the party congress. And it
sharpened considerably the attitude of Lenin and of his party
towards oppositions in general and towards their relations with the
trade unions in particular. Indeed the 'opposition' now was speaking with the authority of a strong political action behind it – and its
representation at the Congress was, at least in the view of Lenin
and Stalin threatening to join forces with 'factionalist' tendencies
like those of Trotsky and Bukharin. On the other hand the rapid
coalescence, to the sounds of canonade and counter-canonade in
Kronstadt, of a real opposition in which workers, sailors and
soldiers had taken a clear political stand against the government,
was too obvious an omen for the man who had written *The State
and Revolution*.

What is, however, of greater interest for the present discussion
is the theme of the basic debate in which the fundamental and permanent *leitmotivs* of the dispute between the two apparats are
clearly heard. The claims of the trade unions, after the Revolution and despite the fact that they were led by a trusted member of
the party, were based on article 5 of the Programme of the
Communist Party of 1919 which reads: 'The organizational

[24] See his: *The Communist Party of the Soviet Union*, loc. cit., pp. 198–212.

apparatus of socialized industry should rely chiefly on the trade unions which must to an ever increasing degree divest themselves of the narrow craft-union spirit and become large industrial associations, embracing the majority, and eventually all of the workers in the given branch of industry. The trade unions being, on the strength of the laws of the Soviet Republic and established practice, participants in all the local and central organs of industrial management, should eventually arrive at a *de facto* concentration in their hands of the whole administration of the whole national economy, as a single economic entity. The Trade Unions, ensuring in this way indissoluble ties between the central state administration, the national economy and the broad masses of working people, should draw the latter into direct economic management on the widest possible scale. At the same time, the participation of the trade unions in economic management and their activity in drawing the broad masses into this work are the principal means of combating the bureaucratization of the economic apparatus of the Soviet power and making possible the establishment of truly popular control over the results of production.'[25]

To this categoric text, of which a year before he had been one of the authors, Lenin opposed in 1921 only the weak and dishonest theory that what it *really* meant was that the trade unions, *after* they had divested themselves of the narrow craft-union spirit and *after* they had embraced the majority and 'eventually all' of the working people, would only achieve a *participation* in economic management; the specific and cardinal matter in this sphere being, according to Leninism 1921-vintage, '*not* administration, but the *ties between* the . . . administration . . . and the *broad masses*'.[26] The trade unions therefore, according to Lenin were only 'a school of technical and administrative management of production'. Armed with this new definition he attacked both Trotsky's thesis on 'the role that has to be played – and is being played by the levers known as the trade union apparatus', and Bukharin's thesis that 'industrial democracy' (an expression which Lenin abhorred) meant that nomination of candidates to managerial and responsible posts must be made 'with an eye not to their political staunchness, but also to their business efficiency, administrative experience, leadership and

[25] Text as quoted in Lenin's *Collected Works*, vol. 32, pp. 65–6.
[26] Ibid., p. 98, italics in the text.

proven concern for the working people's material and spiritual interests'.[27]

For this was actually, and was to become ultimately, one of the main issues between the trade unions and the party: the question of 'mandatory nominations' (a phrase again coined by Bukharin) by trade unions to management bodies. For Lenin this was the worst kind of 'syndicalist deviation'. It was also, if implemented, the beginning of the end of the party dictatorship. For as he exclaimed with admirable sincerity 'what is the good of having a party if it can't appoint the people in the management'. Lenin believed that the party had to do three things if it was to survive (for he acknowledged publicly the deep crisis in which the party found itself at the time). First it had to 'put the lid' on any opposition including and especially that of the workers; second, to impose in the leadership of the trade unions Bolsheviks who would understand without further failures that the role of the trade unions was only to be a school and a transmission belt; and, thirdly, to consolidate firmly and exclusively in the hands of the party the right to appoint people in managerial and responsible positions – in other words the nomenklatura. This technique proved itself adequate, in conditions of dictatorship, for the purpose of crushing the independence of the trade unions, and it has been followed by all Communist Parties in power ever since.

They have not, however, succeeded in solving the main problem, namely the relations with the industrial workers as such. In spite of the total control of the trade union leadership by the party, and by the state as the main employer[28] the unmistakable fact remains that whenever the party gets into great, especially economic, difficulties it is some kind of 'syndicalist' opposition which reappears first. Thus in East Germany, in the crisis of June 1953, in the Poznan events of 1956, and in the Hungarian rising of the same year, the workers led, or played a massive part, in the initial rebellion; and in Yugoslavia the slow melting of the party into broader and less political and ideological organizations has produced the corresponding re-affirmation, or attempt at re-affirmation of the trade unions.

[27] Lenin's *Collected Works*, vol. 32, p. 81.
[28] See *infra*.

Two examples will suffice: East Germany and Yugoslavia. In East Germany, in June 1953,[29] after the Politburo published its vacillating text on the new course on June 9, industrial strikes against party organizations in the various enterprises occurred mainly in the 'red' districts: East Berlin itself, the industrial strongholds of Bitterfeld, Halle and Merseburg (and especially in the big concerns Leuna and Buna), Leipzig, Magdeburg and Görlitz. The total number of workers on strike was estimated by Ulbricht to be some 300,000, but more probably it was nearer 400,000. The slogans of the strike and of the protest-action, were, at the beginning, merely professional, directed against the norms, and the wages. But they soon became social: 'We want to live like human beings', 'Set the slaves free', and a strong class-consciousness was revived in old socialist slogans, expressions and the disciplined behaviour of the workers in demonstrations. Moreover one of the main targets was the leadership of the FDGB (the communist 'Free German Trade Unions Association'). 'What do we get from the FDGB?' asked an article in *Neues Deutschland* and answered 'We must take our interests into our own hands'. Mass withdrawals from the communist controlled organization soon followed, and on 17 June workers were throwing away their membership cards and insignia in the streets. The tendency to disintegration spread quickly from the rank and file to the leadership of the official trade union. 'In the conflict between the interest of the system and the newly reasserted will of the workers,' says Jänicke, 'entire trade union organizations dismissed their totalitarian leadership and reassumed the classical oppositional functions of the trade unions against the state as representative of the "ruling class".'

How deep the rot had gone could be measured retrospectively in the two kinds of measures which were taken by the Ulbricht regime once it returned to the saddle after the passage of the Soviet tanks. A massive purge of the trade union-apparat followed, in which the leadership and the cadres of the metal, construction and timber, energy and fuel industries, and transport and communications, were almost entirely changed. In all it is estimated that in the purge 71·4 per cent of the leading cadres of the FDGB were changed. The other campaign undertaken by the party was directed, significantly enough, against the politically sinful tendency towards the

[29] See Jänicke: loc. cit., pp. 42–52.

alleged, but also real' 'Sozialdemokratismus' shown by the rebellious workers. Four hundred thousand members of the SED Party who had formerly been members of the Social-Democrat Party were purged. The witch-hunt of the socialists, afterwards also called 'reformists', continued with fury – and the suspicion that illegal groups of socialists were active in the factories and the party organizations, became more widespread.

The German example is typical for the sudden reappearance, in lightning circumstances, of the 'trade-union spirit' and 'socialist consciousness' believed to have been buried under the strong dictatorship of the party and its process of re-education. The Yugoslav example, on the other hand, of which more will be said in later chapters, is noted here precisely because it describes the contrary evolution: that of the slow and gradual withdrawal of the party from direct industrial control and the slow and gradual reappearance of the industrial representation of interests. In Yugoslavia the part played now, and to be played in future by the trade unions as a representative body, is somewhat obscured by the fact that the workers seem to be primarily interested in direct participation in the decision-making processes of their enterprises and concerns. In this case the Union of the Workers Councils might become, in the future, a stronger body than that of the trade unions. Yet it is significant that the old trade unions have again, in the recent economic and political crises, become the spokesmen, and the organizers, of the positive opposition of the workers to the plans, budgets and industrial legislation of the government. 'First and foremost the (Yugoslav) trade unions were committed as a body to the process of evolution which is in progress in Yugoslavia and within their sphere of activity was aimed, not at stability, but at promoting change in definite directions.'[30] In the discussion of the Plan of 1965, the trade unions carried the brunt of the opposition against the policy of growth and reinvestment of the plan, and were able to enforce substantial amendments to the plan. And in the discussion of the purge of the security police apparat and its leadership, it was Vukmanović, President of the Central Council of the GN, the leader of the trade unions, who most pointedly denounced the inevitable collusions and confusions between the security police and the party. A few days later, on 9 July 1966,

[30] *Trade Unionism in Yugoslavia*, London, 1964, a report of the British Trade Unions delegation which studied this problem in the winter of 1963.

speaking at a session of the Central Council of the Yugoslav Trade Union Federation about the task of the trade unions in the democratization of the national life, he declared that 'The situation is more favourable for us now. We have not only the general political climate, but also the resistance to the introduction of self-management is no longer so active.' But whereas his conclusions were ambivalent in the sense that he recommended an intensive collaboration between the trade unions and the party in the new climate thus created, subsequent speakers expressed more strongly a distinctly new feeling in the trade unions. Andrey Verbić, for instance, stressed 'the need for a country-wide reorganization of the trade unions and for the de-professionalization of political functions in trade union leadership'; he pointed out that it was the trade unions officials directly employed in production who showed most independence, 'but', he concluded, this skill 'called for a good trade unions apparat in the trade unions councils'. Thus, whereas within the League, the head of the Yugoslav trade unions, and a representative of the combined leadership of the League and trade unions, criticized the League and its part in the entire affair, in the trade unions debate he was outpaced by even stronger critics of the League, seemingly even more impatient to achieve the emancipation of the trade unions.

The party and the local administration

The administration, in a broad sense, can exercise three categories of 'checks' on the party's power of decision-making, according to which meaning is given to the word 'administration'. One is the usual range of checks which any administration exerts on the actual policy-makers by altering or rejecting the legislation or decisions for the implementation of which it will be responsible. This is common to all states, but in apparat-states the 'administration', unprotected by either the legislative or the judiciary powers, feels the brunt even more. It can, therefore, be expected to develop, in a sort of self-defence, attitudes of its own, different from or even opposed to those of the party. Here again in the Eastern European countries the administration, as a body, had enjoyed, at least between the two world wars, a period of modern constitutionalism, which left upon its former employees, and upon the population, impressions which the Tsarist administration had never made in Russia. (Indeed in the countries or provinces of Central and

Eastern Europe which had formed part of the Hapsburg Empire, the discipline learned from its excellent administration could never be forgotten.) Such administrations could not but look with contempt on the party's initial improvisations – and on its incompetence at all levels. One can therefore assume that there is, apart from the natural antagonism of the executive-apparat towards the main, political, one, a mutual jealousy between the two apparats in communist countries – exacerbated by the fact that, in Russia perhaps more than in most of the East European countries, the party considers itself as a distinct and superior body. This has led some commentators to believe that the separation created at the top, after Stalin's death and Khrushchev's fall, in Russia and in some of the European communist states, between the offices of Prime Minister and First Secretary, would crown, as it were, the separation between the two apparats facing each other as two distinct entities.

But, to carry this idea further, and to speak of an organized struggle between two watertight and opposing corps is to overlook the fact that such a broad and vague organization as the 'administration' does not have an exclusive personnel (as do some of the apparats like the political police, the army, the State Planning Commission, and the Prokuratura); but, that on the contrary, its personnel is the most interchangeable with that of the party; that it is divided horizontally into the top administration and the petty bureaucracy (with two different attitudes and mentalities); and that most of the component apparats have a bilateral relation with the party which deserves to be examined separately.

The other range of checks is formed by those exercised by the regional, or in this sense, local administration, upon the central administration. These checks, as will be seen, are particularly relevant in federal states.

And, thirdly, there are the ranges of checks exercised by the local administration in its third meaning as self-administration, through which the new organs of 'direct democracy' exert at all levels, but especially and more distinctively at the low, basic, levels, direct checks on the party's leadership which must not be too apparent and which in any case must 'wither away'. Of these three categories of checks this section will deal only with the last two.

Regional-central relationship. This is the influence of the regions or of the Federal Republics on the politics of the communist states in this, geographic, sense. Federalism, as observed before, acquires, in the context of a communist state, an entirely different meaning from that which it has in a pluralistic-constitutional state. The federal structure is, generally speaking, the boldest experiment yet made to combine diversity and unity in a state. It is the obvious solution whenever an attempt is made to establish supra-national or indeed continental associations of formerly sovereign units. The powers of the regional or federal administrations cannot be expected to increase under political regimes which by their very aims and methods tend towards even stronger, tighter and better organized centralism. On the contrary, as Carl J. Friedrich has shown in a study on the subject,[31] federalism broadens and stimulates the functioning of opposition. The natural antipathy of the provinces, of different ethnical, religious and historical backgrounds, originating from what can be described as irredentist-populist attitudes, breeds a constant distrust in the capital and the centre of power of the state, and a strong need for self-assertion. This attitude is accentuated when the central government uses dictatorial methods. Hence, the specific quest, in federal states, for stronger and better institutionalized 'checks and balances', whereby the 'autonomous' and 'sovereign' parts of the association could oppose, control and veto the decisions made at the centre. The general opposition of the province against the centre acts thus as a catalyst of all the other motives of opposition, social, political, ideological and religious; and amplifies them. Thus the basic political process of federalism is incompatible with that of the communist states. But at the same time it renders their power-holders more aware of the dangers of their disintegration under these centrifugal pressures.

In the USSR, as in Yugoslavia, and as in Czechoslovakia (which although it is not a federation has a quasi-federal structural problem with two different territorial and national units within its frame) there was an initial federalist enthusiasm during the formative period of the new 'revolutionary' states. This was based on the assumption of the national equality of all races, peoples and provinces of the state, previously exploited and subjugated by the same central oppressors, and has been progressively subdued and diluted. In all three states the federal powers have been gradually

[31] Carl J. Friedrich: 'Federalism and Opposition', in *Government and Opposition*, vol. I, No. 3, April 1966.

reduced, their constitutional provisions and description subsequently toned down and emasculated. The functional authority of the centre was progressively reasserted and re-imposed. The same is true also of the other European communist states which are not federal: East Germany, which transformed its initial *Länder* (states) into *Bezirken* (provinces), Rumania where the Magyar Autonomous Region was slowly, after 1956, de-autonomized, etc.

From this point of view in all the European communist states the most characteristic situations prevail in Yugoslavia and Czechoslovakia. This does not derive only from the fact that, unlike Soviet Russia, they are small territories, and that their reduced size renders federalist or quasi-federalist 'co-existence' more difficult by the contiguity of the components and by the scarcity of their resources. Nor is it only due to the fact that the quarter of a century which elapsed between the birth of the USSR and their own birth as communist states with federal structures, had been for Yugoslavia and especially for Czechoslovakia a period of experiments in constitutional and political pluralism. Moreover, one must remember that under the dramatic circumstances of the Second World War and of the disintegrating influence of the Axis upon the states of the Versailles Treaty, former parts of both Yugoslavia and Czechoslovakia (Croatia and Slovakia) were set up by the invaders as separate national states. Thus both these states now contain within their territories units which have very recent memories of their national 'independence' and sovereignty. Even if it was achieved in ugly and precarious conditions, it gives in retrospect the measure of the possibilities of another kind of national emancipation. In both countries therefore the balance of federal decentralization is watched by the central power-holders as a potential threat, and by the local nationalists as a hope of ultimate self-determination.

Under the 1948 constitution, within Czechoslovakia, Slovakia was provided with a Slovak National Council and a Board of Commissioners as separate organs. None of these organs carried an element of sovereignty – but they were for all intents and purposes meant to be agencies of independent government. The Slovak National Council, however, never did become an independent Slovak Parliament – above all because in the conditions of political dictatorship which prevailed since 1948 no Parliament, either in

Prague or in Bratislava, played any part at all in the political life of the country. The Board of Commissioners which also had a chequered existence, with confused attributions and controversial administrative competence, was finally abolished in 1960, by the new constitution, and replaced by an intricate system more adequate for the new centralization.

Like in Yugoslavia, as will be seen, in Czechoslovakia Slovak nationalism was compensated by other means by the central government for the direct losses in 'federal' or 'regional' representativeness. One of these ways was to integrate the two Communist Parties more fully. After the 'anti-nationalist' purges carried out within it the Slovak CP in 1950–3, was given, after 1956, much better treatment and now carries greater influence within the Czechoslovak Party as a whole. The appointment of many of the Slovak CP's leaders to high party and state positions, among them that of Prime Minister, was a logical extension of this policy and yet another means of compensation. Finally, the ultimate scope and direction of 'decentralization' and of 'local administration' were changed, through the new economic and administrative reforms. Instead of leading to further provincial, or regional or indeed republican autonomy the new decentralization addressed itself principally to the local units of administration in the whole state, regardless of the geographic location, thus stressing the importance of the inferior administrative unit against the superior ones. And the new representation, in a considerably more decentralized administration, laid the accent, in particular, on professional and quasi-corporatist nation-wide lines, which thus cut across the traditional regional and quasi-federalist patterns.

In Yugoslavia the same problems and the same trends (as those which influence developments in Czechoslovakia) can be detected more clearly because it has a federal constitutional structure. Serbia, Croatia, Slovenia, Macedonia, Montenegro and Bosnia-Herzegovina were defined in the 1946 constitution as six sovereign federal 'people's republics' united in the federal state.[32] The 'sovereignty' of each of these six republics was as complete in the Yugoslav constitution as in the early Soviet constitution. Each Republic had an ultimate right of secession. Like the leaders of the

---

[32] Within the Republic of Serbia there are also other, but non-sovereign autonomous units: the autonomous province of Vojvodina and the autonomous region of Kosovo-Metohija.

CPSU immediately after the First World War, the leaders of the YCP adopted the federal system after the Second World War for three main reasons. One was the ideological one. The other had the political aim of rallying all the nationalities of the heterogeneous state. The third, of a mixed ideological and political nature, was the hope that the initial federal nucleus might be enlarged later by the accession of other 'sovereign republics' such as Albania, or might serve as a model or basis for a larger Balkan, or Danubian federation. But soon afterwards, the basic contradiction between the centralistic communist system of government and the basic independence which federal units should be allowed to enjoy in genuine federal structures, appeared in full light. The party, which as the Partisan Army during the war of liberation had been the main architect of national unity, became in the eyes of the provincial and republican administrations the main agency of the central government, together with the army and the political police. The fact that it had a Croat leader, Tito, and that two of his main aides were a Slovene, Kardelj, a Serb, Ranković, and a Montenegrin, Djilas, seemed to show clearly that from top to bottom it had irreproachable national heterogeneity. But this was a different story from that of the actual federal organization and collaboration – and in this realm the regional or republican party organizations were and are under the strong pressure of the local administrative units, and populations, traditionally opposed to 'Belgrade's rule' whoever the rulers there may be. From 1950 on, and especially since the adoption of a new constitution in 1953, some of the federal pretences were dropped: the Republics lost their 'sovereignty' and their independent right of government, the federal departments were abolished and the Council of Nationalities was absorbed into the new Federal Council. In the 1963 constitution the Chamber of Nationalities became one of the Federal Chambers set up, and its future is even now the key to the reform of the Yugoslav Parliament.

In either the more utopian initial constitutional regime, or in the more realistic one, the Republics and their organs cannot be said to have been dormant or ineffective. If anything the contrary is the case. Their 'checks' on and indeed opposition to the Belgrade one-party government are most effective. They are powerful in the economic realm, where they can become fortresses of ill-will against the central regulations. They are dangerous should they make use of the ultimate weapon: the movement for national emancipation from a government alien to their populations for cultural, national and religious reasons. As will be seen in the chapter in the section on 'dissent' of this work, the fear of the aggravation of the regional nationalism and irredentism inhibits the leadership of the Yugoslav League when faced with proposals for the reform of the present political system. They allegedly fear that the national factors would precipitate so fast in a pluralistic political system that, for instance, a Liberal Party might soon become a Slovene Party, an Agrarian Party a Croat Party – and that the aims of these revived parties would be changed, under the pressure of their electorates, from social-political to exclusively national ones. Even in the present structure the regional-republican point of view prevails in the deliberations on the 'plans' and main 'laws'. The checks of the regional organs are exercised not only to attempt to secure the impartiality of the central federal organ, but also by the Republics against each other. For instance, the contrast between the more economically developed and the under-developed parts of the federal state is one of the main themes of the national debate. The incongruence of the rivalries and jealousies they unleashed by such debates benefits the central administration to a certain degree. It strengthens its main contention of the need for an organized consensus within the entire state, without which it could so easily be disrupted.

In a situation as advanced and as clearly realized as that described above, any attempt at re-centralization in Yugoslavia by granting greater powers to the central organs or by setting up new coercive organizations would have been useless even in the fifties. Decentralization, essential for carrying on and developing the economy of the state, had to be achieved through other ways than the federal blind alleys. One of the ways was the weakening and ultimate abolition of the coercive and repressive central organizations – and the setting up, in contrast, of democratic and legalistic central organs. Thus, the Prokuratura and, more recently, the political police, which were both associated, in popular antipathy against them with 'Belgrade' and the 'Serbs', have had their power gradually curtailed. At the same time, the Constitutional Court of Yugoslavia, which in theory should crown the authority of the constitutional courts of the Republics, might, if it acquires in practice more power, become the strongest weapon yet that the individual citizens as well as the national communities have ever had in communist Yugoslavia against the arbitrariness of the central government. Another way is the nation-wide professional representation attained through the new chambers, and elections for the Political Chambers, the Administrative Chamber, the Chamber of Economy, the Chamber of Education and the Chamber of Social Welfare and Health. These are all specialized high organs of consultation and legislation and are the ultimate link between the professional sub-divisions of the councils and commissions of the local organs of administration: the communes, the towns and the districts.

Local self-administration. An entirely different means of decentralization is the establishment of the communes as the main 'seats of power'. Article 73 of the 1963 constitution stipulates that the 'self-management of the citizens in the commune is the political basis of the socio-political system' and article 96 makes it clear that 'the commune is the basic socio-political community'. In the new and genuine importance given to the nation-wide local administration the present Yugoslav power-holders believe that they have found the answers to the main questions posed to their regimes. The commune is, first, the one essential organ of self-administration, and thus the only alternative to the state. Secondly, for the same reason, it is the channel through which social integration is attained and an end is put to political 'alienation' and indeed to any form of political activities. The state, and the party, wither away, as it were, through the communes. This interpretation claims that self-administration and self-management have already led to social-political integration. It puts the Yugoslav school of thought ahead of all the other communist doctrines. According to it the commune and the channels of hierarchy which link it directly with the Federal Chambers, should immediately become the new network of decision-making centres. They should therefore deprive the central *and* regional-republican administrative authorities of their dual and sometimes conflicting powers; they should cut across the old regional-central checks and counter-checks, controls and counter-controls, through an independent system of national administration. Decentralization is thus a vertical process reaching down to the uniform organs of local administration, rather than, as previously, a horizontal one spreading sideways to the specific regions of republican administration. Federal organs and republican organs together should, in theory, act as channels of co-ordination of this process of decision-making by local self-administration. Whether this theory is utopian, realistic or even potentially realistic should now be considered.

What is the mechanism of decision-making in the organs of self-administration? How much is it under the domination of the party, or how much has it, of late, and in at least some of the European communist countries, shown more independent tendencies? Some answers to some of these questions emerge from several more recent studies, and especially from the original research produced in Poland and Yugoslavia, and in Western Germany on the German Democratic Republic.[33] Indeed, perhaps the best way to draw some conclusions on this still very elusive question is to find the common denominators between the studies undertaken in the three states,[34] bearing in mind, however, that the interpretations will be different in each case.

In Yugoslavia, progressive decentralization, federalism, and general depolitization have had a direct impact on the growing importance given, at least since 1950, to local administration. This

[33] The Western literature on this subject is very scarce. Even on the subject of local administration in the Soviet Union, specialized authors like Rigby, Churchward and Marcus Wheeler are, at the time of writing, still at work on as yet unpublished studies. To be sure some of the monographs on some of the European communist states contain, as a matter of course, a section or chapter on this aspect of the respective society – but these concentrate mainly on the institutional aspect. West German political sociologists, taking advantage of the possibilities offered to them by the vast material available on the German Democratic Republic, have published serious works on this subject too. (See especially a well-documented study in Ernst Richer's, *Macht ohne Mandat*, loc. cit.) But the substantial research undertaken by the Polish Institute of Philosophy and Sociology, under the leadership of Professor Jerzy J. Wiatr, and by the Yugoslav Institute of Social Sciences, under that of Dr Anton Vratuša has now begun to show rewarding results. Apart from the material published by them in their respective countries the two institutes are also engaged in a quadrangular project with the Indian Institute of Social Studies, and with the University of Pennsylvania. I was privileged to be able to consult some of the preparatory papers of this project.

[34] See also: on Yugoslavia: Anton Vratuša; *The Commune in Yugoslavia* (loc. cit.); Zivko Vladislavjević: *Saveti narodnih odbora, organizacija i funksionisanje*, Beograd, 1963 and Radosin Rajović: *Proces Stavaranja opstirskih pravnih propisa*, Beograd, 1962; and on Poland: Jan Szczepanski in *Studia Socjologiczne*, 3, Warsaw, 1964, and Zygmunt Bauman: *Struktura wladzy spolecznosci lokalnej*, in *Studia Socjologiczne*, 12, Warsaw, 1962, and last but not least, K. Ostrowski and Adam Przeworski (eds) *Local Political System in Poland*, Warsaw, 1965, containing studies by J. Wiatr, W. Narojek, Wanda Harz and by the editors, to which references are made in the text.

importance was enhanced by the fact that in the more recent constitutional organization, even the self-managed enterprises in the territory of a commune were more fully supervised than previously by the communal self-administration. And it was further enhanced by the weakening of the political police following the events of June 1966, a weakening which was one of the direct causes of the progress of decentralization, and which indirectly, as it reverberated on to the League, undermined the latter's relation with, and the position of its individual members within, the organs of self-administration.

In Poland the political importance of local administration is less emphasized than in Yugoslavia. This is because the Polish United Workers Party, acknowledges not only the social-economic forms of pluralism, but also, and somewhat hypocritically, political pluralism under the theory of the hegemonic party.[35] It keeps in existence other subordinate political parties or groups. In contrast with Yugoslavia, the Polish party doctrinaires stress the factor of the influence of the party over the local administration not only more insistently than in Yugoslavia, but sometimes with an insistence which is not warranted by the real situation. In other words, the party in Poland wants it to be known that it is the Party which controls the self-administration. Finally, in the German Democratic Republic the local administration is so organized as to remain, in spite of the periodic attempts at decentralization, the proper 'transmission belt' or to use Richter's[36] expression: 'Nachgeordnete Exekutive'. This means that in principle the local administration suffers a 'double subordination' to the superior administrative organs as well as to the representative organs (local assemblies or main chambers). But in reality, in East Germany, the party keeps the entire administration under its tight 'kontrol', more successfully than, for instance, in Poland.

The following are the characteristics of the working of local administration in most of the European communist countries, taking into account the differences discussed above and with special regard to the extent of genuine decision-making *in* and *by* the local administration.

(*a*) *The units of local administration fight against their subordination and against their limited importance.* The power of the local

[35] See *supra* pp. 14, 44–5 and *infra* pp. 248–51.
[36] *Macht ohne Mandat*, loc. cit.

administration to make decisions is, first, limited to some matters only and to the geographical territory over which it exercises jurisdiction. But the communes are growing in size. The tendency of late in all the communist countries, including Soviet Russia,[37] has been to enlarge the size of the basic unit of the local political system. In Yugoslavia where there were before 3,811 communes, there are now only 550. This means that the basic territory of each of the new, consolidated, communes is roughly eight times larger than the average of the old and scattered units. In Poland it is the middle unit, the *poviat*, which is the basic unit. It groups under its administration the villages, too small to achieve economic and administrative coherence. Secondly, the competence of the local organs is in principle limited to such matters as protection of public order and safety, local industry, agriculture and forestry, local construction and housing, trade, roads and road transport, education and culture, health and social welfare, finance and social organizations. Finally, inside the unit of the local administration itself the executive is submitted to the 'double subordination' of, on the one hand, the central administration and the government, and on the other, of the representative, elected, organs, ranging from those of the commune itself to those of the National Chambers or Parliaments. This hierarchical dependence is aggravated by the executive process. Only a few of the decisions taken or resolutions adopted by the local administrative units (in a rough statistical assessment not more than a quarter of the total number of decisions taken in one year) are afterwards implemented by the authorities in charge. For the latter must either in their turn await superior approval or cannot, for practical (economic or organizational) reasons, implement them, or more often, simply show indifference towards the local units.

There are various ways by which the local units of administration, can make their own views or claims accepted and implemented. One is to act as pressure groups upon the central organs and the national deliberative bodies. This can be done either through direct intervention, by correspondence or by visits of delegations to the hierarchic authorities; or indirectly, by the influence of their own, official or ad-hoc, representatives or intermediaries on the central administrative organs, the Parliament, and the party. Another is to press for the 'vertical administrative processing of

[37] See L. G. Churchward, *Soviet Studies*, April 1966.

their postulates'.[38] This, again, can be achieved either by forming 'a common front of local community'[39] which afterwards uses all channels of influence to pass the petition, or by persuading one or two persons in 'high positions' and interested, for personal reasons, in a project, to use his or their personal connections and authority in order to make the competent superior organs consider it favourably. Yet another means is to make 'decisions to influence decisions'.[40] Here pressure is exercised on institutions which are located on the territory of the community but not under its jurisdiction.

But by far the most efficient means of realizing and extending the autonomy granted by the constitution and the special laws is by affirming the control of the local community over its own means of autonomous existence: administrative, economic and especially financial. The budget is the main battleground on which the fight for influence can be lost or won on such important matters as planning, economic and social development, trade, employment, housing etc. These real means matter much more than the legal ones. The budget of the unit of the local administration should be emancipated from the control of the superior organs of central administration; and should be made to include all incomes and revenues from its territory. The fact that, as a rule, the share of the central budget in the local community's budget is almost half, profoundly affects the dependence of the latter on its superior organs. In Yugoslavia, where decentralization is much more advanced, the communes have fought against this dependence. The more recent laws have granted them more fiscal independence. They have also been able to incorporate in their budgets the incomes and revenues of the enterprises located on their territories. The fact that the importance of the intermediary unit, 'the district', has been greatly diminished, unlike that of the 'voivodship' in Poland or of the 'kreis' in East Germany has helped considerably to this end.[41] With greater financial autonomy and with ample resources behind

[38] Narojek, in Ostrowski and Przeworski, loc. cit., p. 31.
[39] Ibid.
[40] Ibid., p. 99.
[41] 'The communes are free to pool their resources to deal with their own affairs within their jurisdiction. This is why all smaller constituent republics have already liquidated the districts . . . The budget of the Communes has become progressively more dependent primarily on the earnings of its population, and on the consumption within its territory.' Vratuša, loc. cit.

it the local unit is in a better position to present its own plans for the plan, and especially to solve the vexing problem of investments and re-investments which, until now, have been directed almost exclusively by the central administration.

It is this issue, of both real and symbolic importance for the local unit, which remains the main bone of contention between the two systems of administration. This is where, to use the terminology of the German Democratic Republic, the 'Lokalegoismus' or 'Lokalpatriotismus' clashes, even in the most decentralized communist countries, with the 'Zentralismus'.[42] For, whereas the local unit endeavours to keep the entire 'surplus' revenues for its own purposes, and develops a tendency to build new factories neglecting the financing of schools, hospitals, roads etc. which are considered to be within the competence of the state – the latter, in turn continues to ask the local units to hand over all 'surplus' or 'profits' for redistribution on the 'national plane'.

(b) *The participation of the 'people' in the decision-making does not carry enough weight.* The assumption that in the system of 'direct democracy' the 'masses', or 'the people', or 'the citizens' or any such abstract categories, control the communal administration by making and carrying out decisions, is and will remain a fiction. It is true to say that whatever communal deliberation can be achieved takes place in the meetings of the commune assemblies or the voters' meetings. But neither the attendance, nor the procedures of decision and of the ensuing implementation justify the assertion of the existence of an 'all-people's' government, even within a limited range of competence and a restricted sphere of deliberation.

Thus in Yugoslavia according to Zdranko Mlinav[43] there are three distinct categories of local community members: (a) 'there is a small percentage of individuals who take most of the initiative . . . and are quite frequently active in several parallel social activities. In one specific local community with ca. 2,000 inhabitants, we found only 30–50 such individuals. (b) There is a group of persons who undertake no initiative and who are extremely passive, and (c) the majority of the population represent a kind of intermediate category: they rarely take the initiative by themselves and usually follow actions which are undertaken by others; these persons

[42] Richter, loc. cit.
[43] 'Some problems of social integration of local communities' in *Problems*, No. 7–8, Ljubljana, 1963, and No. 13, 1964.

account for roughly two-thirds of the residents of the community.' The same author notes that 'voters' meetings which are the most developed form of institutionalized expression of the needs of the community . . . decide only the less important questions . . . Local self-government is less effective when the problem is so complicated and specialized that it can be understood only by a limited circle of professionals and when the general level of education of voters is low. Such specific situations encourage centralization of the decision-making process in the hands of the professionals. . . . A similar question concerns individual attitudes towards engaging in public life. We often meet traditional, patriarchal conservatism: "Politics is not our business, there are others who are more qualified for it".'

In Poland, it was found[44] that 'there are certain factors which limit the opportunities for full representation of the interests of the inhabitants. Some of the factors are irregularity of control, a low professional standard of committee members, a lack of interest in the fate of voted conclusions, the opportunist approach of committee members to problems which would necessitate a conflict with the management of controlled establishments and, finally, the attitude of management in the controlled institutions, which makes the work of councilmen difficult.' In a particularly negative example of the study, 'The population of Insk (a small town in the Szczecin Voivodship) seems to be dissatisfied with its situation in life and conscious of a sense of neglect. It is a community torn by inner conflicts, distinguished by asocial attitudes, not exhibiting any active interest in the future of its town . . . a community with no real leadership which would be recognized by its members. The town people's council is a stage for strife between various groups. The internal opposition claims that the chairman is totally unable to manage the council and to undertake any initiative or decisions.'

Indeed, this leads to the further problem of the initiative or the initiators in the communal decision-making. An intensive study carried in the Yugoslav commune of Skopia Luka in 1963–4 shows that out of the total of 1,627 decisions, 119 were made by the voters' meeting, 464 by the community assemblies and 1,044 by the councils of the community assemblies – but that the councils and the social-political organizations (the League, Socialist Alliance) were proportionately the main initiators of the decisions. As far as the

---

[44] Wanda Harz: *Opinions and Demands upon Local Authorities* in Ostrowski and Przeworski, loc. cit., pp. 44 and 53.

contents were concerned it was found in the Polish as well as in the Yugoslav studies that more than a half of all resolutions and decisions were concerned with procedural and organizational matters, less than a third with budgetary ones and a quarter with economic and political matters. And, finally, although this too is a common feature of the local administration in both states, the Polish studies showed more clearly that the actual initiators and decision-makers formed in reality an elite, which in turn was composed of certain persons or categories of persons.[45] These were the regular employees of the councils: presidents and secretaries, directors of departments or sectors, directors of establishments dependent on the praesidium of the council – almost a third of the total. Another third was recruited from the directors and higher staff of industrial plants, trade establishments, the National Bank, building establishments, etc. The other third was divided between on the one hand the regular employees of the party and on the other the schoolmasters, trade-unions representatives, judges, and prosecutors, employees of youth organizations etc. But with this we come to the next point.

(c) *The representatives and agents of the party and of other apparats tend to compromise between their conflicting loyalties.* The members of the Polish United Workers Party are said to constitute a definite majority in the local elite. 'On the average, 78 per cent of them belong to the party' says Narozek, and these official statistics are repeated in most of the communist states of Eastern Europe. Even in Yugoslavia the percentage of the functional elite who are members of the League would not fall far short of the official figures for League membership. Two questions arise from these figures. One is the relation between the party-apparat and the local administration within the community itself. And the other is the attitude of the members of the party, who hold responsible positions in the local administration and are faced, sometimes, with a choice between their two loyalties.

In Narozek's description the 'party organizations constitute the strongest political power on the local stage'. Their strength is drawn from the direct contact which they have with the policy-making and decision-making circles of the central apparats; and from the fact that they man the principal responsible posts in the local apparat. 'The influence of party organizations on the policies

[45] Narozek, loc. cit., pp. 35-6.

of state agencies, social organizations, working establishments and institutions is exerted . . . through party members holding important posts or through deputies to the representative bodies. The participation of party-members in collegial presidia ranges from 50 to 80 per cent; party members in the councils themselves form 40 to 50 per cent of all the councillors.' But the fact is that if this internal control worked as smoothly in a state of democratic centralism like Poland as these figures imply, there would be no conflict either within the local administration itself, or between the local and the central organs of both government and party. The proof of the conflicts, on sometimes quite deep issues, between the local administration and the central organs is to be found in the range of pressures and complaints emanating from the local organs, some of which have been mentioned above. It can also be found in the range of reproaches and admonitions sent constantly by the government and party to the local organs accusing them of faulty execution, lack of discipline and delays in implementation. In these conflicts, closely scrutinized by the narrow circle of the population, the position of the councilmen is bound to be difficult. 'In such a situation,' says Narozek, 'the solidarity between councilmen and the inhabitants is much greater than on any other subjects, especially when the inhabitants turn to councilmen with complaints against administrative bureaucracy. Councilmen understand that their interests are doubly conflicting with those of the administration: on the one hand they feel that the executive power is slow to fulfil their demands, and, on the other hand, as the result of the committee's insufficient range of competence in relation to that of the administration, the departments take decisions without consulting the committee.'[46]

These dual attitudes which members of the party, as holders of responsible positions in local councils or committees constantly adopt, reverberate afterwards within the party organizations and the party itself. 'The party in Poland,' says Wjatr, 'is a broad representation of the interests of the working people, not only of the workers but of a broad front of socialist classes and strata which find place within the party and which attempt to realize through the party their interests and aspirations . . . Thus the party becomes the forum of conflicts resulting from the new socialist relations.' On the one hand membership of the party has become now, and especially

[46] Loc. cit., p. 11.

in the smaller communities, almost a necessary formality, at least for all those who wish to be appointed to responsible positions. On the other the conflicts of interests, and of values, which appear more often at informal meetings or functions cut across the otherwise indifferent mass of party members. One wonders what is left of the enthusiasm and the single-mindedness which a 'mobilizing' party should have. Especially noticeable is the attitude of the younger generation of members. They are more versed in the pragmatic tasks of administration and economy than in ideology. They form an entirely different layer, and bring with them a characteristic aloofness into the relation between the local party organizations and the party as the 'leader of the society'.

The way here is shown by Yugoslavia. The decrease of both the ideological and the political importance of the party was formally acknowledged when it was transformed into the League. Now there is a distinct possibility that the League itself will be slowly absorbed into the yet broader and vaguer 'Socialist Alliance'. The slow dilution of the former party mentality of omnipotence is, in any case, noticeable. This necessary change started in Yugoslavia when that country, excommunicated by Stalin, was left to build its 'socialism' by itself. It was then faced with the immediate problem of survival through efficiency. Since then too, the party has had to subordinate all other issues and ambitions to that of rendering viable the new state and the new society. By now, the local self-administration and the self-managed enterprises, are within the local control of the community. These are collective organs in which the representatives of the League could and should be kept in check by the representatives of other bodies.

(*d*) *Broadened consultative councils of the local administration overlap with broadened consultative committees of the party-apparat and form new centres of decision-making at all levels*. It has been mentioned before that the communal assemblies, voters' meetings and local people's councils tend to 'integrate' in their activities as many residents of their administrative territories as possible. They also endeavour to secure the collaboration of all people who by their competence or their skill can help to solve the specialized problems with which modern techniques face governments and their sub-agencies. Thus the 'responsible posts' in the local administration are occupied now mostly by members of the 'elite', recruited merely on their education and background.

This elite, which until now had accepted, if only formally, some links with, if not full membership of, the party, is now, in most of the European communist countries, invited to work with the organs of local (and for that matter central) administration even if they are, and prefer to remain, non-party members. (This situation is prevalent often in Yugoslavia, especially in Hungary, and now also in Czechoslovakia and Rumania.) Their collaboration can be on a contractual basis through a permanent job or commission, or on a consultative basis, whereby the particular individual could continue his profession but would come as an expert to the meetings of the local organs. Thus people's councils and communal assemblies tend to form broader or enlarged consultative organs around them. In most of the European communist countries they also enlarge their sphere of action by recruiting into their 'pressure groups' persons of repute or specialists from other and superior levels. Indeed even in Soviet Russia the 'standing commissions' of the Soviets which have greater autonomy, and better and more direct contacts with the higher hierarchical organs, are also closer to the persons or sectors of population of the respective local unit most interested in the particular problem facing the decision-makers.

On the other hand it has also been noted in previous sections that the party organizations and the party organs, at all levels, rely on the collaboration and advice of all experts available in the unit, or in the country. At the level of the Central Committee there are now the powerful 'Commissions' which give the Central Committee expert advice and great guidance.[47] At the level of the local administration unit, commune or *poviat*, the party conference elects a committee. In turn the latter forms a bureau. The bureaux require the collaboration, or advice of the outstanding personalities to be found in the respective administrative unit. The *Aktivs*[48] are the most frequent appendage of the bureaux. They have tended recently and especially in some parties to become

[47] See: A. J. Brown: 'Pluralistic Trends in Czechoslovakia', *Soviet Studies*, April 1966.

[48] 'The same objectives are pursued through the *aktivs*. Here, the sections and commissions of a Soviet, that is the working committees that are set up to handle particular problems, seek to enlist volunteers or 'active elements' from among the citizenry to participate in their work. At the same time this work is expected to engross the majority of the voluntary participants sufficiently to make them permanently interested as well as proficient in the problems of the Soviet.' Towster, loc. cit., p. 207.

non-party-Aktivs. They are centres of information, consultation and influence in which the party employees together with the best personnel available either in the local administration or in the enterprises, are called to solve the problems and to discuss the projects and plans.

But the fact is that in an administration based on elites, technical intelligentsia and experts, there are not always, indeed almost never, enough persons to form at least two distinct teams – one composed of the experts of the party and the other composed of the experts of the local administration and of the enterprises. More often than not these two external consultative bodies are formed by almost the same persons and groups of persons. This overlapping, as well as the dual identity of most of the state officials, who are also members of the party, and vice-versa, reduce in reality the actual numbers of persons engaged in decision-making to a much smaller figure than that of the functions, permanent or provisional, for which they account. Thus one can visualize the presence, in each community, of a functional group of people who look at the problems to be decided upon in a more pragmatic business-like way and who form the real, if not institutional, decision-making centre. Their decisions are afterwards endorsed, publicized and implemented through the three channels in which they occupy, separately or cumulatively, the responsible positions: the party-organs, the administrative organs and the enterprises and economic units.

2. THE SOCIAL CHECKS

The social classes, sub-classes and groups of a communist society indirectly question the *raison d'être* of the 'classless society' by the very fact of their survival. Thus the peasants, the workers and the 'new class' of the intelligentsia affect the action and programmes of the communist governments and parties by their almost instinctive politics.

The party and the peasants

The countries of Eastern Europe, as well as Russia or for that matter China had a predominantly agricultural population. This is an aspect well known to students of communist sociology and, indeed, communist philosophy who study the intrinsic differences between classic Marxism, and Leninism-Stalinism or Maoism. In the special case of the European communist countries, this aspect, and especially that of the relations between the peasantry as a political sector of the population and the party, has been successfully analysed in many monographs both on these individual states and in more general works.[49] The object of this sub-section is to look summarily at the politics of the peasantry *vis a vis* the party. This is in contrast to the understandably more usual analysis of the relationship from the viewpoint of the party.

The relationship of the Eastern European peasants with the party, can be divided into three different phases over the last twenty odd years. They were all characterized by a strong distrust of the party. But it was only in one phase, the middle one, that the basic conflict flared up with unmistakable and violent overtones.

The first phase, 1945–8, was that of the attempt by the communist parties to win over the peasants by offering them what they were expected to desire more than anything else: a land reform with a new expropriation and distribution of the landlords' lands. This was, of course, the reproduction of the Leninist revolution's initial step in agriculture – even if it was in both Lenin's and his successors' minds only a step backward in order to make two steps forward. Indeed, as the collectivization of agriculture is a condition *sine-qua-non*, of the Leninist-Stalinist doctrine, this initial move by which the appetite of more peasants for more land would only be whetted, contradicted the ultimate and real aims. But the move was necessary not only to repeat, as it were, ontogenetically the phases of the Russian revolution, which was still thought, in 1944, by the Russian as well as by most of the East European communist leaders, to be the universal pattern for their own revolution. It was necessary also for immediate political reasons. The peasants were by far the largest sector of the voting population of these countries, with the exception of Czechoslovakia. In the initial period during which

[49] A very short bibliography should mention at least: David Mitrany: *Marx against the Peasant*, London, 1957; Hugh Seton-Watson: *The Pattern of Communist Revolution*, London, 1955; George D. Jackson, Jr.: *Comintern and Peasant in East Europe*, 1966, and two studies which, although specially focused on two individual countries, project the problem on a general plane: Henry L. Roberts: *Rumania, Political Problems of an Agrarian State*, Yale, 1951, and Andrzej Korbonski: *Politics of Socialist Agriculture in Poland, 1945–1960*, New York, 1965.

the Communist Parties alone, or in bogus-coalitions with other parties, were seeking some kind of popularity this enormous mass of potential voters could not have been overtly antagonised. Besides, the parties which were the outstanding rivals of the Communist Party were the peasant or agrarian parties. These parties were doomed to be banned and abolished. But that could not be done without first at least trying to weaken the strong links which they had forged over the last half century or so with the peasants of their countries.

To be sure the post-Second World War agrarian reforms had different echoes in the different countries of Eastern Europe, according to how well the land had previously been distributed. In Rumania, Yugoslavia and Bulgaria, for instance, the second, 1944–5, agrarian reform had far too little land to distribute, as the result of pre-war reforms, to those peasants who had not previously acquired, or had lost their land. As such the move could not therefore, in these three countries, stir the mass of the peasants, the majority of whom already owned their plots of land. But even in Hungary and Poland, where the proportion of big estates in the total agricultural surface was greater by far, and where the landless peasants might have been impatient with the agrarian parties which represented especially the small-holders, the general attitude of the peasants towards the advances of the party was still one of distrust and suspicion. 'The chief difference (between the Soviet and the Polish revolutions) is considered to be the attitude of the peasants to the reform as such. A large part of the Polish peasantry distrusted the communists . . . Consequently there was really no revolutionary zeal to destroy the landowning class . . . the fact that land was not nationalized is said not to have been accidental but to have resulted from the much higher development of individual peasant ownership in Poland than in Russia' notes Korbonski in his excellent work on this subject.[50] But the reform was a significant political success. It neutralized, for a while, if it did not gain, the allegiance of half of the population. It also helped to destroy one of the important centres of opposition, the land-owning class, and led eventually to the destruction of the only effective political opposition party.

In its turn, the suppression of the peasant parties, thus facilitated, was needed for the start, around 1947, of the ultimate

[50] Loc. cit., p. 93.

purpose: collectivization. It is now known that not all Eastern European communist leaders were convinced at the time of the opportuneness of collectivization. But the Russian tutors were. The signal for intensive collectivization was given in all these countries in 1948. This was the moment when Stalin decided that the 'people's democracies' of Eastern Europe must be transformed into straight dictatorships of the proletariat. This was also the moment when he realized that the leadership of the two most advanced Eastern European Communist Parties, the Yugoslav and the Polish, were preparing to refuse to copy the Soviet blue-print in agriculture.[51] This became one of the principal tenets of the newly asserted ideology of the inter-bloc organization COMINFORM, then set up against the 'deviationists'. The main deviationists, the Yugoslav communists, were outside the bloc, excommunicated. But inside the bloc deviationists like Gomulka, the First Secretary of the Polish Party were to be dismissed and denounced. (One of the main accusations against him was precisely that as late as 1947 he had maintained that the Polish party 'did not need to imitate the Soviet farm policy' and that it had 'rejected collectivization because in Polish conditions it would be economically and politically harmful'.)[52] The orders were given in the Soviet bloc states to proceed at once with collectivization. This was also the signal of the more violent phase of political and social struggle between the peasantry and the party.

The party's campaign for collectivization, as is known, followed different paths and had four different results in the different countries. In Yugoslavia collectivization was dropped in 1948, partly as a result of the open fight with the CPSU and with the COMINFORM. One of the main laws of politics in a foreign power dominated country is that the government in power there either leans on the support of the foreign power, or on that of its own people when the latter believes that the foreign power is

[51] 'To underestimate the experience of the CPSU in matters relating to the development of socialism in Yugoslavia is a great political danger, and cannot be allowed for Marxists, because socialism cannot be developed only in the cities and in industries, but must also be developed in the villages and in agriculture . . . Where, as in Yugoslavia, there is no nationalization of the land, where private ownership of the land exists and land is bought and sold . . . the Party is disarming itself for the struggle with the main difficulties in the development of socialism.' In the letter of the CPSU to the CPY, 4 May 1948, in the *Soviet Yugoslav Dispute*, London, 1948.

[52] In an article in *Nowe Drogi*, I, 3 May 1947.

preparing to overthrow the government. In view of the outside danger the Yugoslav League needed to have its rear covered at home – and to mobilize the 'national' support of the population, two-thirds of which was formed by the agricultural producers.

Collectivization was carried out, without provoking social upheavals, in Bulgaria and Czechoslovakia as early as 1957 and in East Germany in 1960. In Rumania it led, in the first and brutal phase (1948–51) to armed resistance by the peasants in the villages. For almost ten years afterwards the cat-and-mouse struggle went on under the form of 'co-operativization by persuasion'. In 1962 it was brought to an abrupt end. It was announced that collectivization had been totally achieved. But by then the Rumanian communist government and party, already at loggerheads with the Russian government and the CPSU needed to have 'achieved' collectivization so as to be doctrinally irreproachable, and to be able to proclaim itself a socialist republic, for which, according to the book, socialized agriculture and industry are essential requirements. In Hungary, for a short while in 1956 after the revolt, and in Poland, for good after Gomulka's coming to power also in 1956, the collective farms set up in the previous decade were disbanded by the peasants in revolt. The doctrine of collectivization 'on the Soviet model' was rejected in theory and in practice. But in Hungary, in 1961, collectivization was fully achieved. And in Poland the relations between the party and the peasants remained ambiguous. Only in Yugoslavia the League, in quest of social harmony, continues unabated the policy of consolidation of private land-ownership.

One thing which must be remembered here is that, until now, collectivization, from an economic point of view, has been a failure, both in Russia and in Eastern Europe. Although it co-incided with, and to a certain degree helped in communist states to intensify mechanization, the agricultural output in these countries is only now beginning to rise *above* the low average indices of the pre-war under-capitalized and under-mechanized East European agricultures. Moreover, in all these states, the small and economically secondary sector of the 'private plots', shows brilliant results when compared with those of the state – or collective – sectors. This, of course, points to the importance of the human element in the operation. For, it is difficult to assess which is the cause and which is the effect: whether the system oppresses the individual producers, or whether the latter, *en masse*, sabotage the system.

'It is impossible to say what the peasants think of all this: the evidence is biased on either side. Peasant-like, they may want to see how it works. Two points seem, however, self-evident. The process of collectivization, as part of an economy planned and controlled from urban centres is at the same time binding the villagers together as they have never been before on a professional and class basis. The second point is that there is nothing ultimate about a collectivized farm. A factory cannot be taken apart and its machines turned back into hand tools. But a socialist estate is as easily broken up as a "feudal" estate, and a "brigaded" farm labourer can as easily carry on as a peasant again.' These conclusions of Mitrany,[53] although perhaps argued somewhat too forcefully, are generally valid for the normal political attitude of the enlightened peasantry in the European communist countries. The strong consciousness of the peasants as a persecuted social and political class makes them expect the erosion of the system and resist both the threats and the persuasions of the communist party in power. Thus, the Polish Workers Party failed to win over, in the years of collectivization and after, the two groups from within the peasant class which, on the face of it, could have been attracted by the party's revolutionary agricultural policy. These were the landless peasants and the new generation of farmers' sons. 'Contrary to the Party's expectations' states Korbonski,[54] 'the small peasants proved to be most resistant to the official policy. Their participation in the co-operatives was extremely poor and so was their membership in the party.' The ZMP, formed from four separate organizations in 1948, failed even at the peak of its action to recruit as members more than 14 per cent of the young peasants, even though its membership had risen between 1948 and 1954 to two million, most of whom were young people from the villages.

But the main weapon of the peasantry against the communist government, and for that matter against any government, remains, as already mentioned, its participation or refusal, usually silent, to participate in the production processes. The barometer of the relation between the peasantry, whether collectivized or not, and

[53] Loc. cit., pp. 229–30.
[54] Loc. cit., p. 189.

the government is still to be found in the index of production and of delivery to the market of agricultural goods. Bound by 'quotas of deliveries' or by 'collective contracts', the peasants can still condition the essential supplies. It is a truism, fully confirmed in the recent history of communist states in Eastern and Central Europe that trouble starts in the cities when the markets are empty, and especially when bread and the essential commodities coming from the countryside, are lacking. This is how the troubles started in East Berlin, in 1953, and in Poznan and in Budapest in 1956. Since the beginning of the sixties a great effort was noticeable in all European communist states to give more attention and more help to the agricultural sector of the economy. Investments and mechanization have been intensified. But the greatest effort has been made in the direction of improving relations with the men themselves. All sorts of economic, social and, of course, political devices are now used to stimulate the interest and sympathy of the farmers. The main operation of 'political agitation' and 'persuasion' is carried out by the party in the countryside.

Politically, the East European peasantry, which before the war had its parties and its governments, tends unmistakably to reconstitute its own social representation and organized pressure groups and ultimately its own parties. In cases of possible political pluralization in Eastern Europe, in this decade, it is more than probable that agrarian parties will reappear, in one form or another. Agrarian or peasant parties have been the traditional political representation of the peasantry. Politically handicapped by the fact that they lack the concentration in towns and factories of the industrial workers, the peasants can only act slowly and indirectly in the political conflict. The regular electoral procedures fit their political rhythms and habits. The same habits explain also the traditionalism and conservatism of the peasantry.

But as long as agrarian parties do not reappear the peasant class has successfully relied on the political support of two non-political organizations. One is the Church, or indeed the churches. The peasants are more linked to the church through their own faith than are the towns-people. On the other hand, the Church's doctrine runs, like the peasants' natural interest, against expropriation and the subservience of the individual to large economic machines and organizations.

In Poland the Catholic Church, which is, by force of circumstance, the main political rival of the party, draws its great popular strength from the backing of the silent masses of the peasants in distress. But, as will be seen in the chapter on dissent, this basic alliance is founded not on social and economic postulates (although the Church was operative in resisting the doctrine of collectivization) but on the general, national and political postulates opposed by the Church to the communist doctrine. The other natural ally of the peasantry is the army, which draws its yearly contingents from the enormous reservoirs of the rural population, and which is therefore a better, and more sympathetic judge of the feelings of the peasantry.

The party and the workers

If the peasants are, politically, the most handicapped class of the communist society, the workers should be, in the general theory of the 'dictatorship of the proletariat' and of the 'state of the workers' the most privileged. They are, according to this theory, the rulers and the symbol. They should hold, as a group, the main posts in the state. Yet, in reality the communist parties, from the moment they come to power, fight a most determined and tenacious war against the 'workers' opposition'. This war is the result of the basic contradiction between the ideological myth that the working-class is in these states the 'ruling class' and the determined efforts of the party, the actual rulers, to eradicate the ultimate class aims, and even class instincts of the workers. To put it in a nut-shell, the party prevents the working-class from doing what it most wants to do, to assume the responsibility and direction of the management of industry and the economy.

The 'workers' opposition', as a political instrument was banned in the same way as any other opposition. The organ of representation of the workers, the trade unions, was occupied from within and turned into a transmission-belt of the state-employer. The discontent of the workers, thus deprived of these necessary safety-valves, flared up in most of the European communist countries more violently at times of acute crises. It actually sparked off the most dramatic upheavals, notably those which took place in Pilsen and in Berlin in 1953, in Poznan in 1956 and in Budapest and Warsaw in 1956. On all these occasions, the workers were the first to put forward the national, political and economic claims common to all layers of the population (and of which the Poznan slogan 'Bread and freedom' is the most characteristic). But, just as Lenin had bitterly prophesied as early as 1912, the claims for better wages and conditions always ended in the final all-embracing claim to self-management. Indeed, whenever the communist regimes, under the pressure of national revolutionary movements, have shown signs of disintegration, the workers in revolt have reacted almost instinctively by setting up 'workers' councils'. In countries like Poland or even Hungary and the German Democratic Republic, these lasted for a longer or shorter time. But, clearly on Soviet orders and with the exception of Yugoslavia, which does not take Soviet orders, the workers' councils were eventually closed down in all the European communist states.

Yugoslavia is the only communist state in which 'workers' councils' function openly. It is also the communist state which presents self-management as its main social and economic system. On this system and on the communes, the entire working of the society is now centred. By introducing the 'workers' councils' in 1950 the Yugoslav communist leaders and government answered the need for a more efficient and more productive industry. They believed that they had found the short cut to the future organization of the communist social and economic life. This was not and is not an accident and it is the principal difference separating Yugoslavia from all the other communist countries, European and non-European alike. The difference spreads to such aspects as relations between workers and party and government, participation in decision-making in the industrial and economic sphere, and eventually to the principal political conditions. There is no stronger weapon in the Yugoslav ideological defence against either the Soviet bloc, or especially now, China, than the fact that it can claim that it is a society which is based on self-administration and self-management. The main argument is that these institutions alone create direct democracy; and alone prevent a communist state from becoming the most tyrannically centralistic and dictatorial of all states.

The Russian party, as the ideological founder, answers this claim by professing a traditional scepticism towards workers' self-management. It recalls the early years of the Russian Revolution and of workers' control – which already in the spring of 1918 had shown its inadequacy, the extent to which it lagged behind and was intrinsically more difficult than 'expropriating the expropriators'.[55] The phase of Lenin's open fight with the trade unions and their 'workers' oppositions' followed in 1919–20 (and was described in an earlier section).[56] This marked the end of the open political and ideological claim for workers' control and self-management. In the meantime, until the start of the first five year plan in 1929, factories and plants were run by the compromise system of the triangle; representatives of the party, the trade unions and management interlocked in a difficult attempt to co-ordinate their decisions and orders. A resolution of 1929 introduced 'one-man management' in principle, but that too remained only on paper until 1934. For, in reality, the manager himself was submitted to the 'functional' system whereby all departments of an enterprise had the right to issue their 'functional' orders and decisions. It was only after the Seventeenth Party Congress in 1934 that the 'functional' system was also abolished. The last remnants of the internal controls of workers upon the manager were abandoned. From then on the manager was submitted to no control from inside the enterprise itself. He was instead, exclusively and for that matter very strongly, submitted to controls from outside and from above: party, state and police controls. This experience of Soviet industrial life was afterwards considered to provide a sufficient model for all other European communist countries, with the exception of Yugoslavia.

The other communist parties also answer the Yugoslav challenge on this point by pointing out that not only does self-management lead in any case to disorder and chaos in industry – but it does not really give the workers the much talked-of power of decision. The Yugoslav system would therefore be, in such a cynical view, a nuisance for production and a source of confusion for the economy – as well as a farce. For, in this same view, the alleged self-management amounts only to the manager and the party and the state organs taking the decisions, while the 'workers' councils' remain only a façade. Their meetings would be called

---

[55] 'Our work of organizing proletarian accounting and control has obviously . . . lagged behind the work of directly expropriating the expropriators . . . The art of administration is not an art that one is born to, it is acquired by experience'. Lenin, quoted in Fainsod, loc. cit., p. 89.

[56] See *infra*: 'The Party and the Trade Unions', pp. 113–20.

upon only to endorse in public the decisions taken elsewhere in private.

One should try to examine, if only briefly, two aspects of the political relations set up by the functioning of the workers' councils. One concerns the process of decision-making in the Yugoslav workers' councils. How independently are the decisions made, or how much are they prepared beforehand and manoeuvred from above by the party – and state agents and representatives? The second question concerns the extent of pettiness and egoism shown by the workers' self-management in conditions of freedom. In other words, how justified are the Communist Parties in Russia and elsewhere in asserting that real workers' self-management leads always to such economic selfishness and narrow-mindedness that the entire industrial operation is threatened with ultimate dissolution and collapse? These two questions, to be sure, are only part of the vast and important problem of the 'workers' councils'. This is by now one of the best studied subjects in the Western as well as in the Yugoslav social literature.[57]

The Yugoslav system of 'management by working collectives' was set up officially in June 1950, two years after the split between Yugoslavia and the Soviet bloc and as a direct consequence of Yugoslavia's newly-obtained freedom of ideological and political action. In this system the working collectives or collectivities, which group all the employees of the enterprise, administer it directly, if the enterprise numbers less than 30 employees, or, when larger, through an elected 'workers' council', managing board and a director. In principle all enterprises are free to decide upon their own business. But so far as their external relations are concerned they have to be co-ordinated within the economic plan for investment and production. The state can dissolve them in

[57] The main works on the subject are: J.U. Dunlop: *Industrial Relations Systems*, New York, 1959; Adolf Sturmtahl: *Workers Councils*, Harvard, 1964 (indispensable for the general historic introduction as well as for the chapter on the Polish experience); Albert Meister: *Socialisme et autogestion, l'expérience Yougoslave*, Paris, 1965 and Jiri Kolaja: *Workers' Councils: The Yugoslav Experience*, London, 1965 (two studies focused on the decision-making processes). Among the Yugoslav works: Institut Drustvenih nauka: *Radnicko samoupravljanje*, Belgrade, 1963 is probably the most complete and up-to-date, but the official and academic literature on the subject is very rich. On the German Democratic Republic: Rudolf Becker: *Die sozialökonomische Funktion der Produktionsberätungen*, in P.C. Ludz (ed): *Soziologie der DDR*, Cologne, 1965.

case of grave inefficiency. The state[58] appoints the director, sets by law the minimum rates of wages, and also by law or by decision restricts the distribution of the income from the enterprises to the surplus obtained only after funds for investment, social purposes and maintenance have been deducted.

As far as the internal relations are concerned the workers' councils are managed, from within, by an intricate mechanism which forms a sort of battleground for the conflict of influences between the protagonists of the old 'triangle': the party, the managers and the workers. It is true to say that, on the Yugoslav stage, the forces which clashed on the stage of the emerging 'industrial democracy' of the Soviet Union have not only changed their names. Since their very nature has been substantially altered, their mutual relationships also have undergone deep changes.

The Yugoslav party itself, evolved into the broader and more public-minded body of the League. The managers, as time went by, were less and less like the uncouth, inexpert and rough revolutionary workers originally appointed by the party 'to expropriate the expropriators' and to eliminate and persecute the 'bourgeois specialists', but incapable of going further than that in the realm of the administration. In the 1950s they were already mostly young graduates of the various technical schools and universities, and were already, and have become even more in the last decade, bent on the pursuit of administrative success rather than of political ambition. And the 'workers' in the newly liberated enterprises, disillusioned with and actually betrayed by the communist trade unions, were much more interested in securing direct results from the self-management of the enterprise on their own conditions and for their own aims, than in the elusive and indirect professional representation by unions or other institutions.

According to Mr Kolaja whose study[59] is the most up-to-date and also the one which focuses most clearly on the problem of influences and counter-influences in Yugoslav 'industrial democracy', six organizations are involved in the management of an enterprise: the workers' council itself, its managing board; the managerial group, or the director; the League of Communists;

---

[58] i.e. by a communal committee composed of members of the enterprise and by representatives of the commune.
[59] Loc. cit., pp. 4–6.

the labour union, or the syndicate, and the youth organization. The functions of each of these organizations in an enterprise are different: that of the League is described as 'educational' and is therefore kept in the background. The labour union is the official initiator of all activities in the sense that it organizes the election of the workers' council in the enterprise and then guides it during the organizing phases. In turn the workers' council elects the managing board, the executive group as it were, headed by the director who is a member *ex officio*. The youth organization is also represented in the workers' council, but its influence, when at work, is directed especially to the socio-political education of the young workers; in any case the youth organization's influence on the enterprises was always slight and is very much in decline. The most important relationship by far is that between the workers' council and the director. The former act, *mutatis mutandis* as the shareholders. The latter has as his main duties the implementation of the decisions taken by the council, the observation of legal prescriptions and the representation of the enterprise in its relations with other enterprises and with the authorities.

Taking into account the differences between various enterprises, the members of the workers' council are, usually, equally divided in numbers between representatives of the managerial and white-collar element, and of the skilled and unskilled workers. (The foremen, as a special, characteristic, and more and more influential group, are divided, for these exclusively statistical purposes, between the two categories between which they form the social link and the professional transition.) At least half the members are also members of the League of Communists. The same proportions are generally speaking valid also for the 3–10 members of the managing boards. The director, usually a skilled worker or the graduate of a technical school, is usually, also, a member of the League of Communists. The ultimate decision on his appointment or dismissal is taken by the people's committee of the local commune.[60] The secretary of the League's organization within the enterprise, who is the direct representative of the party, is also usually a man with some professional qualification or background. He intervenes in discussion at meetings – and has his own separate

[60] Sturmtahl, loc. cit., pp. 112–3 and Meister, loc. cit., pp. 65–6, give a more complete description of his functions and conditions of appointment.

meetings with the director and with the representatives of the labour union and the youth organization.

Generally speaking the workers take an interest in the activities of the workers' councils only when and if they directly affect their work and remuneration. As has been seen their representation in this body amounts to only half. At the meetings, although the 'workers have not failed to make use of the opportunity to speak out, they have not played a large part in deciding issues which were of keen concern to management because they were not particularly interested in these matters'.[61] When interviewed by Mr Kolaja on the question of 'who has the greatest influence in the enterprise?' their answers were as follows:

		Influence attributed to:			
	Director	Workers' Council	Labour Union	League of Communists	Don't Know
First in influence	27	45	2	4	0
Second in influence	29	22	11	11	5
Third in influence	10	4	33	19	12[62]

When, however, questions directly related to their work conditions or earnings arise, not only do the workers participate actively in the decision-making processes by trying to contact and to influence the managerial groups – but when they are dissatisfied with the decision taken they go so far as to organize a sit-down in the factory, or simply to strike. (It can be recalled that during 1965–6 11,000 workers were on strike in Yugoslavia.)

How much do the League and the government actually influence and pre-direct the decision-making by the fact that they are openly active in every enterprise, and by the fact that the top personnel are also members of the League and ultimately appointed by the administration? As regards this first question Mr Meister, shows that in 1958, at least, party members still held 31·2 per cent of the responsible posts in the workers' councils and 41·5 per cent in the managing boards in the entire country. They therefore played the leading part. Yet Meister believes that this leadership can be obtained only through patient techniques of producing consensus and through serious compromises made by officials absorbed in solving, efficiently and smoothly, daily problems at the local level. 'When it created the workers' self-management'

[61] Kolaja, loc. cit., p. 57.   [62] Ibid., p. 34.

he says, 'the League created more or less independent power-centres which could at any moment find themselves in opposition to it. At the enterprise-level the League is no longer the unique party. Each workers' council is a place where opposition can be manifested on concrete issues, and rather against the means than against the aims of the regime.'[63]

Mr Kolaja's conclusions are that the League, although less in the foreground than the party in the other communist countries, is still the ultimate political authority. It 'exercises its influence in a workers' council less upon the director and upon the workers' councils than upon the labour union and the youth organization, which are more often concerned with maintenance problems than with production . . . Thus the functioning of the whole social system results in a new division of labour and this in turn contributes to the equilibrium of the system . . . The Yugoslav enterprise today is a mixture of areas of autonomy – especially for management, and areas of control – especially for labour.'[64]

The Yugoslav workers' councils, might one day be reframed, either in some larger form of communal activity, or in the trade unions which, in a more pluralistic regime, could be revived and could reassume their representative functions. But the fact is that in the decade or so of their activity they have set up in the relationship between the centralistic political authorities and the decentralized economic enterprises an irreversible trend. Plural checks have been established for good, and failing some major political upheavals they should lead only towards further and more general pluralization. The influence of these economic developments on the political plane is undeniable – and the two evolutions are interlocked.

We come now to the second question. How true is it that, once self-management is achieved, the workers show an unmistakable tendency to withdraw into the narrow spheres of professional and economic claims and grievances – and to separate them from the main, national, preoccupations? The workers' councils, like their predecessors, 'the trade unions', have succumbed only when they have failed to substantiate their economic claims by a more or less independent political action. Lenin's curse on the workers' organizations, that they could not see further than their own

[63] Loc. cit., p. 84.
[64] Loc. cit., pp. 68–9 and p. 76.

narrow interest, has had many echoes in the history of the past fifty years. They have often been pushed back by the parties into renouncing political claims for the sake of exclusive professionalism. Moreover, within this professionalism itself the main instinctive trend of the workers' councils, or for that matter, of the trade unions, has always pointed towards local and direct interest, and has shown a lack of concern for general activities and problems.

The workers' councils suffered two severe setbacks in the 1950s, both in Yugoslavia and in Poland. These were due to the fact that in both countries the workers' councils have nearly always chosen, when given freedom of choice, to distribute the surplus earnings among the members of the enterprise. They also chose to raise wages and benefits either by reducing the funds for investment and reinvestment in the enterprise itself, or by cutting expenses at the communal, social or national level. This has given the critics of workers' self-management new and serious arguments. In Yugoslavia a correcting trend is shown in the progressive absorption, integration and control of the enterprises in and by the communes. Here it is hoped that the general and particular preoccupations can be more easily blended, and the two perspectives brought closer together.

In Poland (as well as in Hungary and East Germany) the party, forced under the strong impact of the popular movements of 1956 to accept the setting up of 'workers' councils', did so only very reluctantly and with noticeable insincerity. The 'triangular' relation between the party, the technical intelligentsia or managerial group, and the workers themselves was, from the beginning, very difficult. But the party fanned the conflict between the representatives of the workers and of the management. However, here too, the former showed an exclusive and almost obsessive preoccupation with their own immediate interests. According to Sturmtahl:[65] 'For the intellectuals and technicians the councils were to be the managers of the enterprises and, at the same time, cornerstones of a new democratic order. They were therefore to concern themselves primarily with the long-run interests of the enterprises. The workers, however, favoured the councils mainly in the hope that they could produce real wage increases in the immediate future. For them the councils were to represent their

[65] Loc. cit., p. 133.

interests – their only real representation, as the unions had long ceased to be concerned. This combination of two essentially divergent, if not contradictory, assignments in one organization proved impossible. Differences between the two views of the nature of the councils were inevitable. Indeed, the very measures they took for a long-range increase in productivity, and thereby of wages, accentuated the conflicts. The elimination of waste, the reduction of surplus labour, the struggle against pilfering, and the reorganization of the plants hurt a great many workers in the short run and caused, insofar as these measures were effective, a decline in the earnings of working-class families. Attempts to eliminate surplus labour ran into workers' opposition which gave the discredited unions an opportunity to stage a come-back. They appeared as defenders of working-class interests against the councils.'

The Polish party had seen with alarm how the councils were becoming a threat to the party, in the sense that the election campaigns in the councils themselves had become openly anti-communist. It also had serious misgivings from the beginning about the possibility of the councillors becoming efficient managers. For these and other reasons it seized upon the internal conflict thus opened within the enterprises and in a series of rapid measures first emasculated them and then closed them down. In December 1958 the workers' councils were transformed into advisory bodies on economic, financial and technical issues but under the direct guidance and control of the party. The Polish economic crisis of November 1959, which led to cuts in employment, cuts in invest-ment and a stiffening of the production-norms was, in reality, the last stage of the agony of the Polish 'workers' councils'. The resentment of the workers combined with varied political resent-ments of the population against the regime. The discontent was bound to find expression in the non-opposition state in whatever forms of dissent could be utilized or opened up.

The party and the post-revolutionary elite

Because it has been too often and too allegorically described, the picture of this particular political relationship in a communist society has somehow lost shape and proportion. An entire range of works starting with Mosca's and Michels' studies of the political influence of the functional elites, concentrated after

Burnham's *Managerial Revolution* in the West and, later in East Europe itself, after Djilas's *New Class*, on the question of the 'rule' in the communist world of 'the managers' or of the 'new class', or of 'the bureaucracy', or of 'the intelligentsia' or indeed of 'the elites'. Adversaries of the communist regimes, and especially former communists or fanatical ideologists, found in this aspect the cause of all evils. And the larger and therefore less precise, in terms of sociological analysis, the notion of *intelligentsia* or *elites* became when projected on to the political plane, the denser the confusion grew. By now whereas it is generally assumed that a privileged social group rules the communist societies, the theories about who form it and how it rules are still controversial.

But the vast literature on the subject amply confirms that in a communist society the people who occupy the 'responsible' or 'leading' posts (in the apparats themselves, in the institutions and agencies, in the fields of production, in agriculture and especially in industry) exercise, as a social layer, powerful checks on the state. That they form a distinct social layer[66] can be deduced from three main characteristics. All these persons receive above average wages, living conditions and social prestige. Nepotism, intermarriages and social environment mean that members of the same families, and especially subsequent generations, occupy similar or better positions. Indeed, whereas the technological expansion of contemporary societies offers increased possibilities of employment in such posts for newcomers from the 'working classes', there is no evidence that the established elites have lost or might lose their positions or might decay socially. Finally, the main social difference in a communist society remains that between the manual and the non-manual workers, the latter being a minority, with the foremen at the threshold between the two worlds. The contrast in standard of living shows startling discrepancies between the top layers of the non-manual workers and the bottom categories of the manual – and is further aggravated by the differences between town and countryside.[67]

[66] The intelligentsia 'has become a social stratum that owns the means of production on a par with the working class and the peasantry', V. S. Semyonov, in G. V. Osipov (ed): *Industry and Labour in the USSR*, London, 1966, p. 132.

[67] Concern with this unbridgeable abyss is shown more and more, not only in the Polish, Yugoslav and East German sociological literature, but also in Soviet Russia. This is one of the recurrent themes in a series of Soviet essays published under the title: *Industry and Labour in the USSR*, loc. cit. Thus: 'Essential

This permanent social dichotomy, which in some respects is aggravated in communist societies, has in itself a direct effect on the political process: the nearer people are in a centralized state to the centres of power the more likely they are to exercise influence on the political decision-making. The 'they', who as far as the vast numbers of anonymous and powerless 'we' are concerned rule the country, live in the smart districts of towns and have white hands. This political 'they' includes the party, the police and all the potentates and professionals who, together combine in a supreme parallelogram of power dictating 'their' orders and imposing 'their' solutions on the great majority of the population. Such a broad view is correct in its oversimplified way. No one would deny that politics is made by elites in communist societies.

Less clear and more difficult to detect are however, the relationships within the ruling sphere itself. It is easy to identify exactly the different forces which, by consensus or by conflict, coalesce ultimately in the policy-making. To differentiate between the Stalinist party and the Stalinist political police, from this point of view, is as difficult as to differentiate between the Yugoslav local party organization and the Yugoslav people's committee. But probably the most difficult distinction to make in the political relations of social groups with the power-holders (or the main-party-apparat) is that between 'the elites' themselves, in their different roles. The ultimate political influence of such abstract categories as managers, bureaucracy, creative or technical intelligentsias, elites, etc., is almost impossible to assess separately. All these concentric circles overlap in the final policy-decision-making. They overlap, as already mentioned, even in personnel. The same people act, in these rarefied heights, in more than one capacity, carry more than one responsibility at the same time, and have

distinctions between intellectual and manual labour, in the last analysis, are social distinctions. There are, in the main, two groups of people in the system of social production: the group engaged in manual labour (workers and peasants) and the group engaged in intellectual labour (technical intelligentsia). In other spheres of social life (state administration, science, art, etc.), intellectual labour (labour of the intelligentsia) is characteristic; manual labour holds an insignificant place in these fields (chiefly service personnel concerned with the cleaning of premises, transport, etc.). The different positions and roles in social life under socialism are marked by certain differences in earnings. Earnings of brain workers, especially those engaged in state administration, are to a certain extent higher than those of manual workers.' A.N.Maslin and G.V.Osipov, loc. cit., p. 183.

simultaneous loyalties. One could treat the party, on the one hand, and the bureaucracy, the technical intelligentsia or the managers, on the other, as separate entities, only if the latter categories, too, had an exclusive personnel, a crystallized *esprit de corps* and if not programmes, at least postulates of their own.

But these conditions are found only in the party. Its personnel is exclusive, in the sense that even when it is lent to other apparats or institutions, the party loyalty is understood to remain the bâsic one. It has a powerful *esprit de corps*. And it lives and dies by its ideology. The party is, or should be, or has been the political elite by definition, and its leaders in the past have always insisted that its homogeneity and purity are its two main conditions for survival. This was the case of the Bolshevik Party as a revolutionary opposition party; but was not entirely the case with the other communist parties, since, even in opposition, their authentic homogeneity was marred by the extraneous controls of the Comintern or of the CPSU. But, once in power even the CPSU was infiltrated by the political police and lost some of its integrity. The European Communist Parties lost theirs even more, as they were from the very beginning under the double control of both the Soviet institutions and their own political police. But then in the measure in which they strove to become broad mass-parties and purely national organizations they had, at least, to try to become more representative of all layers of society. They had thus to accept the idea that one day they might become 'debating bodies' where conflicts of economic or social interest could clash in the open. In these bodies 'the intelligentsia' should be recognized as a powerful group with a characteristic and dominant influence.[68]

The ever-increasing influence of the elite or intelligentsia lies in the fact that being the *trained professionals* and the *exclusive experts* their knowledge, advice and ultimately leadership is required by and in all apparats. The main (party) apparat, the state, army, police and all other apparats, institutions and agencies, and the economic enterprises, industry and agriculture are by now all led by them. Their power is ubiquitous, even if diffuse.

[68] Z. Bauman's studies on the social aspects of the Polish Workers Party are the most penetrating of all those published in any communist country. His statistical analyses and the research in depth which he and his students carried out in the factory organizations in Warsaw reveal the increasing activity and influence of the technical intelligentsia on the basic party organizations. See further p. 159.

Their influence, already overwhelming, is achieved by means of inter-penetration and inter-infiltration of their functions with the political functions, and by the imposition of their expert knowledge on the decision-making processes. But this influence and eventual leadership is not, or at least not yet, the result of consciously motivated actions and claims. It is rather the constant result of personal duplicity, conflicting loyalties, attitudes and techniques of compromise, founded more often than not on some pious individual notion of 'common', 'revolutionary' or 'national' cause.

The motive force behind these elites is drawn from their reaction against the power of the apparats. If they function outside the direct control of the apparats, whether in modest machine-tractor stations, or advanced atomic laboratories they resent its orders from outside, and if inside an apparat they resent its direct orders, especially those of the main apparat, the arrogant party. Being in charge of responsible posts they resent the interference from outside in their responsibilities. This is as true of the 'technical intelligentsia' already in the service of the state or of the party, and therefore within the apparats, as of the 'managers' in charge of firms, factories, farms and other enterprises which even if they ultimately belong to the same common entity have, or should have, administratively greater independence, and whose relations with the apparat should be determined by the results which their enterprises can show under their management.

The more dogmatic European Communist Parties such as, in this respect, the Polish, the Rumanian and the East German try to bridge the gap by ensuring that the majority of the experts are active members of the party, and are thus seasoned to accept the orders from above and prepared to advise genuinely from below. (This belief has its counterpart in the widespread belief of the intelligentsia in the first decade of existence of the European communist states that it is better to influence the party from within than to try to fight it from outside.) The more modern parties like the Yugoslav, the Czechoslovak and especially, from this point of view, the Hungarian, have adopted the opposite line and have claimed that as long as a man is competent, shows good will and above all is successful in handling the tasks or especially the enterprise to which he was appointed, not only is it immaterial whether he is or is not a member of the party, but in the Hungarian case it is positively recommended that he should not be. This quotation from a leading article of the Hungarian party newspaper, *Nepszabadsag* of 8 January 1963[69] throws light on this attitude. 'Giving more and more important leading functions to non-party persons is a known and approved principle of our party's policy. This principle also applies to functions pertaining to public life. The consideration of maintaining rigid proportions, which might diminish the number of able non-party candidates eligible to hold public office, is harmful for our progress and contradicts the principles of socialist democracy. The main requirements for the candidates – be they party members or non-party persons – are political ability, professional knowledge and good relations with the workers.'

Although the dogmatic approach leads to further confusions and mutual bitterness, both methods cannot but converge at the end. The quest for economic efficiency will continue to be the *sine-qua-non* objective which will lead to the same pragmatic attitudes. For, in the first case, in the average Polish Workers Party's factory organization (or *branch*, as it is called now) in 1960–1, the membership, including the activists, was formed by 2·24 per cent of the managerial-engineering staff, 1·25 per cent of the administrative staff, 3·31 per cent of the foremen, 0·95 per cent of the skilled workers and 0·60 per cent of the unskilled workers.[70] This shows beyond doubt, as Professor Baumann concluded, that : 'the present politics of the Polish Workers Party appeal more to the people with higher education'. (From this point of view the inclusion of the foremen in the intelligentsia is justified from both a sociological and a political point of view.) In terms of political relations, this means that either the party is and will be, at all levels, under the growing influence of the intelligentsia with its anti-ideological and anti-political biases and focused on the practical problems of economic efficiency and political viability; or that as in the case of holders of responsible posts in Rumania or Bulgaria, this membership amounts to a formality which does not alter the balance of influence between the intelligentsia and the party.

In the second case, in Yugoslavia, Hungary and Czechoslovakia where now the experts and managers are recruited on the basis of their objective qualifications and without the party strings attached

[69] Quoted in an excellent study by A. J. von Lazar 'Class Struggle and Socialist Construction: the Hungarian Paradox', in *Slavic Review*, vol. xxv, No. 2, New York, June 1966.

[70] Data from a lecture given by Prof. Z. Bauman at the seminar of Political Sociology at the London School of Economics on 13 May 1966.

to their jobs, the parties themselves seem to believe that the more decisively they exercise their influence on the future managers during their education the greater will be the chance that it will last afterwards. The final result is that, for both sides, efficiency and success now count more than authority and allegiance. From this point of view it is more than significant that the economic reform in Czechoslovakia, which is the boldest and at the same time the best-organized and thought out, was first proposed and then imposed by a group of party economists. When Ota Sik published in September 1963 his manifesto 'The remnants of dogmatism in political economy must be overcome' in the party's monthly, he was director of the economic institute of the Academy of Sciences and an important Central Committee member. His reforms hit, among others, the party apparatchiks who were in control of the economy under the previous regulations. The battle in the party itself raged around the proposed reforms for almost two years, during which the 'political-first' conservatives attacked the 'efficiency-first' progressives. The State Planning Commission, which, before, was the symbol and the mainstay of the centralistic apparat of the economy, fell however into the hands of Sik and his reformers and by January 1966 their plan for economic reform was made into law.

But the relations between the managerial staff of the economic enterprises and the party are modified and refined by the fact that they are set in the frame of the old triangle: party – managers – workers. The more autonomous the enterprise becomes the clearer this triangular relation appears. Moreover, the larger the unit of economic autonomy becomes the more articulate becomes the relation between the three main factors of management. And the units are now definitely increasing in size. In Poland, Hungary, Czechoslovakia, East Germany and of course Yugoslavia the *trusts*, with different names in each of these countries[71] replace the

[71] In East Germany the Association of State-owned Enterprises, VVB (Vereinigungen Volkseigener Betriebe), in Poland the 'combine', in Hungary and Czechoslovakia the Trusts, in Bulgaria, the 'amalgamated enterprises', are the new bigger groupings which are themselves expected to associate into even larger units called the 'unions' in Bulgaria or the 'sector' in Czechoslovakia, etc. This entails a change also in the workers' organizations: the former workers' councils, as in Yugoslavia and Poland, or production committees or production councils as in Bulgaria, Czechoslovakia, East Germany or Rumania will have to be re-adjusted and re-shaped to fit the new dimensions of the managerial units.

former individual enterprises as the units of organized management; and 'associations' with different names supersede the former individual workers' organs of the enterprises.

During the Stalinist period the managerial staff, harassed by the controls and demands of the party, the police, the ministries and the state-administration, were more often than not in sympathy, if not in solidarity with the workers. Both categories were persecuted and buffetted by 'those' who fixed norms prices and targets regardless of the practical conditions and possibilities. In self-defence against this tyranny the managerial and engineering staff preferred to fake the statistical data and the accounts and balance-sheets, and this was done with the complicity of the staff and workers together. Under the Stalinist system of one-man management the manager himself was a party agent who covered his own inefficiency and technical inadequacy by his ability to 'transmit' the terroristic orders from above to the enterprise for which he was 'responsible'. Mutual incomprehension, extended hostility between the apparatchiks on the one hand and the enterprise-personnel on the other, persecution by the apparatchiks and sabotage by the workers, and eventual inefficiency and chaos were the results of that conception of management even in periods when absolute 'growth', easier to obtain by any means, was the only criterion. The natural triangular functional relations were reduced to a bilateral relation of coercion-disobedience, with everyone involved in it being subjected to the two contrary pressures.

With the introduction of the Yugoslav self-management, and with the increased autonomy of the enterprise which it brought about, the part played by the manager changed. Although appointed by the state, or by the commune, and although usually a party member, his responsibility was real. Under his management the enterprise had to show genuine results, and his competence had also to be real if he was to impose himself on the 'council', the managerial group and the representatives of the party, trade unions and youth organization in his establishment. Better men had to be found than the old party-hacks, better training had to be given and better conditions offered in order to compete with the fewer risks and greater advantages offered by direct state employment, especially employment by the party. The improvement in the conditions and, therefore, of the quality of the managers in Yugoslavia, and afterwards in the other European communist countries which followed the Yugoslav method of decentralization through self-management, proved to be a continuous trend. By now the great majority of the best students of the Yugoslav, Hungarian and Czechoslovak universities go, year after year, into 'business', for which they are also much better prepared,[72] if not especially groomed, in the reformed schools and universities. They are attracted by the managerial career because of its better income[73] and facilities, because of the privileges and special status attached to it, because of the freedom which it eventually entails within its 'responsibility', and because of the neutral political and ideological position it offers in countries where the younger generation feels current tensions and senses future internal conflicts. Because of their special living conditions, their caste-like behaviour (including inter-marriages) and their growing importance as their societies become increasingly dependent on technology, the 'neutral' managers can become a sizable group in the society, and can acquire also a political consciousness of their social and economic importance.

Here, however, one has to take into consideration two facts. The first is that even now their initial links with the party and its control over them are still very strong. The second is that, within the 'economic complex' the individual or groups of managers align themselves, from the point of view of the main lines of economic policy, with the vested interests of their particular groups of businesses. The main cleavages are between agriculture and industry, and within industry itself between heavy and light industry. It is known for instance that the representatives of the heavy industry groups are very often lined up with the representatives of the army, the security police and the conservative wing of the party. They oppose the natural alliance of the agriculturalists, the economists, the managers of the consumer-goods industry, and of the retail-

[72] In Poland the Fourth Congress of the Party in June 1964 reorganized the National Management Centre set up in 1958, and asked that all the supervising personnel in the economy 'from the foreman to the director should be trained or retrained according to a new intensive education-programme'. The victims of this reorganization were mostly the persons appointed by the party as prototypes of what is called in Poland 'social advancement'.

[73] In Hungary and in Czechoslovakia the salaries of the managers and of the managerial staff went up abruptly – but even in 1965 there were complaints that the best people could not be attracted by industry because they 'profess that if one cannot earn more through greater effort, then it is better to live quietly with less work. *This attitude is unfortunately a mass phenomenon.*' Bognar, loc. cit.

trade organizations and the progressive wing of the party, when major economic problems are under discussion.[74]

But in the triangular reaction thus re-created the party can either reconcile, or intrigue between, the other two groups: the managerial or intelligentsia group, including the foremen, and the workers' group, including the skilled, unskilled and the seasonal (peasant-workers). In countries like Yugoslavia where the party

[74] A good description of the different groups' reaction to the economic reform in Czechoslovakia, is given by J.M.Montias, in *Survey*, April 1966, p. 589. 'The question bandied about in Prague these days is whether the forces in the party that favour a liberal interpretation of the January directives, that support a real deconcentration of economic power, will prevail against the conservative opposition. It is said that in the party presidium itself only Josef Lenart, who was once employed by the Bata Works when it was a private firm and has retained some understanding of the complexities of efficient management, wants a thorough overhaul of the system. His fellow-members, and above all Novotny himself, are going along with the reform so far as a necessary evil but hardly from internal conviction. It may be significant, in connection with the attitude of presidium members to the reform, that one of the initial impulses for change in the system came from the Soviet Union itself, when Khrushchev threw his support behind proposals for decentralization at the time of his visit to Prague in August 1964. Unfortunately, the views of the new Kremlin leaders on the Czech reform have not been reported.

'The ministers in charge of industrial branches are said to be against decentralization, as are most influential officials of the Planning Commission, although it is also said that there has been a change of heart in the part of some of these functionaries, especially among those responsible for price formation.

'Many economic administrators, unable to envisage the workings of a decentralized system, are reluctant to embark on fundamental changes without years of preparation and study. They hamstring the reform more by their inertia than by outright opposition. A strong current against the reform emanates from party officials in the provincial National Committees, who foresee that their power will be curtailed if enterprises are cut adrift from administrative regulation. District party secretaries represent an important minority in the central committee of the party; together with various conservative allies, they are said to form a strong enough opposition to block any proposals for the creation of a market-type economy. At present it seems unlikely that there will be significant changes in personnel at any level; this is liable to frustrate the intentions behind the new model. If, as is rumoured, those in charge of its operation are the very people who were most strongly opposed to its introduction, the scheme will be undermined from within.

'Enterprise directors are not all happy about the prospects for reform either. Many directors who are getting large bonuses now without great exertions are worried about the uncertainties of the future; some who banked their career on their party connections and on their understanding of the rules of the game in a command economy know they will be at a relative disadvantage when it comes to competing with men of middle-class background with experience in running a firm according to business principles. Many rank-and-file workers, in so far as they care at all about the reforms, are apprehensive of greater wage differentiation, which might leave them at least relatively worse off than before.'

itself has over the years gone through a steady change of mind and of approach, the de-politized and pragmatic new members or activists feel that the party's main task should be to smooth the ways of the different categories and groups and bring everyone to work within the broad and vague new framework. But in other countries the die-hard ideological, conservative or, to put it in a nut-shell, the Stalinist opposition, within the party and the security police, is not easily reconciled to the changes in the general political situation and orientation. This opposition can launch in such countries a successful counter-attack against the 'new masters' or indeed the 'new class' of the pragmatic, anti-ideological, technological and pro-Western experts and managerial groups, by inciting the workers in the new production organizations against them.

In Hungary, the process of emancipation of the managers from the party's tutelage has come more rapidly and, as it were, more cynically than anywhere else. In the new triangular relation thus re-opened some insistent voices are heard claiming that the trade unions should be resurrected and made to face their new tasks within the new dimensions, and, even more surprisingly, that management should be 'humanized and modernized'. Thus an article in the Hungarian trade unions journal *Munka* stated in April 1966 that : 'In the changed circumstances the demand of the workers that they participate more in the work of leading the enterprises will increase . . . and it will require a changed and increased political significance for the trade unions as social-political organizations and as class-organizations.' But the most outspoken, and as such the most characteristic attack from this point of view came from the veteran Stalinist Andras Hegedus who in his study on 'Optimization and Humanization – on the Modernization of Management System' focused his observations on the fact that the new managers, or leaders, were not democratic enough.[75] They did not give enough consideration to the superior/subordinate relationship. They were not popular with the workers and were not public-minded, in the sense that they did not allow the party press to inspect the factory as often as it wished and to interview the managers. Therefore, in many instances 'particularist interests may

[75] 'The working masses know practically nothing of their leaders. Personnel changes are often wrapped in mystery. New directors, not infrequently, come to companies so that only the best-informed top-managers know of their previous activities and not even a piece of gossip reaches the majority of the employees.' Budapest, 1956, p. 49.

easily prevail against the all-social interests'; as such the workers' right to have a say in certain matters should be widely put into effect.

The future orientation of the relations between workers and party and managers in the transitional industrial life thus opened might change in the distant future. But there is no doubt that the technological advance in general, and the progress of automation in the field of industrial production in particular, will give a further lead to the technical elites in these already industrialized societies. Cybernetics exert on the minds of the present communist leaders the same fascination as electrification had for Lenin and industrialization for Stalin. The combination of rapid technical and economic advance with a concentration of power and leadership[76] excites their imagination. More than ever before the politicians look at the scientists, the pioneers of increased productivity, as well as those of the outer spaces, in the hope that they will give their political regimes and their ideologies the key to final victory. The entire utopian background of the Marxist-Leninist philosophy, its humanistic undertones and its voluntaristic overtones have found new hopes in the new ways opened by science. It is therefore predictable that, squeezed between the quest for efficiency in the economic field, and the further estrangement of scientific knowledge from the realm of the understanding of the average man, the party politician will give more and more recognition and scope to the intelligentsia and the elites. This is a basic and irreversible trend.

As for the 'elites' themselves their political influence in the political life can be observed, as these notes suggest, in the checks which they, more than any other group in the society, can exercise in all fields, and at all levels, on the decision-making and policy-making of the communist societies. At the same time, however, they have not as yet a common basis for action, an ideology of their own or even social and political consciousness. The main pressure of the elites in all the quarters where they can be found, is naturally and instinctively directed towards *institutionalization* or *reinstitutionalization*. Both for their creativity and to achieve the efficiency for which their services are so much coveted, the elites need *institutional order* and *institutional freedom*. In the realm of dissent, as will be seen, the intelligentsia is one of the main forces pressing for some institutionalization of dissent, if not of opposition, so that freedom

[76] It is often forgotten that *government* and *cybernetics* have the same etymological root in κυβερνητικος the Greek word for 'rule'.

of opinion could be ensured. In the realm of checks the influence of the elites can make itself felt only through the channel of institutionalized checks, the separate powers of the constitutional-pluralistic regimes: the legislative, the judiciary and the communication-media. Even in the very modest way in which these seem now to be starting up in the European communist states, they are at the same time the effect and the cause of the influence of the elites in public life.

3. THE CHECKS BY THE CONSTITUTIONAL AND CULTURAL BODIES

In a pluralistic-constitutional state the two main checks on the government, or executive, are exercised by the legislative and the judiciary organs. Cultural bodies, like the churches, the universities, the academies and other such centres enter into the process of decision-making either directly, as institutions which are expected to check on measures of their competence, or indirectly through the influence which they exert on public opinion. The press and the other media of information and communication are rightly described as the 'fourth estate'. They have their own and very effective 'checks' on the activities of the government, even if here the expression 'check' is taken in a slightly different meaning.

In the Apparat communist states the principle of the separation of powers is denied. The function of the legislative and judiciary organs, and of the institutions of culture and information is transformed into a duty of implementation. In an ideal Apparat, or for that matter *totalitarian* state, the function of all these bodies is that of 'transmission belts' and of agencies of state-control. But then it can be said that the history of any 'ideal' Apparat or totalitarian state is precisely the history of the failure of the central 'monolithic' power to prevent institutional checks from being reformed. In other words, whatever the efforts of the regimes themselves to improve, from within the Apparat, the working of mutual checks between the apparats (and great attention is now paid to this improvement in all European communist states), what counts for and is demanded by the various layers of society is the institutionalization, or, in the case of the European states, the *re*-institutionalization of the constitutional and public checks. This reinstitutionalization affects especially the old and as it were classic organs, institutions and powers, listed above, which correspond functionally to the basic needs of these 'checking' activities. They, as in the principle of communicating vessels, are the first to be animated by the process of institutionalization.

There is now an active reinstitutionalization going on in the European communist states. The principle itself of the separation of powers is re-discussed and re-assessed.[77] On the other hand the renewed activity of the Parliaments, under different forms in Yugoslavia, Poland, Czechoslovakia and Hungary; the reconsideration of the role of the other 'political parties' in Poland and from an entirely different point of view in East Germany; the growing importance of the courts, and especially, as in Yugoslavia of the constitutional courts, which seem to be reassuming some of their lost independence and authority; the use made by the regimes of the cultural bodies such as the universities, academies and other such centres for their own decision-making, and the acknowledgment of the churches as, at least, opinion-forming bodies; and the fact that the press and, perhaps to a lesser degree, radio and television now provide a more genuine service of information than in the obscurantist Stalinist years, are among the principal signs and symptoms of this trend.

But, in general, and from the special point of view of the organization of the material in this book, institutionalization or reinstitutionalization is the effect of the pressure of *public opinion* and it is always accompanied, if not preceded, by the growth of the *spirit of legality*. These two phenomena must be observed and discussed before institutionalization can be studied. It is therefore essential to examine first the question of whether, and what kind of, public opinion exists in these states; what are the means by which it can articulate and manifest itself and eventually bring pressure to bear on the power-holders; what are the compromises reached during the period on the outstanding issues of establishing legality; and how during these new and intermediary stages public opinion can postulate its dissent until, properly institutionalized, it takes the form of public debate. It is at this point that the mechanism of checks by groups or institutions merges both with the mainstream of 'politics' and with the activities of dissent to which this analysis now turns.

[77] See for instance: Pavel Nikolić: 'Notion and classification of the systems of power in the modern states', in *Annals of the Faculty of Law of Belgrade*, January–March 1966.

THE MANIFESTATION OF DISSENT

In the introduction to this book dissent was described as the conflict of values which originates from the incompatibility of outlook, opinion, beliefs and indeed even interests among people of different allegiances and mentalities, living together in the same community. In other words dissent is any attitude, whatever form it takes and however it manifests itself which is contrary to the attitudes expected and required by the, in this case, conformist and centralistic, power-holders. The questions which the present part will endeavour to answer are : How does dissent come to be manifested in a communist Apparat-state particularly in the European communist states? Are the main centres of aggregation of dissent active? In such states, where dissenting political organizations are banished, these centres can be only non-political bodies, like churches, universities, reviews, and national-cultural groups. And is there a noticeable tendency for the manifestation of dissent to progress, by becoming institutionalized, from unorganized and instinctive protest against coercion to more organized activities within the political organisms of the system – the party itself and the Assemblies? The evolution of dissent is parallel to that of institutionalization. Institutionalization, in its turn, appears in the history of any polity only after a period during which public opinion brings pressure to bear on the power-holders. The first question to examine therefore is whether public opinion exists now in the European communist states, and if so, of what kind.

I. PUBLIC OPINION AND DISSENT

Public opinion is still a controversial notion. It is also *the* imponderable part of politics. Perhaps the name itself, vague and somewhat old-fashioned, is responsible for this. Sociology, and for that matter the socialist school of thought, insists that it should be spoken of in the plural, as 'public opinions' because the various sectors, groups and classes of the population have different *Weltanschauungen*, different, and more often than not opposed to each other. Political science, and for that matter the liberal school of thought, insists that public opinion should be assessed and identified by means of referenda or, now, by means of scientific polls; and that only in the measure in which it expresses itself clearly and consistently should it be considered as a determining political factor. Historians insist that the appearance of the notion of public opinion as we understand it today is in itself a historical development which occurred roughly towards the end of the eighteenth century in Western Europe, and a little later in America.[1] Bearing these observations in mind, there is still no way of approaching the question of whether public opinion exists in a communist country, and especially in the European communist states dealt with here, without knowing what is meant, in this context, by public opinion. In this sense public opinion can be said to exist in those states where there is sufficient information, and where the population is sufficiently interested in general problems, to make most sectors and classes of the society feel that they should all obtain fuller information and greater control over the power-holders.

This approach obviously links the existence or non-existence of public opinion in a given society to its symptoms of inward *awareness* and *dissent*, rather than to the exterior signs of *expression* and *influence*. If one were to judge by these latter symptoms one would reach a conclusion which did not differ very much from the aphorism usually held to apply in such matters: 'There is no public opinion in communist states because the government would not allow it to come into the open'. This attitude is unwarranted now in most of the European communist states because in all these countries the party in power knows now that people react to its behaviour and measures with sufficient speed and impact to force it sometimes to alter them; and from a more special point of view, the majority of the European communist states, unlike Soviet Russia, have

[1] Four more recent books, which have in common their blending of the sociological, political and historical definitions of public opinion have helped towards this summary discussion of public opinion in communist countries. They are: Alfred Sauvy: *L'opinion publique*, Paris, 1956; Jurgen Habermas: *Strukturwandel der Öffentlichkeit*, Neuwied, 1962; A. H. Birch: *Representative and Responsible Government*, London, 1964, and R. R. Palmer: *The Age of the Democratic Revolution*, Oxford 1965 – the two last quoted works containing two admirable sections, political and historical respectively, on the subject.

permanently established public-opinion polls. But even if this were not so, it would be a mistake to start from the premiss that the existence of public opinion is proved only by its full articulation and free expression. This would render useless the present endeavour to find out *how* public opinion is *formed*, or re-formed, in countries where it is believed not to exist at all, or any longer; and to discover whether its pressure, even if undetectable on the surface, is felt by the power-holders.

From this point of view it is in a sense immaterial to distinguish whether the process under observation is the emergence or re-emergence of public opinion. (Emergence was the case for instance in Western Europe in the eighteenth century, in Russia in the nineteenth and currently in most African societies. Re-emergence of public opinion is what happens in societies where, as in Napoleon's France or Franco's Spain, or indeed the East European countries after the first years of a period of dictatorship, punch-drunk public opinion regains its strength through different means and manifests itself through different channels.) For in cases both of emergence and re-emergence what matters is *when* and *how* the power-holders begin to reckon with this imponderable – and why this happens. And what matters, too, is to find out, as the sociologists remind us, who are the people who form the re-emergent public opinion. For in most cases of re-emergence, after a revolution or a dictatorship, the new public opinion is formed by different people from those who formed it when it was suppressed, both in terms of social classes and in terms of generations.

Taking thus first the factor of awareness, there is little doubt that the awareness of the population of the European communist states is now acute, especially among the leading and urban strata, even if *they* have changed in the meantime. It is more acute and had more continuity than in Soviet Russia, let alone China, or even Germany under Hitler, where pre-Nazi German public opinion was atrophied by the impact of sheer terrorism, war, and the effect on the nation as a whole of the regime's propaganda without the more modern techniques of international communication to counterbalance it. The best example of change in the structure of public opinion in the East European countries was that which occurred immediately after the war when in countries like Poland, new territories, a new generation and new 'ruling' classes gave the communist regimes in the first years the advantage of having no prepared public opinion to face. They increased this advantage by persecuting and actually reducing to impotence the former urban 'bourgeois and petit-bourgeois' circles which were the most vigorous element of pre-war East European public opinions. But later the functions of public opinion were taken over by those who had moved into the positions and roles of the previous occupants. Since then the process of re-formation has continued uninterrupted, although its pace has varied at different times in different countries. In Poland and in Hungary in 1955–6, and in Czechoslovakia and Rumania in 1963–4, for instance, public opinion re-formed very quickly, but these phases had been preceded and were followed by slower and more difficult ones.

One factor which helped this rapid re-formation is the communist parties' belief in, and need for, ideological persuasion of the population. It is not true that a communist government is indifferent to the mental processes and moral attitudes of the population over which it rules, like a pre-war Latin-American or Balkan dictatorship. Mobilization of the forces of society is the lifeblood of communist administration. Hence for communists one of the most important elements in the operation is the mobilization of the minds, the good will and the 'fervour' of the people (to use the formula of the Chinese communists). The danger with the communist regimes lies, on the contrary, in their *excessive* concern with what they would call in a distorted context 'public opinion' rather than with their indifference towards it. For what they want is to mould it so much and so well that it would adhere to and participate in the aims and programmes of the party, or for that matter of the world-communist movement. The Agitation-Propaganda Department – a name which could not be more self-explanatory – is one of the most important, developed and permanent departments of the entire organization; and Lenin, Stalin, Mao or Tito have always shown, each in his own way, a genuine care in the shaping of its policies for such precise notions as 'persuasion', 'engineering of the souls', 'fervour' or the 'guiding' of the 'people'. The importance which they gave these notions in the entire operation of running the state is in itself significant. The 'new citizen', brain-washed since his earliest years in the severe schools, and with his beliefs and ideas constantly checked and oriented throughout his daily life by the care of the 'Agitprop', is expected to become part and parcel of a 'public' which says what it thinks provided the party knows in advance what it thinks.

It is known now that these hopes of the Communist Parties of East Europe have been brutally disappointed. Most of the studies on these countries rightly present the failure of ideology as the most important aspect of the failure of communist power altogether. While the 'iron curtain' was still down, the rest of the world could not know what changes the new regimes, with their ruthless techniques adopted from the Russians, had produced in the mentalities and attitudes of the people. It was known that the former 'elites' had been decimated, their most influential members scattered in prisons, concentration-camps and in exile. But not much was known about the new elites formed by the new 'ruling class', the workers, and especially by the youth of all classes. Young people had already undergone several years of communist indoctrination, which in all East European countries had followed the obscurantist years of the war and of the immediately pre-war quasi-fascist dictatorships, and they could have been entirely different from their parents and especially from the elite which they were now replacing. But Berlin in 1953, and Poznan in 1956 proved that the workers opposed the Stalinist regimes. And Warsaw and Budapest in 1956 proved beyond any doubt that youth, from the students to the young workers and from the Komsomols in the village to the university graduates newly appointed to 'responsible posts' totally rejected Stalinism. Moreover, whereas they believed, in a general way, that socialism was preferable to capitalism and that for national reasons their regimes represented progress when compared with the pre-war regimes, they still rejected Marxist-Leninism as a 'school of thought'.

Among the main reasons for this dismal, and indeed cardinal failure, of the communist governments in Eastern Europe, at least four well-known and well-analysed in most of the works on communist East Europe should be mentioned. One is the fact that, in any political system in the world, direct political propaganda does not influence people's way of thinking. This is as true in the democracies, where no poll has shown any relation between a party's propaganda and the election results, as it is in all kinds of dictatorship, where, on the contrary, people develop a characteristic allergy against controlled media and techniques of information. Secondly, in the first decade or so the local Agitation-Propaganda Departments chose to use the most appalling methods of Stalinist terrorism and, what was worse, with an unwarranted zeal for Russification. This created a double, political and national, revulsion in the new 'public opinion' of countries not only like Rumania, or Hungary where the population was traditionally anti-Russian but also in Bulgaria or Czechoslovakia where it was pro-Russian. Yet a third reason is that the regimes themselves met with great difficulties and failures, ideologically as a result of the general collapse of Stalinism which was acknowledged at the Twentieth CPSU congress and in the big Sino-Soviet debate; and practically as a result of the economic and administrative mess in which each of them soon found itself. Finally, in the absence of decent *national* media of communication the 'people' kept themselves informed through the *international* media. This, of course, divorced public opinion from the regimes even more, since it enabled the public to compare the regime's assessments of internal and external developments with the reality.

Indeed, one of the main differences between the formation of contemporary public opinion and that of previous epochs, even that of the period before the Second World War, is the increasing part played by international public opinion in national public opinion. This, of course, is even more noticeable in the case of the European communist states. This is due partly to their cultural interpenetration with the continent and with the world at large, and partly to their dependence, as small or middle-sized states, on international developments.

International public opinion nowadays acts in two different ways upon governments and governed alike. First, and most important, it forms through international oganizations ranging from the greatest, the United Nations, to the smaller ones of lawyers, publishers, writers etc., a controlling link between public activities in all countries. Of this both governments and peoples are aware. It is true that in more important matters communist governments show little concern for the reaction of 'international public opinion' or for the protests of international organizations. The most outstanding example of this was the repression of the Hungarian revolt in 1956 by Soviet Russia, and by the Kadar government subsequently appointed by Russia in defiance of all injunctions of the United Nations and with total disregard of the disgust created in the entire world. Moreover it is also true that the communist governments gain more by using United Nations and other international media for their own propaganda purposes than they lose by the impact of the conflicting propaganda of these international organizations reaching their countries through their national media.

Nevertheless, it still remains true that the awareness of the existence of international watch dogs has a profound influence on the behaviour of all communist governments. This influence is weaker in the case of China, which in any event is not a member of these organizations, and strongest in the case of the European communist states. These states belong geographically to the continent of Europe and have the deepest cultural links with the Western part of it; they depend to a considerable extent on trade with countries other than Soviet Russia and those of the Soviet bloc; and their political history has been conditioned by their links with international, and especially European, developments. They came into existence when a new balance of power was struck on the continent between the Western and the Eastern powers and they achieved full sovereignty and independence when the three Eastern empires collapsed and, afterwards, during the existence of the League of Nations. As such they are in reality, and in times of peace, more dependent on 'international public opinion' than their governments would now like to admit.

But international public opinion also acts on national public opinion because of the openness of the communication created by the new media. Press, television and, specially, radio are now universal and they provide complete and simultaneous information to all parts of the world. Radio transmits information about events in the whole world to anyone who is interested in any part of the world, and especially in those countries where dictatorial regimes suppress the free national means of information. In such conditions, and especially in the all too frequent periods of international tension, the radio-transistors have become the most efficient agents of communication. During the Stalinist period, the communist governments subjected the national information-media to abject conditions and instituted a total censorship of foreign publications. They tried, as in Soviet Russia, to 'jam' the transmissions of Western stations and to persecute, by law, those who listened to them. Evidence now fully examined shows that this was of no avail: regardless of the technical difficulties and of the legal risks, people continued to listen intensively; and, generally speaking, people continued without any interruption to be informed of all national and international developments. Moreover, by creating difficult conditions and making people more determined, the communist governments achieved the opposite result from that intended: undue amplification by hearsay and rumour. In the three major crises of the European communist states, that of Berlin in 1953, of Poland in 1955-6, and of Hungary in 1956, the 'people' exaggerated the versions of the events broadcast by RIAS, the 'American radio' or 'Radio London'. These versions were distorted through oral repetition, and bore little resemblance at the end to what had actually been transmitted.

Starting from this premiss the Yugoslav government was the first to grasp that it was better not to 'jam' Western transmissions. Like Gomulka's government in Poland later, and, still more recently, Gheorghiu-Dej's in Rumania, it also had an interest in letting the population obtain more information from other sources about its conflict with Soviet Russia than it could afford to divulge through its own media. By now everybody in every communist European state can listen to any radio station in the world which it is physically possible to hear.

By now, too, other contacts are so well established with other sources of information from the outside world that radio itself is becoming a secondary medium. The media of the regimes themselves, under the double pressure of evolution from within and of fear of losing all influence on the population, have had to improve. The volume and accuracy of news, the fairer and more balanced comments, the deliberate effort to achieve standards equal to those of Western information and culture, have made current Polish, Czechoslovak, East German, not to speak of Yugoslav, newspapers entirely different from what they were in Stalinist times; and this is also true of local radio and television which feel even more the competition with foreign stations. Also the amount of information imported – foreign books, foreign periodicals or indeed foreign professors and lecturers – has increased and is increasing in geometrical proportion every year. This alone explodes any ideological framework or any censorship the regimes might still try to keep. Finally, there are the possibilities offered, in conditions which vary from time to time and from country to country, to residents of these countries to travel abroad: East Germans to West Germany, Hungarians and Czechoslovaks to Austria, and Poles and to a lesser degree Rumanians to France, Britain and Italy. To see with their own eyes, to speak with other people and to bring back with them books and publications of their choice has now become perhaps the most efficient source of information for members of communist states. In this sense the new 'public opinion' is now informed as it should be; for it is able to judge a development soon after its occurrence against a background of impartial, accurate and independent assessment.

This leads to a further question: who are the people most likely to acquire by these means the information and background which is essential to this new awareness? It is obvious that in the conditions prevailing in the communist European states, those who are most likely to absorb a large amount of information are also those who can exert the most efficient 'checks' on the party. They are those who have already been described in the previous part of this book: the leaders of the other apparats, the top layers of the two working classes, the foremen, and, above all, the elites, technicians and creative intelligentsia. Therefore, the circles of society whose standard of living and of prestige are high enough for their members to have the means of information, to travel abroad and to keep in contact with the outside, non-communist, world are the same as those which by virtue of occupying the 'responsible posts' are best informed also about the internal situation, most consulted by the party and government, and ultimately in the best position to help or to hinder the administration by providing or withholding their co-operation. In Western Europe in the eighteenth century it was the merchants, the magistrates, the members or former members of the courts, and other groups of lower strata whose numbers and importance were increased by social mobility, and who, by obtaining more genuine information and by establishing closer and closer exchanges of news between themselves, were in a position to press for further improvements and reforms in the functioning, or nonfunctioning, of the political system. In the communist European states of the twentieth century another section of society is in the same position: it is the experts, the technicians, the artists and intellectuals, the managers, the executives, the students, the foremen, the leaders of workers and peasant organizations and the occupants of the higher positions of the various apparats who form the larger sphere of public opinion.

This view has led the majority of authors and commentators to believe that this movement, once started, creates an impetus of its own; that the intelligentsia presses naturally and, as it were, functionally for greater freedom; that it makes breaches through which the national pressure for freedom will sweep forward and demolish all other obstacles. This is an over-simplified view. It is over-simplified, first, because it overlooks the fact that, as yet, the re-formed and re-emerging East European public opinion has not asserted itself as an overwhelming factor in the policy-making of these countries. It also overlooks the fact that like all public opinion, the still inchoate public opinion described here is not always *against* the government or the power-holders. Public opinion is not always against the government as a whole – on the contrary it tends to be divided into a variety of opinions and attitudes according to the different issues with which it is faced. In the case of the reforming public opinion of the communist European states this is even more noticeable. There the mixture of political vested interests in the regime and of functional and ideological disagreement within it produce very involved and complex relations for all individuals and groups who formulate public opinion.

Moreover in these countries there are now *limited, non-communist* grounds of congruence between the opinions of some sectors of society and those professed by the governments. The Rumanian communist government, by its characteristic switching from Marxist-Leninist attitudes and semantics to sheer nationalist, even chauvinistic ones, rallied behind it a new and active 'public opinion'. But at the same time the Rumanian government itself is now committed to maintain this new attitude and to observe these new principles if it wants to keep this backing. The same is true of the new *modus vivendi* between the Czechoslovak government and Czechoslovak, and especially Slovak, public opinion on the issues of economic and administrative reform based on decentralization.

It would therefore be erroneous to think that the 'pure need for freedom' or the 'self-generating idealism of reform' lead to an immediate and total coalition of all *cognoscenti*, of all those who show a higher awareness, against the power-holders on all issues and at all times. Many of these people and of these categories are also acutely conscious that their present privileges are inevitably linked with the present regime and many of them have reasons to approve of it as well as reasons to dissent. Yet there are deep and widespread grounds for dissent which might catalyse many sectors and groups, attitudes and orientations, into a coherent public opinion, pitted against the power-holders and bind them together to press common claims and general demands upon them.

The motives of dissent

In states ruled by communist parties (that is parties which are proletarian, authoritarian, atheistic and internationalistic) there are four main motives of dissent. The political grievances of all individuals or groups who demand that freedom of expression of opinion and of information should be granted, restored or enlarged form the first category. The social and professional grievances of classes and groups which claim that the government discriminates against them and impedes their professional or commercial activities are another. The religious grievances of worshippers who claim that the state interferes with the practice of their faith play an important, direct and indirect part. Finally, the most virulent are the nationalistic grievances either of the people as a whole, when they see the sovereignty of their country curbed or overruled for the benefit of a suzerain power, or of ethnic or regional groups which claim that the central administration oppresses or neglects them. Indeed in moments of crisis, all these grievances take the form of a general claim for 'freedom'. But of them all, the nationalistic grievances provide the broadest common ground. This remains true even if they are expressed in many different ways. For some, these emotions conjure up the image of a golden past which could be brought back if the old regime was restored. While others, the younger ones – this is very much a matter of generations – regard both the failed past and the transitional present as of secondary importance, and are intent on bringing into existence the promised 'society' or 'nation' of the future.

In this sense, of course, the claim for 'freedom of expression' goes together with that of freeing the economy. To be sure, there is an important difference in this respect between the opposition in developed and undeveloped countries. But in the European communist states the various layers of contemporary public opinion criticize both the economic and the political restrictions. And they are naturally inclined to give priority to the latter. Contemporary public opinion in each of the European communist states crystallizes these grievances into claims against arbitrariness, against subjugation and against interference with religious belief.

Against arbitrariness. The claim for freedom – and for order – is basically the general revulsion against, and fear of, arbitrariness. Both the 'citizens' of an entire state, and those who share any responsibility for it, aspire towards a basic order to be respected by everybody, and which offers a minimum of protection to everybody. Arbitrariness is that same spectre which haunts a man at work during the day when he does not know whether he will be able to 'fulfil' his overwhelming tasks, and at home during the night when he does not know whether, to use a *cliché* of all totalitarian states, he will not 'hear the knock on the door'. Here again it may be noted that in conditions of total arbitrariness there can be no question of public opinion establishing itself gradually. There may be quick upsurges of anomic indignation and hatred, driving the population into emotional and violent reactions. But there can be no considered advice from professional groups if they are constantly dragooned into fulfilling tasks which they know to be either impossible or against the national interest. No consensus can be achieved with men who see only one solution for all their troubles: the end of the terroristic regime.

The quest for justice in a society must always end in the establishment of an independent judiciary, which alone can keep in check the arbitrariness of the executive. But this, in its turn, brings into question the entire structure of the state – the unity or separation of powers, the doctrine of the state and the concept of legitimacy. It is the crux of the main political debate. But this debate cannot be brought into the open at once because it might seem too far-fetched and too abstract to mean enough to those submerged in the worries of daily life. This is why the battle fought by an incipient public opinion in a communist country is usually limited to the objective of 'legality', or even 'socialist legality' – which means that even within a communist state there should be some degree of order, and respect for that degree of order. This does not mean only the indispensable restoration of some authority and independence to the courts and the magistrates. It means also respect for the legal and statutory provisions governing all relations of authority between subordinate and superior, regardless of whether these are individual relations or whether they are relations between the state administration, the enterprises, the apparats and whatever other collective bodies may be involved. The notion of legality, or of socialist legality, contains therefore two inter-related aspects: that of the laws and institutions and that of the political climate.

The climate of legality has been changing steadily in the communist European states since Stalin's death. There were of course dramatic setbacks for the entire region, like that which followed the crushing of the Hungarian revolution; and there are striking differences between the various states, Yugoslavia, Hungary, Czechoslovakia and Poland being the most advanced. But Poland, which had been in the lead is now showing greater reluctance to grant further reforms and is, from this point of view, being outdistanced by other communist countries. A characteristically paradoxical situation prevails in East Germany where the brutality and ruthlessness of the system and its regulations is accompanied by great meticulousness and concern for legal procedures at all levels of authority and especially at the lower ones. The eradication of corruption, whether undertaken sporadically or consistently, creates another paradoxical situation. For whereas in any dictatorship corruption is a lubricant which helps towards the humanization and the attenuation of the unabated pressure on individuals, it is also one of the main obstacles to the establishment of a true legality. But if one looks back to the last decade of the fight for legality one finds again that it is the rule of and by the political police which was, and still is, the main target of this campaign against arbitrariness. The process of curbing the political police started in Soviet Russia in 1953 and in Poland and Hungary in 1956. It came to the fore again in 1963 in Poland as one of the points of conflict between the progressives and the Partisans; and in Yugoslavia in 1966, where the political police waged a strange counter-attack against the spreading of the climate and institutions of legality. In all these countries it was this stronghold of Stalinism that was affected first and most directly by the change in the climate of legality.

As far as new institutions of legality are concerned, the country in which the most profound and characteristic changes have recently occurred is Yugoslavia. There, a Federal Constitutional Court[2] started to function in February 1964. It had been established by the Constitution of 1963, which in its article 241, makes it responsible for resolving 'disputes on rights and duties between the

[2] See a very good study by Winston M. Fisk and A. Z. Rubinstein *Yugoslavia's Constitutional Court*, in *East Europe*, New York, July 1966.

Federation and a republic, between republics and between other socio-political communities in the territories of two or more republics'. But the court must also protect 'other basic freedoms and rights, whenever they are infringed by individual edicts and deeds'. In theory the constitutional court is an independent organ of the Federation. The Federal Assembly, the Federal Executive organ, the Supreme Court of Yugoslavia and the other supreme courts of the Federation, the Federal Public Prosecutor, the republican constitutional courts, the assembly of a commune or of a self-managed enterprise can submit to the court cases in which legal and constitutional points are at stake. The main object of the constitutional court is to look into the constitutionalism of the relations between the state and the self-managed enterprises and into those between superior organs of the state administration and the self-administered communes. But in more far-fetched interpretations, especially of article 4 of the special law on the constitutional court, which states that 'everyone can request constitutional court proceedings', it is said that even private 'citizens' can submit questions of constitutionalism to the court. The case of the individual farmers and landowners from a Dalmatian commune whose land was returned to them by a decision of the Constitutional Court, when they took their case against expropriation by the commune before it, provides an encouraging example.[3]

The constitutional court, as created in 1964, presented two ominous flaws. One was that the President of this 'supreme and independent' organ, Blazo Iovanović, was and is also a member of the Executive Committee of the Central Committee. This coincidence was aggravated by the fact that there is no provision stating that the President or the judges should *not* be members of the League. The relation between an independent judge and a party which demands total dedication from its members is equivocal. The other drawback was that, according to the law, the judges of the constitutional court are elected and dismissed by the Federal National Assembly but 'on the recommendation of the President of the Republic'. These personal and political claims on the members of an organ pretending to be supreme and totally independent were rightly criticized, and denounced as a sign that this was yet another façade-institution controlled from within by the power-holders. This may be so. But it may also be a transitional phase and

[3] Fisk and Rubinstein, loc. cit.

arrangement. A dictatorial regime in transformation often allows the formation, within the structure of its dictatorship, of institutions contrary to its own basic principles on condition that for a shorter or longer period it can keep political control. Regimes which, under the pressure of public opinion, grant rights, laws and institutions contradictory to their basic rules, always hope that they will remain ineffectual and empty of substance. But institutions have a life of their own and more often than not they survive the regimes which established them only as façades.

Indeed, the greatest importance of the constitutional court of Yugoslavia is that it was, and remains the first case of the reappearance within the structure of a communist state of a functional organ of legality. The fact, for instance, that the court issued its own memorandum on certain facts of significance for constitutionality and legality[4] is characteristic of its functionalistic expansion. The court is one of the instruments of the institutionalization, which alone can precede and lead to a new constitutional pluralism. It is thus also a milestone along the way of the reforms now demanded by Yugoslav public opinion.

The other European communist states have not yet followed the Yugoslav example. But, by now, in practically every one of these states it is fully understood and openly argued in the current 'great debate' that the pressure of public opinion leads towards institutionalization, which in turn leads to legality. 'Without public opinion, in its institutional aspect, for example without the press as an instrument of its formation and expression, the actual mass media cannot work and the constitutional system cannot function. The point is to normalize the constitutional relations, to introduce a procedure whereby an act of the public prosecutor or of any other judicial or administrative body could be sanctioned by court decisions in the case of a violation of a provision of the law or of a breach of some administrative regulation', claimed the journal of the Law Institute of the Czechoslovak Academy of Sciences in 1966.[5]

Against subjugation. Another main motive of dissent is that of

[4] 29 October 1965. It recommended the adoption of a unified civil code, particularly with regard to property rights, of a law concerning the responsibilities of state employees, and criticized the Federal Executive Council for often exceeding its authority.

[5] Pavel Peska: *The Future of Constitutional law and of Constitutionalism,* 5/1966, translated in *RFE Czechoslovak Press Survey, 1806–1966.*

nationalism. The quest for legality faces the Communist Party with the dilemma of whether to abandon its basic principle of the 'unity of power' for the old 'separation of powers'. The quest for national independence and sovereignty faces the party, as a basically internationalist party, with the dilemma of whether to abandon its basic principle of world communist allegiance and adopt instead the old national aspirations and egoisms. This is another range of issues, like those concerning legality, behind which the entire population will swiftly rally. The East European peoples are thus particularly suspicious of the communist parties, known to have been part and parcel of the International, and to have come to power only when Soviet Russia, a foreign power, began to dominate the Eastern part of the European continent. This suspicion was aggravated by the fact that the worst outrages, and the last to be forgiven, of the communist governments under Stalin, were perpetrated against the pride and sensitivity of these most nationalistic peoples. The blind submission of the new power-holders to the orders of the metropolitan or proconsular organs of the Soviet administration shocked the populations more than anything else. The one example – Yugoslavia, under Tito – of a European communist state daring to resist and defy Soviet Russia, electrified all the other peoples of the region.

Indeed, whenever any of these governments showed a genuine determination to resist further encroachments of Soviet control over national affairs, and to shake-off some of the servitudes imposed by Soviet Russia during the period of initial collaboration, they immediately found a genuine response from large sectors of the population. This was already obvious in the case of Yugoslavia in 1948, and Poland and Hungary in 1956. Regardless of the fact that each of these countries had a different background, they all had in common the spontaneous trust shown, and the backing given, by large sectors of the population until then resolutely hostile. But the backing given to a Communist Party, or to that wing of a Communist Party which claimed to be in conflict with Soviet Russia, was accompanied, if not conditioned, in all these cases by characteristic demands for changes in the communist social and economic system. These the party promised to make. They amounted, in fact, to breaches in the initial programme and ideology of these parties, set up under the inspiration of the CPSU and implemented under its supervision. Allowing the peasants to abandon collectivization; letting the workers set up the workers' councils; giving more creative freedom to the intellectuals and artists and allowing them to reject the *tabus* of socialist-realism or of the primacy of Russian culture in their own national culture; all these measures were granted or promised by the rebel parties in order to enrol greater popular support. These reforms also amounted to the implicit or explicit confession by the rebel party, or party-wing, that the Soviet example was not always or even generally relevant to that particular East European state, and, for that matter, to East Europe. This is also what the CPSU saw in these changes: gross ideological deviations and failures for which the Yugoslavs, out of the Soviet reach, were publicly criticized, in 1948, and again in 1958. But the deviations were corrected, partly in Poland and totally in Hungary, as soon as the collaboration with Soviet Russia of the new governments of these states was re-established in 1956–7.

But even in the Yugoslav, Polish and Hungarian cases it was obvious that although these reforms were necessary if the 'national communist' government was to gain some popular backing, they were not the ultimate reason for the support of the population. The ultimate reason was still the hope of most of the people that the way to national and political dignity and freedom would begin with the termination of communist Russia's control over the country. Terror, arbitrariness, economic exploitation, social persecution, were all attributed to the 'Muscovites' from the Communist Party and from the security police. By weakening, if not abolishing the 'Muscovite' control over the affairs of the party and government, a trend would begin which would lead to national and political emancipation.

The logic of this approach was confirmed in the case of the Rumanian party and government in 1963. Its quarrel with the Soviet government and the CPSU originated from its ultimate refusal to bow to the decisions of COMECON, first, to institute a supranational planning board for all the economies of the region and, secondly, to allot to Rumania and Bulgaria in the new regional planning the parts of permanent agricultural and light industry producers. But this turned out to be the top of an iceberg, the basis of which was formed by the past grievances of the Rumanians against all the persecutions and discriminations to which they had been subjected in Stalin's time and by their firm resolution that they should not be repeated.

When, in 1963, the Rumanian communists won their battle against Khrushchev on the COMECON issue, the process of de-russification in the country as a whole was already well on the way. According to the official interpretation, it had started within the top layers of the party itself and of the mighty political police, as early as 1952, when the purely 'Muscovite' troika of the leadership, Ana Pauker, Vasile Luca and Teohari Georgescu had fallen. It had appeared more clearly since the autumn of 1958 when the new, anti-COMECON, economic plan was prepared – an event which in its turn had taken place only a few months after the withdrawal of the Soviet troops from Rumania. The new 'native' leadership of Gheorghiu-Dej, Maurer and Ceausescu, had cautiously prepared the ground by spreading among the rank and file of the party and apparats, and through them to as wide sectors of the population as possible, the story of the 'resistance' put up by the party against 'the Russians'. The purge of Muscovites from within these ranks and their steady replacement by young Rumanians already trained in a pragmatic spirit of national achievement, completed the attempt to find the pulse of broader layers of the population.

This attempt proved to be successful and sufficient. For, unlike the Yugoslav, Polish, and Nagy-wing of the Hungarian party, the Rumanian party did not promise, or indeed grant, any social or economic concessions. On the contrary it embarked on a resolute and accelerated scheme of Stalinist economic policy, 'achieving' collectivization before the original target date, and continuing an ambitious plan of autarchic industrialization. Yet the party began to become popular with some sectors of the Rumanian population and by now the Communist Party of Rumania is notorious for the way in which it emphasizes and indeed, over-emphasizes the nationalist argument. This movement shows that the bridge which was thus built between the isolated party and some sectors of the population was based on the latter's supreme interest in shaking off the Russian subjugation of the country. Even within the framework of a dogmatic, Stalinist, economic and political doctrine re-emergent Rumanian public opinion sensed that if the breach with the Russians was real it should then lead the power-holders to grant further 'national' concessions against the formerly Russian-controlled terroristic security police; against the formerly

Russian-dominated obscurantist Agitprop control of cultural life; against the formerly Russian-inspired dictatorial and bureaucratic methods of government of the party-apparat; and against the formerly Russian-imposed anti-West policy of the communist government. The fault for all these was placed courteously and shrewdly on the past 'Muscovite' influence.

Against interference with religious belief. The final major motive of dissent in the European communist states to be mentioned here is the feeling of the faithful against the atheistic party and its militantly atheistic philosophy. Here again the party would eventually be faced with a categoric dilemma: for if it allowed religious worship to continue for ever, then a vast enclave of people of a different outlook, and indeed faith, would be thus for ever maintained in what should be the ideologically homogeneous body of the communist society. The Christian philosophy of life and its social, economic and political teachings, separates the individual communicant member of the Church from the active member of the party indoctrinated in the Marxist-Leninist philosophy of life. The hierarchies of both institutions, the party and the Church, are both fully aware of this. The relationship between church and state since the communist party came to power in the East European countries, has been a cat-and-mouse game, with ups and downs, acute phases, compromises and shrewd tactics on both sides; but the basic dissent always remains.

Here a difference should be noted between the countries with a predominantly Roman Catholic population and the others. The Catholic Church has, for two reasons, a particularly bitter conflict with the communist government. One is that unlike the Orthodox Church (predominant in Russia, Bulgaria, Rumania and Serbia, but not in Croatia or Slovenia) it is separated from the state. The Orthodox Churches have on the contrary recognized the authority of the state – and the hierarchy and clergy are appointed and paid by the state. The second cause of difference is that the Roman Catholic Church has another centre of command (for the same reason Zionism is also not tolerated by the communists), located geographically in Rome. Although in principle Rome does not interfere with the relations between the individual Catholics and the authorities of the respective state in which they live and worship, it influences the attitudes of the congregations at large. These two causes, namely the separation of their church from the state together with the existence of a second authority means that Catholics suffer a deeper psychological dichotomy than the Orthodox or Protestants. Their allegiance to God and to Caesar is, in any case and in any state, in much more open conflict than in the case of worshippers of other faiths in which state and church appear to converge, at the worldly pinnacle of power, forming a 'closed universe'.

It is therefore understandable that whereas there is a basic dissent between all Christian believers and atheistic power-holders, in the case of Catholics it is enhanced by the militant attitude of the Roman Catholic Church itself in its world-fight with the anti-Christs. Dissent against the communist governments was for this reason always more strongly expressed in two predominantly Catholic countries: Poland and Hungary. In these countries, the citizen-and-worshipper felt more reason to oppose the communist regime, and the hierarchies took up adamant positions in the major political-spiritual issues. In doing so they were inspired by the thought that they were defending the faithful under their jurisdiction against the aggressive atheistic state and that their ultimate responsibility was to God and to the Universal Church, through Rome, and not to the respective head of state or administration. The primate of Croatia died in prison; the primate of Hungary is an extra-territorial refugee in the American Embassy in Budapest; and the primate of Poland was again in 1966 refused a passport to go to Rome. (The Protestant Church in East Germany of which the supreme hierarchy is located, not in the territory of the state, but in West Germany, distinguishes itself by its pugnacity in the educational and civic issues raised by communist policy.)

The communist power-holders have alternated between violent campaigns of liquidation of the 'opium of the people' from within their societies, and periods of compromise and cajoling. The most typical example of this remains the long lull under Stalin during the Second World War. He then 'mobilized' the Orthodox Church of Russia for the defence of the Fatherland and, for this all-important task, allowed the Churches more freedom than at any time since the communists had come to power. After the war, of course, the party fell back into its virulent, but ineffective, threats against and denunciations of religion. In Poland, Rumania, Yugoslavia and in the Hungary of Nagy, the 'national common cause' against Soviet Russia provided a new bridge between the party and the

Church. Generally speaking, there is now in every country an uneasy compromise between the two weary warriors. The state tries not to interfere too much with religious activities; but it watches the flux of religious attendance and worship as one of its barometers of political climate. The Church tries to protect the essential moral purity of its worshippers, but tries to avoid unnecessary mass-actions which would only give the Communist Parties grounds for mass-repression.

In this difficult and precarious compromise, public opinion, both international and national, played and plays a very important part. Internationally, the Roman Catholic Church, under the influence of modern Catholic opinion, has advanced steadily towards social-economic positions which render its philosophy less incompatible with some of the basic principles of 'socialism', if not of Marxism-Leninism; and Catholics both inside and outside the two major West European Communist Parties, the Italian and the French, have exercised their influence by trying to sharpen the edges of the philosophy of these parties on spiritual and religious matters. They and other groups and schools of thought have brought their parties to accept their different philosophies with greater open-mindedness and generally to be more tolerant of the idea of pluralism. As for national public opinion in each of the European communist states, it has acted in this matter too as an active intermediary between the two opposing bodies. Public opinion in these states has pressed and is pressing the government to recognize the Church as yet another institution of the social and national, if not political, life. They ask it to institutionalize the Church's activities by allowing the worshippers to worship, and the clergy to carry out their duties, freely – provided that, on the other hand, the Church, clergy and worshippers themselves observe the religious limits of their activities.

This is, very briefly sketched, the impact of the basic political, economic, national and spiritual causes of dissent of the population on the rule of a communist party. They form with a great number of other, smaller and derivative causes of dissent, a sufficiently broad basis in political society to rally together sizeable parts of it, and to crystallize their common points of disagreement into a collective opposition to the government in power. This process is helped by the fact that in all European communist countries there is, by now, enough information available to educate public opinion, to counteract the information provided by the governments, and to increase the demand for more and better information to be made available to all citizens. Finally, the pressure of this growing body of public opinion is mainly exercised in one direction and towards one purpose: institutionalization. How this is done and to what this is leading, or has already led, is a matter which should be now examined.

2. AGGREGATION

The growing body of public opinion and the various dissents crystallize around current issues and aggregate at rallying points. This is how they form a unified public opinion and a common dissent. This dissent later becomes opposition – whether political or not – by a process of institutionalization.

The process of aggregation is a haphazard one. In distress, anger and confusion, anomic crowds gather around any body, person or institution, which seems to say the words they want to hear, or which they themselves had not until then clearly postulated. The same process is noticeable, on a larger or smaller scale, and in slower or quicker rhythms in the manifestation of opposition in all dictatorial states. Institutions and personalities, who might or might not consciously intend to lead attitudes and movements become, for shorter or longer periods, the spontaneously elected standard-bearers of the aggregating multitudes. Sometimes these standard-bearers did intend to seek support for their own determination to criticize some, or the whole, of the power-holders' way of ruling. Sometimes they are just picked up in a rather accidental way by unco-ordinated trends of opinion and an unsolicited leadership is bestowed upon them: *les meneurs sont menés*, as the French saying goes. But in all cases there is mutual influence and stimulation between the leaders and the led. This reciprocity gradually produces further clarification of attitudes and resolution of tempers.

There is a wide variety of centres of aggregation, ranging from the very short lived to the permanent. In the European communist states, where the previous institutions of opposition, and especially the other political parties, the natural channels, have been banned, the tendency is to find new non-political centres which can gradually and involuntarily take some indirect political positions. Only five main centres of aggregation will be discussed here: the churches, the army, the universities and the cultural reviews and groups; and finally the personalities. The present limited examination will look at a typical example of each centre of aggregation in the particular East European country where it is most detectable and easiest to observe. But some general conclusions can be drawn which are valid, with inevitable variations, for all seven states under discussion.

The Roman Catholic Church in Poland

Apart from their oecumenical role the churches have played in most countries of Eastern Europe the part of spiritual, cultural and national leaders of peoples in particular need of protection in their instinctive, ethnical and national, defence against different conquerors. They have shown themselves in Poland, Rumania or Bulgaria particularly, intent on achieving national emancipation and sovereignty. In such countries the priests have been spiritual mentors, cultural teachers and national, if not political leaders, of all these peoples during their long centuries of struggle for the preservation of national identity and unity. In times of national distress the historical reflex of these peoples is to gather around the churches where they will receive individual consolation and collective inspiration. This applies not only to regular churchgoers, but also to people who, in normal times, ignore the church in which they were baptized. (Incidentally, baptism remains the universal practice even now in Eastern Europe.) This applies also to all social classes, although, again, in normal times, the peasantry and the bourgeoisie would provide greater percentages of church-attendance than the workers or the intelligentsia. But in times of distress the need for individual relief and for national encouragement brings renewed majorities of the Eastern European people to the church.

In Poland the Roman Catholic Church, which in 1966, in dramatic conditions, celebrated its 'millennium' (to be touched upon later in these pages), undeniably played in the history of the nation the part of defender of national unity. It did so throughout the different political and constitutional phases which punctuated the dramatic history of this, as of many other, East European countries. At each of these stages, as for instance during the first four centuries of the Piast dynasty, or when the Swedish, the Russian, the Prussian or the Austrian armies occupied or carved up the territory of Poland, her Primates became again the natural leader of the people and Czestochowa, the shrine of the Black Madonna, the rallying place of the nation. After 1945, in spite of the pre-war and war-time rather lukewarm attitude of the hierarchy towards opposition to Hitler, the Church was still popular.[6] But, in any case, soon after the Russian-inspired communist government began encroaching on the national and political freedom of the country, and especially after the abolition of the other political parties, the Church was invested again with the role of exponent of the main national grievances. From 1945 to 1948 the communist-led government did not dare to take any grave steps against the Church (the administrative and military oath was still religious), but such measures as the repudiation, in 1945, of the concordat between the Polish government and the Vatican and the introduction of civil marriage undermined the external and internal status of the Church. In turn the Church tried to keep as aloof as possible from direct political entanglements, and its main paper, *Tygodnik Powszcheny*, observed an attitude of neutrality.

But in 1947 the internal political struggle had reached the point when the Communist Party, under renewed Russian orders, launched an all-out offensive in all directions in order to achieve the dictatorship of the proletariat. The then Primate, Cardinal Hlond protested in a famous pastoral letter of April 1947 against 'the revolutionary manoeuvres on a grand scale', and his letter drew a prophetic and clear sighted rejoinder from the Democratic Bloc, the communist front-organization, to the effect that 'it is the leaders of the Catholic Church who have assumed the role of opposition to the people's power in Poland'.[7] In order to undermine the political influence of the Church the Communist Party resorted to its usual technique of creating from within the Church two organizations which, while under its control and in its pay, would channel the faithful in its direction. One was the 'Progressive

[6] Here two very reliable authors, Korbonsky: loc. cit., and Hiscocks: loc. cit., differ in opinion, the former thinking that this attitude had cost the Polish Church much, the latter maintaining that its 'prestige and influence stood high'.
[7] Quoted in Hiscocks, *Poland, Bridge for the Abyss* (London, 1963), p. 132.

Catholic Movement' *Pax*, founded by the strange Boleslaw Piasecki.[8] He was granted enormous funds so that *Pax* could establish itself as a publishing house and a going industrial concern. The other group was that of the 'patriot priests' under which name a small percentage of the Polish clergy expressed more favourable thoughts and attitudes towards the government than the adamant views of the hierarchy. Both organizations, as happens always in the difficult conditions of political life in a dictatorship, carried with them also some innocent members of the public who by temperament, convictions, or opportunism preferred to stick as long as was possible to the 'middle way'. The main grievances of the Church against the party arose on four main issues: religious freedom, general freedom, education and collectivization.

Already in 1946 the Church had advised the faithful to vote against the communists on these four issues. After 1948 when collectivization loomed on the political horizon, the tension between the government and Church grew. It was brought to a very sharp crisis by the Vatican decree of July 1949 excommunicating Catholics who actively supported communists. The party seized the Church's lands, dissolved its welfare organization *Caritas*, proceeded to mass-arrests of priests, monks and nuns, and suspended its monthly *Znak*.

After Cardinal Hlond's death in 1948, a 47-year-old Archbishop, later to become Cardinal, Stefan Wyszinski, was in charge of the Church. He was the son of a church organist and had shown in his early years a great interest in the social aspects of religion, advocating a progressive attitude and sweeping social and economic reforms in his writings. During the war he fought in the underground and was then made Bishop of Lublin. With the rapid radicalization of the party after Gomulka's fall, and with the sterner attitudes taken by the Vatican, Wyszinski realized that the Church was heading for very difficult times. In April 1950 an agreement was signed between the episcopate and the government whereby it was recognized that 'the principle that the Pope is the most competent and the highest Church authority refers to matters of faith, morality and Church jurisdiction; in other matters, the Episcopate follows the

[8] See Lucian Blit: *The Eastern Pretender, The Story of Boleslaw Piasecki*, London 1965, in which the author produces evidence to show that this former fascist leader was later saved from Polish prisons by General Serov, at that time Deputy-head of the NKVD, and was used as the principal agent of the Russian services in the Polish church.

Polish national interest'. The episcopate recognized the 'Recovered Territories' as part of the national territory. Finally, and this was one of the government's main objectives, the episcopate undertook to 'explain to the clergy that it is not to oppose the expansion of co-operatives in the country's agriculture, since all co-operatives, by their very nature are based on the ethical premiss of human nature'. In exchange for these substantial concessions the government undertook not to interfere with public worship and the traditional processions of the Church, or with the religious education in the Church's schools and university.

But agreements between two opposing centres of influence such as the party and the Church, cannot last long, especially in conditions of intense and stifled political struggle. During 1952 and 1953, the worst Stalinist years, relations worsened in the entire communist bloc. The party continued the persecution, the mass-arrests and suspended the Church's main publication *Tygodnik Powszcheny* because it had refused to commemorate Stalin's death. (A year later it was handed to Piasecki and his *Pax*.) On 8 May 1953 all the bishops of the Catholic Church sent a memorandum to the government protesting against the new measures and stated that 'we have not the right to put on the altars of Caesar that which belongs to God. *Non possumus*.' Wyszinski personally in a Corpus Christi sermon said that the Polish Church would defend its rights 'even to the point of shedding blood'. He was arrested in October 1953 together with eight other bishops and hundreds of priests. 'As has so often been the case in Polish history, the Church became the symbol of resistance to oppression.'[9]

This was shown more and more by increasing attendance at the churches and by the increased contacts between the persecuted clergy and the oppressed population. All this was possible because the churches remained open. No communist government had yet dared to close all churches, and a Polish one would be even less likely than the others to do so. This was demonstrated with striking clarity on 26 August 1956. The atmosphere of crisis caused by the Poznan incidents and the turmoil within the party due to the split between the Muscovites and the National-Communists – who wanted to bring Gomulka back in spite of Russian opposition – had roused the population. Once again a religious occasion was used as the means of a massive political demonstration. This was the

[9] Hiscocks, loc. cit., pp. 164–6.

three-hundredth anniversary of the shrine of the Black Madonna of Czestochowa. Some million and a half people attended. 'The picture of the Black Madonna was taken in solemn procession round the monastery. In the centre of the procession there was carried the throne of Cardinal Wyszinski, empty except for a large bouquet of red and white flowers, representing the national colours of Poland. The occasion was much more than a religious celebration. Since the Church had been persecuted by the Communists the great majority of Polish workers had given it their support or sympathy: one of the demands of the Poznan workers had been for the release of Cardinal Wyszinski. The gathering at Czestochowa, therefore was the second large-scale demonstration by the Polish people of discontent with the regime, and it was on a much larger scale than Poznan.'[10]

On 21 October 1956, Gomulka was liberated from his detention, and was re-appointed, in spite of a desperate attempt by the Russians to resist the move, General-Secretary of the party. A week later Wyszinski was freed from arrest and resumed his duties as Primate. A new and dramatic situation was thus set up: the country was divided politically between the Secretary and the Cardinal. One headed the government and its phalanxes. The other headed the opposition and its crowds.

The two men, both of strong characters, wills and intellects, both inclined to be stubborn, knew each other well. In spite of their conflicting positions and creeds they shared much common ground, social and intellectual affinities, and, above all, strong national feeling and anxiety for Poland. In 1956 they were both convinced that an open clash between the two bodies which they headed could only play into the hands of the Russians. Indeed the Russians had already seized, in Hungary, the opportunity of a civil war to bring back their own troops of occupation. Both Wyszinski and Gomulka are convinced that the geo-political position of Poland, between Russia and Germany, is her greatest historical and political handicap. Gomulka undertook drastic reforms in all directions and fields when he returned to power in 1956. National de-russification was the theme: the farmers were allowed to disband the collective farms, the workers to establish workers' councils, the universities and circles to organize their own activities; basic improvements in the elections for and the functioning of the Parliament (Sejm),

[10] Hiscocks, loc. cit., 201–202.

were promised and partly effected. The Cardinal and the Church behind him were sympathetic enough to these reforms to decide that the Church should collaborate with the new regime. An actual truce was established.[11] This worked smoothly until 1960 in spite of the fact that the Gomulka regime was becoming obviously less liberal, and with greater difficulty between 1960 and 1965 as the stubbornness of the communist regime increased. It was broken at the end of 1965 on the very issue on which the political agreement was based: the attitude towards Germany.

What the Church wanted to obtain during these years of 'national reconstruction and consolidation' was, first, its own 'reconstruction and consolidation'. Communist and Catholic writers although in open polemic in Poland, both recognize that this had been obtained. Thus, the Catholics:[12] 'Poland has the reputation of a country of filled churches. This is a fact. This observation is supported by the statistics of religious practice. Above all, one must emphasize the very high (95 per cent) percentage of people baptized in the Catholic Church out of the population total. There are almost no cases of children of Catholic parents not being baptized, particularly if one disregards the fact that baptism is nowadays often delayed. Parish registers show, however, that there is some delay in baptizing children, in comparison with fifty years ago, when they were baptized on the day they were born or the day after. One may point out, however, that the old registers may not be precise. The parents may have given the day of baptism as the day of birth, in order to please the parish priest who would insist on having a child baptized on the day it was born.'

The same source shows that the average attendance is rather high: in 80 per cent of the parishes the number of those present at Mass amounted to between 65 and 80 per cent of the congregation. From a social point of view 'the traditional division into rural and city religiousness does not fully apply here, and the differences which did exist a few decades ago are becoming more and more indistinct. First of all, there is no basic difference in religious practices. In this respect, only three main industrial centres are different (Warsaw, Lodz and the Silesian Basin) in which, because of the

[11] In the election of 1957 the Church advised the faithful to vote although the electoral law and procedures favoured the Polish Workers Party.

[12] 'What is Polish Catholicism like?', a study by J. Majka in *Znak*, Warsaw, March 1966.

specific conditions of the formation of religiousness, the index of practices is much lower. Certain new industrial centres are approaching the above areas in this respect. In other Polish workers' areas, and in particular in Silesia, a traditional type of religiousness has been formed, adapted to the new, urban and industrial working and living conditions. The new, post-war wave of urbanization has not resulted, at least thus far, in a mass decline of religiousness.' As far as age-groups are concerned, although the inquiries conducted found it more difficult to stress the participation of the younger generation, a 'survey conducted by the Centre of Study of Public Opinion at the Polish Radio Network about the religious attitudes of youth, but from the point of view of membership in political organizations (and hence it cannot be representative for the whole of youth, since it appears from the same survey that members of youth organizations are less religious) showed that 78·2 per cent of those polled claim to be Catholics, and 4·3 per cent are atheists.' It also appears from the above survey that 70 per cent of the group under study has no doubt as to the basic tenets of religion and feels obliged to fulfil the basic religious duties; 74·5 per cent believes that religious education of children is their duty; and 76·4 believes that one should not abandon one's religious beliefs for a person one loves; yet 26·7 per cent did not condemn abortion and 41·8 per cent condemned it under certain circumstances.

'The problem of the religiousness of students is somewhat different. A survey conducted over a period of three years among Warsaw students indicates that 70 per cent of them maintain a contact with the Church through religious practices and beliefs, although half of them practice only irregularly.' The communist sources, on the other hand, are now bitter about the activities of the church since the war.[13] 'In fact, not only are the faithful citizens in our country unhampered in fulfilling their religious needs, but the Church enjoys a situation in many ways superior to that it enjoyed before the war. The number of parishes in 1966 amounted to 6,558, while there were only 5,224 before the war. The Catholic Church is using a large number of formerly Protestant and Orthodox church buildings and the number of Catholic churches is 13,000, while there were only 7,257 before the war. The number of priests is larger by two-thirds than before the war (over 17,000) and the number

[13] 'About the relations between the church and the state', a study in *Nowi Drogi* (the Party's theoretical monthly), Warsaw, April 1966.

of nuns has increased even more (to 28,500). Priest seminaries, the Lublin Catholic University, the Academy of Catholic Theology in Warsaw train cadres for the Church. There are Catholic publications, 71 periodicals issued in about 600,000 copies, hundreds of books are written by Catholic writers. The income of the Church in Poland, not counting income coming legally and illegally from abroad, reaches billions of zloty, which helps maintain the income of the clergy, and especially of the bishops, at a level much higher than that of the highest state officials. Despite all these well-known facts, the Episcopate tries to spread lies about the "suffering" Church, about the "persecutions", although it is hardly becoming.'

From a political point of view the Church has tried since 1956 to institutionalize, within Parliament and through elections, its own political representation. This was even more necessary in view of the fact that the party maintained its own bogus – Catholic organization (*Pax*) which usurped the rights of the true Catholic position. The story of the *Znak* group will be dealt with at greater length in a further section of this chapter, in which the broadening of political representation within the present institutions of the communist state is discussed. But here it must be said that soon after the beginning of the new regime in 1957 *Tygodnik Powzscheny* reappeared with its genuine editorial board, and its circulation jumped at once to 50,000 copies. So also did the monthly *Znak* which afterwards became the name for the 'group' which in the newly-elected Parliament consisted of five deputies totally independent of the Polish Workers' Party and responsible to the Catholic Church. The group made its position very clear from the beginning by accepting in a realistic way that they were not, and could not be, in the conditions prevailing in Poland, a party, but a group. They would try to establish a *modus vivendi* whereby all Poland's cultural and national forces could be used for her reconstruction and progress. They accepted as a fact, and indeed as an inevitable fact-of-life of Poland, the Soviet alliance; and that whereas they were particularly interested in the progress of democratization and legality, they approved of the main lines of social policy and reforms of the government. 'Despite differences in world outlook between Catholics and Marxists we desire within the framework of the Socialist system to co-operate in everything which is good, moral and creative for the individual and the Community, in all which can lift social conditions to a higher level of economic, cultural and moral life. We do not conceal the differences both in fundamental views and in methods of action and do not wish to minimize them. But that which can unite us in various fields is a very essential matter to us.'

Besides, the Cardinal probably and rightly believed that the general reforms in which Gomulka's Poland seemed to be engaging in 1957, combined with the increased influence of the Catholic Church in these newly improved political conditions would lead rapidly to a change in situation. According to contemporary communist sources, he had in 1957 already visualized the year 1966, the year of the 'millennium', as the climax of the changes thus set in motion. According to these sources he is said to have told priests in 1957 that in 1966, in the millennium year, communism would prove to have been destroyed in Poland, and destroyed by Polish Christianity.

The Gomulka regime, though, broke its general, economic, social, political and cultural promises sooner than expected. By 1960 the Polish people saw with great disappointment how, in all respects and in all fields the reformist and progressive government was being transformed into a sombre, reactionary and harassed administration. Restrictions and orders countermanding the initial reforms were the main reaction of the government and party to this disappointment. In an Eastern Europe in ferment, and in a communist world-movement cut across by new revolutionary and centrifugal tendencies Gomulka's Poland and party, which had been ahead of all these ideas and tendencies, now appeared as fatigued organisms. Inside the country all social classes and professional categories were in turn frustrated by the deprivation of most of the freedom obtained in the thaw of 1956. But the more they showed this frustration and disappointment the more severe were the reactions of the party. Within it the conservative, Stalinist wing was trying to get the upper hand – in the party as well as on the state and the political police-apparats.

The Church was gradually forced to acknowledge the deterioration and to come into the open. It did so in its two capacities: as the natural and traditional 'opposition' on general national and political problems; and as itself in the continuing fight for the maintenance of its rights against the renewed encroachments of the party. Moreover as freedom of political expression was curtailed and as the *Znak* group in Parliament, and the two Catholic journals were more and more harassed into curbing their observations against the government and party, the pulpits – and especially the Cardinal's pulpit – became again the main loudspeakers of the national protest. Indeed as Wyszinski himself said in one of his sermons:[14] 'The Church has led you here to lift from you by sacramental grace the chains of your personal slavery. Once you have the taste of this freedom then the desire is awakened for other freedom, social and civic. We do not defend ourselves against the charge that the Church is a rebel.' But there still remained, in spite of the renewed fight between the two sides of the thus divided body politic of Poland, and between the two leading personalities, the basis of the truce, so important to Polish public opinion: the common fear of raising the dangers implicit in Poland's external position through internal political feuds. The Church had never openly challenged the foreign policy of the party. Yet it is in this sphere where the Church has never taken a political attitude, that the 1965 conflict started, when the truce formerly observed between Church and state has been replaced by an open fight.

On 30 November 1965, the Polish bishops sent to the forty-two German bishops, of both sides of the Elbe, an invitation to attend the 'millennium' celebrations of May 1966. The letter contained most unusual phrases for a correspondence between any official Pole and official German, especially West German, such as the hope to 'bring the two nations still closer together in a mutual dialogue' and especially, 'we stretch out our hands to you in a brotherly and human spirit; we forgive you and ask you to forgive us. And only when you, the German Bishops and Fathers of the Council, seize our outstretched hands as brethren will we be able to celebrate our millennium in a wholly Christian manner and with a clear conscience.'

In Poland relations with Germany, and especially West Germany, form the most important, and at the same time most sensitive question, of foreign policy. In fact the antagonism is used by the communist government as the main argument for its continuation in power and for the continuation of a close collaboration with the Soviet Union. Interference in such a vital matter by a non-political body like the Church could hardly have been an accident. The incident in fact was a double landmark in the internal political history of Poland. It marked the moment when Polish public opinion fully

[14] Quoted in Blit, loc. cit., p. 217.

realized, as did public opinion in other East European countries, that the problem of European integration, involving the internal dissolution of the Atlantic and the Soviet 'blocs', had to be quickly reconsidered. This impinged on and conditioned all other political and economic problems. Indeed, from this point of view too, the Gomulka government was lagging behind some other communist countries, not only Yugoslavia with her overt neutralistic policy, but also, more recently, Rumania, with her new European outlook. Gomulka's claustrophobic policy which kept alive the old German preoccupation was the main obstacle to the change, with its diplomatic and economic implications, needed in Poland's European policy. When the Polish Church acted as it did, it knew that politically it was expressing the views of the majority of the Polish people and it was opening a question in the national debate which until then had been blocked and stifled by the obsolete propaganda of the regime. The second watershed was the realization by the other principal political centre of the present Polish body politic that the opposition, wherever and however it functioned, could now take the offensive again and show up the paralysis and impotence of the government. The letter to the German bishops was not sent by the Polish hierarchy without the full realization that this was, at least from these two points of view, a political act.

The quarrel which ensued was to be expected – but it revealed, as it developed, how deep were the differences between, and how irreconcilable the positions of, the two main centres of political influence. Indeed, the immediate cause of the quarrel, whether it is patriotic or not to address the West Germans in a mood of forgiveness, has become a secondary issue. 'It is difficult' said Gomulka in his speech of 14 January 1966, 'to accuse the Bishops of wanting to give our Western territories back to Germany. No one is accusing them of this because this indeed is not their attitude.' The main accusation directed against the Church was that it wished to link Poland to the West and by doing so to destroy the communist regime at home. 'The deterioration of relations between the Church and the State' stated the main editorial of *Nowe Drogi* in April 1966 on this question 'has two essential aspects – an internal and an external one. The internal aspect means the continuation with greater intensity than ever of the previous anti-social action by the leading circles of the Church hierarchy ... (it wants) to assign to the

Church a role which it never played in the life of the nation and which it does not play in the life of any country, not just in the socialist world but even in the capitalist world.' As for the external aspect the authorized communist comment was that this letter 'is a political document through and through' by which the Polish bishops are trying to transform Poland again into a 'bulwark of the West.'

The answer given by the bishops to these accusations was again to counsel 'patience' and to assure that the Church wanted 'to live in peace and does not want war even if war is declared against us'. But the real answer came from the onlookers. The celebration of the 'millennium' was a 'triumphal progress' for the Polish Primate. Four hundred thousand people interrupted another bishop with cheers when he assured the Primate that 'all the faithful are behind you. The more stones they throw at you the closer we gather round you.' And the entire nation realized, watching the triumph of the Cardinal and the Church, and the discomfiture of the Secretary and the party, that even in these strange and allegorical ways the opposition without name had won a battle against the government.

By sheer coincidence, almost at the same time as the latest state-church conflict was developing in Poland, Dr Scharf's election as Bishop of Berlin-Brandenburg in succession to Bishop Dibelius was opening a heated controversy in the GDR. The Communist Party and the government considered the election as null and void insofar as Scharf, the Chairman of the All-German Council of the Evangelical Church, was not a citizen of the GDR and could not carry out his duties, in their view, in a church province situated in GDR territory. Dr Scharf, who had been arrested several times by the Nazis, and who had taken up residence in East Berlin when Bishop Dibelius had been forbidden by the GDR in 1957 to enter the territory, was put in charge of the East Berlin diocese in August 1961, when the Berlin Wall was built.

Ever since 1962, when it was decided that a new bishop should be appointed, Scharf's name had been under consideration but the Synod of the Bishopric, from both sides of the Wall, could not reach a decision. Some *bona fide* members thought his appointment would jeopardize Scharf's chances to circulate between the two parts of Germany; some, under the party's guidance, indeed instigation, had direct instructions to do their utmost to prevent Scharf from being elected. The efforts of the regime went as far as to announce categorically in January 1966 that Scharf would not be permitted to come to East Berlin if he were elected. Yet on 15 February the Synod, by an unprecedented majority, took the decision to elect him. This defiant attitude of the Church authorities against the state, was bound to bring it into new and serious trouble. But it showed that in the GDR too the Church, which had launched from the pulpit a devastating campaign against the family code and against the education laws proposed by the Ulbricht government, felt able to take up more offensive positions.

The students and the universities

The resistance of university students to government policy, which has been a characteristic feature of political life in Europe since the nineteenth century, has now become a phenomenon of the greatest importance throughout the world.[15] In Indonesia or in South Vietnam, in Latin America and in Spain, in fact, in most oppositionless states the students are one of the first opposition groups to come into the open. But, as the sub-title of this section indicates, students cannot, in this context, be considered separately from the universities. Together they form a political complex consisting of three representative bodies: the students' associations or unions, the teaching staff and the university itself. Sometimes they are all divided, sometimes two unite against the third, but they are inextricably linked in twos, in the political argument with the government. In the European communist states the students and the universities had the reputation of having been in the vanguard of the large movements of opinion which shook the communist regimes more than any others: in Berlin in 1953, in Poland in 1955–6, and in Hungary in 1956 – and they have shown their mettle too in Prague, Bucharest and Sofia at various times during the first fifteen years of communism.

For the purposes of this work the influence of the universities in the politics of two states will be looked into a little more closely: East Germany and Hungary. The first, well studied and analysed

[15] See on the general problem, Jurgen Habermas: *Studenten und Politik*, Neuwied, 1961, and on the students in the sixties Seymour Martin Lipset and George Z. F. Bereday (co-editors): *Student Politics*, special issue of *Comparative Education Review*, June 1966, New York, and in *Government and Opposition*, Nos. 3, 4 and 5, 1966, the series *Students opposition*, introduced by Julius Gould.

in many works[16] provides a clearer picture of the intermingled relations between students as such and the universities, and their interaction with the general political movement of aggregation they started. The second led to the formation of the more dramatic *Petöffi's circle*, which was the centre and pivot of the entire upheaval in 1956. It had been at first virtually a students' affair, but it was afterwards swollen and transformed into the leading forum of the opposition. (In Poland the students' movement intermingled directly with the movement of the intellectuals and artists already grouped around the review *Po Prostu*, which will be discussed in the section of this book dealing with 'reviews and groups'.)[17]

In the GDR, in 1953, the movement of the universities and of intellectuals generally followed that of the workers which the builders initiated so dramatically and surprisingly in East Berlin. On 30 June the German Academy of Arts held a general meeting at which it discussed ways and means for intellectuals and students to recover some of their lost responsibility and to keep as free as possible from state intervention. In a resolution which was supported by all the organizations of scientists, artists, writers, professors and teachers, the main demands were formulated. These have remained ever since the charter of dissent of the intellectuals in the GDR. From the point of view of the present study two of these demands are particularly striking: that the freedom of scientific research and teaching should be guaranteed, and that the administrative and disciplinary powers of the authorities over the students and the professorial body at universities should be more clearly defined, or, in other words, that the autonomy of the teaching staff should be recognized. Wolfgang Harich who, through his treble position in the university, in the party, and as the editor of the newly-founded and very influential review *Die Deutsche Zeitschrift für Philosophie*, played a central part in all these events and who indeed became the leader of the movement of dissent against the cultural dictatorship of the party, openly attacked the 'dictatorship of a small group of functionaries' over the cultural life of the country. The main tenets of the revisionist philosophy were postulated then for the first time in clear terms by Harich himself, by Bloch, the other editor of the *Zeitschrift*, and by the

[16] Especially in Jänicke, loc. cit.
[17] See for a complete account Jänicke, loc. cit.

Hungarian philosopher George Lukacs who, at the time, exercised perhaps a greater, or in any case more open, influence in East Germany than in Hungary. It was also then that the scientists Robert Rompe, and Robert Havemann, who later achieved great renown, made their influence felt not only in intellectual and academic circles, but also on the general public. The repressive measures taken in the autumn of 1953 against the Zaisser-Herrnstadt opposition[18] from within the party were directed also very strongly against the 'liberalizing' intellectuals. The universities, reviews, students' associations and groups of scholars were submitted by Ulbricht to drastic 'reorganizations' and purges.

But as with all movements of dissent in dictatorial countries, this one was only superficially silenced by the repressive measures. In 1955–6, under the impact of de-Stalinisation in Russia, and of the further developments in Poland and Hungary, a reformist faction was formed in the SED led by Ernst Wollweber and Karl Schirdewan. It was not only backed but actually inspired by 'reformist' university professors and teachers like the economists Fritz Behrens and Arne Benary, the agronomist Kurt Viewegs and the jurists Renneberg, Lekschas and Gerats (who worked together on a new theory of *Staatsrecht*), and the philosopher Ernest Bloch. In his report on 'Freedom' at the conference of philosophy in March 1965 he put forward together with Kolakowski in Poland and Lukacs in Hungary the theory of 'permanent revisionism'. This theory was afterwards supported by Professor Bassenge, Günther Zehrn, Richard Lorenz and again Wolfgang Harich; among historians by Professor Jürgen Kuczynski and Streisand, and the entire Institute of Economic History in Leipzig; among sociologists by Klaus Sternberg, Saar, Gülzow and the Institute of Social Sciences of the Humboldt University in Berlin (of which Harich also had been a member); and among scientists by Besenbruch, Herneck and especially, again, Professor Robert Havemann.

The role of the university as a rallying point for dissent can best be seen in the interpenetration between the more politically-minded and group-organized students and the individual professors. The professors were thus opening a vast discussion which afterwards spread to the artists and writers and to the entire intelligentsia, and through them to the party. The latter tolerated

[18] See further: *Channelling, Factionalism in the parties.*

it for a while but prepared itself for a stern reaction. In fact Harich was later arrested and the majority of the above named professors lost their posts. Meanwhile, the students less openly but more actively, were waking up to the new ideas. They acted through leaflets which they distributed among their colleagues and outside the university precincts; they held 'spontaneous' meetings, more and more widely attended, and during which short but cogent slogans like 'the abolition of Russian classes', 'solidarity with the Poles and the Hungarians', 'the end of Stalinism-dogmatism' were launched. They also formed clandestine action groups, of which eight were afterwards identified in the repressive trials organized by the party, the most active and best known of which were the Stauffenberg-Kreis in Jena and the 'National Communist Students Union' in Dresden. These groups comprised not only students but also members of the teaching staff, and their programmes quickly went beyond the professional university claims to become a *Gesamtsystem* of demands for change. They became centres of opposition – and indeed Harich was able to say of such actions and groups in November 1956 that: 'We want our opposition activities to become legal and open; but we must continue to act through the method of factions, and conspiracy as long as the Stalinist apparat forces us to do so.'

The demands, as they ultimately crystallized, became known as '*der dritte Weg*' (the third way) which, on the one hand, stated that a restoration of capitalism was impossible, but, on the other, saw no future for the present dictatorial regime and urged that a 'freely-elected parliament' should become the main organ of sovereignty. The programme, and the slogan, was and is still characteristic of public opinion, as it was forming itself in such states. Indeed, while Wollweber, Schirdewan and Harich himself were soon put out of action by the repression of the SED, it was again the universities which, during the next big political crisis, created by the erection of the wall in Berlin in August 1961, led the strongest reaction. Professors like W. Treibs, Seidemann, D. Katner, Wolfgang Hütt and Hamsch-George were afterwards reprimanded by the party for having militated in the university and, together with the students, for 'a capitulationist attitude'. It was also in 1961 that the Ulbricht regime suffered one of the most severe blows in this field, when the philosopher Ernest Bloch announced that he would not return to the GDR and remained in West Germany. But the leadership of university dissent was taken by Professor Robert Havemann, who for the next three years gradually formulated and clarified his theory of 'dialectics without dogma'. It advocated a reform of the party so that it could 'permit the formation of oppositional fractions in the party' and reform of the constitution so that there could be 'a parliamentary opposition under socialism and the workers could have the right to strike'. At this point Havemann's action merged with the great debate which was being carried on at the time in the GDR on the dialogue between the SED and the SPD. In 1964 Havemann was dismissed from his chair at the Humboldt University, on Christmas Eve 1965 from his new post at the Academy of Sciences in East Berlin, and in April 1966 his name was struck from the membership lists of the German Academy of Sciences. He was charged with having advocated 'an alternative to the existing political order in the GDR'.

If the aggregation around the universities in the GDR was chosen here as the example of a slow and recurrent process, the celebrated case of the Petöffi circle in Budapest in 1956 is an example of the university becoming, in favourable conditions, the laboratory of a much more rapid political catalysis. Its history runs parallel with that of the entire revolution – it formed the centre from which the movement radiated in all directions. On the initiative of the students a proposal was submitted to the party to approve of the creation of a debating club of the DISZ (the Hungarian Federation of Working Youth). It was to provide students and scholars with an opportunity to exchange ideas and discuss problems of common interest. Permission was granted, under strong pressures and after much procrastination on 17 March 1956. What is of special interest from this work's point of view is to see in retrospect how in a mere six months the scope of the debate was changed and the range of the membership was enlarged.

The first period lasted from mid-March to mid-June 1956. The membership was mostly, if not exclusively, limited to party members (indeed one of the arguments most widely heard during this period was centred on the question, who is the party: the leadership or the rank-and-file?) The scope of the debate was limited to general theoretical problems, divided into 'sessions'. The first session was devoted to the direct professional problems of the students. They wanted to emancipate their federation from the tutelage of DISZ and recover its lost autonomy. The economists' debate became eventually a hard-hitting general discussion of the economic difficulties and dilemmas of the communist government. The historians' debate on 'how to write the history of the party' was eventually transformed into a severe criticism of the party leadership. After a debate on problems of pedagogy, there followed, on 14 June, the debate on 'philosophy' where the main address was given by George Lukacs who, since 1949, had been cold shouldered by the party for 'deviationism of the right'. This was yet another milestone. For the first time, Stalinists who had criticized and persecuted people like Lukacs for 'deviationism', were unable, in the contagious atmosphere of the debate, to resist recanting their former dogmatic theories. They made their own, anti-Stalinist, self-criticism, and their public apologies to Lukacs and others.

This new development, and the fact that the audience grew so large that the debates had thenceforth to be transferred to a theatre, and then to the particularly vast 'Officers' Club', led Rakosi to realize how fast the infection was spreading and to try to check it. A week later there followed the debate on 'socialist legality' which was bound to be explosive, but which went beyond all expectations when Rajk's widow spoke and demanded, amid the ovations of those in the hall, that those who had murdered her husband and were 'sitting even now in ministerial seats' should be punished. On 27 June there took place the last debate of this first series which started with the theme of the role of the press and of cultural activities, gave rise to devastating criticisms of the party's terroristic and obscurantist policy from the floor, and finished, at dawn, with a vast manifestation in favour of the rehabilitation and the readmission to the party of Imre Nagy, the leader of the oppositionist faction of the party. Since by then the debates of the Petöffi circle had become the greatest centre of attention of the entire Hungarian people, Rakosi, in a desperate move, suspended the activities of the circle as 'the centre of attacks against the party and the peoples democratic system'.

The second phase started with the lifting of the ban on the circle after Rakosi's final fall in July. The first meeting was held in September, and agriculture was the theme of discussion. It soon became obvious that collectivization was generally blamed as the cause of all troubles in that sector, and that the old Small-holders Party was reasserting its active influence on the re-awakening peasantry. But by then the Petöffi circle was merging, in the heat of the revolutionary developments, with vaster and broader circles of a society in ferment. Thus a meeting at the end of October at the Technical University of Budapest, called to discuss students' problems, was attended by large numbers of members of the technical intelligentsia as well as by workers. It ended by producing the 'sixteen points' among the first of which were the withdrawal of Soviet troops from Hungary, the appointment of Imre Nagy as Prime Minister, the holding of free general elections with more parties allowed to compete, freedom of opinion and of the press – or, in other words, all the points which afterwards became the platform of the opposition, and then the programme of the short-lived Nagy government.

These 'sixteen points' were condensed to ten in a statement of the Petöffi circle published in the party paper on 23 October. In this more essential and more radicalized form they were to be discussed at a university meeting on the same day. Another object of the meeting was to manifest solidarity with Gomulka in Poland. The government first tried to forbid the meeting, and then, in a panic, re-authorized it only half an hour before it was scheduled. The students who marched were quickly followed by larger and larger crowds of people of all categories, and especially workers. They proceeded to the Parliament and asked to be advised by Nagy. Then they turned on Stalin's statue and toppled it over. Having swollen to some 200,000, they went to the radio stations demanding that the sixteen points should be broadcast. When the security police, in order to protect the building, fired upon them, they were joined by contingents of the army, who also brought weapons. The revolution was on its way.

The reviews

Whereas the universities are important focal centres of slow or rapid political aggregation, the reviews, very often founded in university or students' circles, are centres of doctrinal aggregation. Their effect is to concentrate the vague and sometimes ineffectual currents of thought which, once thus reduced to essentials, are then disseminated to wider public spheres than the university meetings and scholarly publications can reach. Usually, when the movement of aggregation and concentration starts to gather momentum one publication, either new or renewed, takes the lead in postulating more clearly and more boldly previously diffuse ideas. This has a valuable effect. On the one hand, it gives that particular publication an enormous success in terms of sales and prestige. On the other, it usually has the effect of inducing the main official (party) publications to open their columns to discussion of the same problems and by the same authors, although the upsurge is usually so rich that scores of new names appear simultaneously. In this way the current is spread through more than one channel. When the time comes to clamp down on the movement, it is the publication which first started it that suffers the rigours and thus becomes the symbol of a period. In Poland, even more than the universities themselves or the 'Crooked Circle' (which in the first phases of the 1955–6 events played a part comparable to that of the Petöffi circle in Hungary), the review *Po Prostu* is the symbol of the spring of 1956. Through the ideas which it threw into circulation, and through its own, and its editor's fate its story typifies the period. Although this story is well known[19] some of the basic elements should be recalled here. *Po Prostu* had been a dull and servile weekly for youth published by the communist controlled Union of Polish Youth (ZMP). In 1955 under the editorship of Eligiusz Lasota, and with a very young editorial board, it quickly responded to the new trend. Through the pressure of the universities, intellectuals, writers, and artists, this trend penetrated even the most august party publications (like *Nowa Kultura* where earlier Wazik had published his startling 'Poem for Adults', thus provoking the dismissal of its editor-in-chief; or, a little later, *Nowi Drogi* itself, which then started a discussion on the 'Polish road to Socialism').

But *Po Prostu*, as the organ of young intellectuals and students, showed greater determination to forge ahead, regardless of the Party's concern. It got away with it partly because it was less easy to repress the enthusiasm of the new and unexpectedly resolute generation. Indeed, the review took direct political attitudes and raised explosive political issues. One of them which added to the rapid aggregation (and to its readership which quickly reached

[19] See especially Jan Kott: 'Les dix années que je viens de vivre', in *Les Temps modernes*, February 1957, and K. A. Jellenski: 'A window on to the future: the story of Po Prostu', in *Encounter*, December 1957.

the unprecedented number of 200,000) was the campaign for the rehabilitation of the Polish Home Army, which had been systematically vilified and persecuted by the Russians and by the Polish Stalinists. The campaign was successful, in part because of the revelations in Moscow about the terrible treatment inflicted by Stalin on the Polish Party. The party leadership, while still criticizing the leaders of the Home Army, totally changed its attitude towards the members of that patriotic organization, who until then had been treated, collectively and individually, as potential anti-Soviet and anti-communist elements. Afterwards, *Po Prostu*, more than any other publication, put its columns at the disposal of all the economists and agricultural experts who were denouncing the Soviet-style collectivization of agriculture as the source of all evils in Polish agriculture and economy. Next there came the concentration on the political problem. *Po Prostu* in its leading articles took up a strong position on the question of the revival of Parliament, which it described in an editorial entitled: 'Initiative, responsibility and legality' as 'not only the legislative organ but the seat of the sovereignty of the people'. Finally, by the end of October, *Po Prostu* was also the most outspoken publication on the problem of relations between Poland and the Soviet Union. Even after Gomulka had started advising the public and the nation at large not to be carried away by anti-Soviet feeling and resentments, it argued that no one had the right to deprive the citizens of the Polish state of the right to criticize the Soviet Union.

With Gomulka back in power and therefore when most of the claims it had put forward were satisfied, *Po Prostu* reached the climax of its popularity. This was reflected in the fact that its editor, Lasota, who was a candidate in Warsaw at the 1957 election, received the greatest numbers of votes after Gomulka. But soon after the election all this was changed. This was due in part to the jealousy Lasota's parliamentary success had provoked; but also to Gomulka's firm determination to eliminate one of the sources of ferment as early in the day as possible. Had everything gone smoothly, *Po Prostu* might have lost some of its justification. As it was it got into deeper and deeper trouble by trying to maintain, from within party-circles, an oppositional attitude to the new policy of the party. In May 1957 Lasota resigned the editorship. In June the review announced a two months' delay in publication. In October it was officially closed down by the government, together with other publications. The students organized meetings of protest in Warsaw and in the country. Many writers and artists of the first importance resigned from the party in protest. But neither of the two big centres of political influence in the new Poland, the party or the Church, had any special reason to support the existence of this independent publication. The protests were thus of no avail. Lasota himself lost his parliamentary seat in the April 1961 elections, which were much more sternly 'organized' than those of 1957.

Ephemeral as reviews are generally known to be, and sad as the example of *Po Prostu* was for dissenters in the other countries of Eastern Europe, reviews have nevertheless remained one of the natural means of aggregation in all cases of ferment, starting, or re-starting, in any of these countries. Both in Czechoslovakia, where in 1963 for the first time since 1948 dissent against the regime began to manifest itself, and in Yugoslavia, where since the adoption of the new constitution in 1963 a broader and sharper national debate on the future of the state has developed, it was around reviews that the clarification of ideas and the crystallization of attitudes took place. In both countries, too, the new ferment showed similar patterns, almost clinically classic: the anxiety of the governments faced with economic difficulties and reforms, a strong supplementary pressure originating from the federal or quasi-federal regions, and the continuation of the quest for a solution to the dilemma of the communist state after the end of Stalinism.

In Czechoslovakia, under the initial pressure of the Slovak communist intelligentsia, the first awakening of public opinion since it was silenced in that country in 1948 took the form of an affirmation of national pride and identity, accompanied by a claim for freedom of opinion. The classic works of Masaryk and Kafka, were re-authorized for publication. The former created an embarrassing situation for the communists through their permanent association with national independence and the political democracy of Czechoslovakia. The latter even more, because Kafka's works prophesied the terror psychology of the totalitarian dictatorships. Both had been banned, and both were returning now with a greater impact and a strange timeliness for their own country. A brilliant generation of writers, philosophers, playwrights, painters and film directors appeared in Czechoslovakia overnight, with the same kind of flowering of talent and creative originality which accompanied, in 1955–6, a similar political period in Poland and Hungary.

With the passing of time, though, the disappointment and weariness of the new thinkers in Czechoslovakia with the entire communist philosophy were seen to go much deeper than in the case of their Polish and Hungarian opposite numbers in 1956. Whereas in 1956 the then young revisionist thinkers in Yugoslavia or Poland defended Marxism-Leninism against Stalinism, a decade later not even Leninism on its own was considered by the 'second wave' of revisionist thinkers as a sufficiently safe line of defence. In Czechoslovakia, in particular, the disintegration of faith showed even deeper traces in the works of the new philosophers. The problem of 'alienation' seemed to the Yugoslav Supek, to the Pole Schaff, to the German Havemann and to the Slovak Strinka to be looming heavily on the horizon of the Marxist *Weltanschauung*. Julius Strinka was severe on communism as it existed in Czechoslovakia and the other European communist countries. In his view it was not much different from Stalinism. He called it a 'conformist Marxism', or 'apologetic Marxism' because it could not move further than consideration of itself as a perfect embodiment of socialism – and because its only defence was to vilify the capitalism of past generations. Like Havemann, Strinka expressed forcefully his belief that the defects of communism were not confined to Stalinism and its aftermath. Both believed that there was something wrong with the entire doctrine, and that as long as new revolutionary forces from within society could not find a way to inject a new dynamism and a new humanism into their fossilized Marxism, these societies and these states would not be healthy. Although the methods and conceptions of the post-Khrushchevian governments in Eastern Europe differed considerably from, and were better than, those of the Stalinist regimes in Poland and Hungary in 1956, which clashed head-on at the time with the indignant intelligentsia, there was nevertheless an equally wide gap between the new intelligentsia and governments in the sixties because of the further estrangement of the intelligentsia from the 'common ground' and from the compromises offered by governments.

The doctrinal gap between *Tvar*, the periodical of the Czechoslovak new generation, and the Novotny government was as wide in 1966 as that between *Po Prostu* and the Gomulka government in 1957. Novotny, like Gomulka, soon realized that if such a review continued to be read by the increasingly discontented and disenchanted intellectual youth of the country, the gloom and pessimism it expressed about the regime and its purposes would have disastrous consequences for the regime. In March 1966 the Czechoslovak government resorted again to the ultimate argument in this kind of battle: it suspended *Tvar* after its editor had refused to take further advice from the party and government. The explanation given by the party for this highly unpopular measure had an ominously defensive ring. It showed openly that the party resented the editor's firm attitude. 'J. Nedved,' it said, 'disregarded the recommendation of the higher party agencies and changed the line, mission and character of this journal, putting it into conflict with the interest of the socialist agency ... This young man and party member had lost his links with the party ... although he persisted in claiming the right to be considered a member of the party. He also wanted complete freedom to act as he wished against the political line of the party.'

In Yugoslavia, too, where the political *mores* are much more flexible and polished than in Czechoslovakia, the intellectuals who gave the party most trouble were those grouped around two reviews: one the very successful and authoritative *Praxis* (founded in September 1964 in Zagreb) under the leadership of Professor Supek, already mentioned; and the other a projected review which, even before publication, induced the government to act hastily and in a manner and style different from that adopted ever since 1963 and the new constitution. With *Praxis*, which its party critics openly called the 'review of the opposition', the top-leadership of the League behaved patiently in spite of the tenacity with which that review stressed again and again that the contradictions of Yugoslav communism could not be resolved without changing the entire political system. In September 1965 the Zagreb Communist Party held a special meeting to discuss the activities of this review which was 'transforming itself into the nucleus of a political group around which all opposing and dissatisfied elements in our society would gather'. In January 1966 Edward Kardelj himself undertook to answer at great length criticism of Yugoslav-style Marxism published in *Praxis*. Later, in the spring, even Tito expressed annoyance at the review.[20] Ominous warnings mounted up. In the late summer of 1966 it seemed that *Praxis* would not be able to appear again. But in spring 1967 it re-appeared, much strengthened.

At the end of July 1966 Mihajlo Mihajlov asked for permission to publish, with three other young colleagues, a review ostentatiously called: *Free Voice*. Mihajlo Mihajlov was the young writer who had been subjected to an unusual prosecution in Yugoslavia for having offended the Soviet Union in his article 'Moscow Summer 1964'. After a trial unique in the history of any communist state, during which he and his defence not only conceded nothing but openly attacked the right of the state to interfere with literary creation, he was first sentenced to nine months' imprisonment but, after a fiercely contested appeal, received only a five months' suspended sentence. On 6 August 1966 permission to found the new journal was granted; but two days later Mihajlov was arrested again and taken back to the prison from which he had just been released. He was then sentenced to one year, and sent to gaol on 12 November 1966. On 21 November 1966 his co-editors Ivin, Batinić and Zenko were also arrested. But they were freed before Christmas together with Djilas himself. It may be that the sharp reaction of the Yugoslav government was due in part to the fact that *Free Voice* announced that it would militate for 'Djilas and Djilasism',[21] a particularly explosive subject. This showed that even the Yugoslav authorities, which try to be as tolerant as a communist regime can be, are particularly on their guard against the influence of periodicals. In April 1967 Mihajlov was tried again, on other grounds, and sentenced to four and a half years in prison.

The army and the partisans

Several aspects of the part the army can play in the politics of a communist state have already been touched upon in this work. Here a few words should be said about the army as a centre of aggregation. In some or most cases the aggregation around the army consists of the conspiratorial action of the army or political

---

[20] In his speech to the 3 Plenum of the Party Central Committee on 25 February 1966, when he said 'We must fight against various ideological deviations as for instance, in the periodical *Praxis*'.

[21] See further: *Personalities*.

police leading to the classic *coup d'état* when one of these apparats takes over the centres of power. In other cases it takes the form of a slow propagation of dissent. The military or police leaders try to build up collective support for the action which they might project.

Yet, public opinion in the communist European states does not look on the communist army, or on the political police, as organisms which could, in moments of grave national crisis or emergency 'save the Republic'. Nor for that matter, is a desire to play this role the main reason why leaders of the army or police in those countries are active on the political stage. The present officer-corps is not as intellectually advanced in the communist countries as to proceed to a thorough re-examination of the simple Marxist-Leninism which they have learned in their formative years, or so well-educated as are the new university scholars and intellectuals. Their own doctrinal background consists mostly of a combination of simple nationalism and simple communism which was sufficient to inspire their action as partisans in the early years. Thus, in spite of the fact that the political appetite of the armies everywhere might have been whetted by the political successes of the army in other countries and continents, the present political self-image, motive and eventual platforms of the officers of the armies in the European communist states are not entirely different from or opposed to the party.

The officers in communist countries, or at least those who can develop more political consciousness and see the political field, were communist-moulded and belonged to the Communist Party. What is more in communist countries the incipient public opinion to which they belong is itself a body with a dual approach. Only the most advanced layers of the intellectuals have lost in the last decade the deep-seated Marxist-Leninist way of thinking. The communist officers are not as intellectually advanced. Their beliefs would seem to be, rather, a mixture of 'partisan' conservatism: the dogmatic state-conservatism, the patriotic national-conservatism, and the social-conservatism of the 'entire people' as against the concept of 'dictatorship of the working class' (a belief which they draw from their familiarity with the rural communities). This, of course, might change with the passing of the generations.

In both European communist states, Poland and Bulgaria,

where the armies have lately shown more political ambition it is the partisan-mentality which has come through more clearly in the guarded and, in any case, confused pronouncements they have made. And the active members have come from the old groups of the partisans, transferred after the coming to power of the party directly into the leading positions of the army and political police apparats.

The main difference, of course, between the political attitude of the army in Poland and in Bulgaria originates from the basic political climates prevailing in these two by no means identical European communist states. In Bulgaria, provoked by the particular severity of the Bulgarian Communist Party, and the general harshness of the political control of the regime, but also by the tradition of politics by *coups* in that country under any regime, the aggregation before the *coup* is bound to be conspiratorial. It is only after the failure or the success of the *coup* that the depth and range of the aggregation can be gauged. In Poland, on the contrary, even a shrunken political debate, as that which the Gomulka government in its repressive mood was prepared to admit, had to be carried on in public if the ideas put forward were to attract the attention of a sensitive and wide public opinion. This was why the 'partisans'[22] scattered throughout the army, the security police and, of course, within the party itself made a deliberate effort in the sixties to attract public support and to aggregate around their own slogans the diffuse, but quickly growing, dissent in the nation as a whole.

In Bulgaria the top of the iceberg was visible in the mysterious and abortive coup of April 1965.[23] A senior member of the Communist Party, Ivan Todorov-Gorunya, a head of the Asian department of the Bulgarian Foreign Office, Tsolo Krastev, and the commandant of the Sofia military garrison, Major-General Tsvetko Anev, were accused of having plotted against the government, the first of them having 'committed suicide before he was arrested'. The fact that it was the army which had been the centre of the conspiratorial aggregation, and that it participated in these developments, was the aspect that most worried the

---

[22] The 'partisans' are a main faction of the Polish Workers Party. See further, 'Factionalism in the parties', pp. 228 ff.

[23] See especially: J. F. Brown: 'The Bulgarian Plot', in *World Today*, London May 1965.

Zhivkov administration. This is revealed by the fact that the very elusive and reluctant references by Zhivkov to the subject were all accompanied by strong assurances that 'our army' was as loyal as ever before and that no clouds could be seen on the horizon of the relations between 'our army and our party'. Yet, if there was one clear connecting link between the three 'rings' thus suspected of having conspired together, it lay in the fact that both Todorov-Gorunya and Anev had been, during the war, not only 'partisans' but also in the same detachment, the Genov-detachment, in which Todorov-Gorunya was the political commissar and Anev the commander.

The common 'partisan' background of the two main plotters had further helped to inspire them because, since 1960, the former and by now aged wartime partisan leaders had been re-appointed to the leading posts in the army. During the Chervenkov period, 1947–56, they had been replaced by younger, mostly Russian trained, professional officers. Zhivkov himself had been a 'partisan' and, once placed by Khrushchev in the leadership of the party, preferred to have his old comrades and friends in the politically sensitive top posts of the army. They were stimulated by this come-back as a group. They also felt that, in comparison for instance with Rumania, Bulgaria under Zhivkov's leadership, was far from showing signs of shaking-off the Soviet tutelage. Thus the 'partisan' group responded quickly to the popular pressure for more patriotism and more dynamism in the conduct of the Bulgarian communist government. For many years the name of the hero of the partisans during the war, General Transki, was the symbol of the hopes of the former partisans, and of the sectors of Bulgarian public opinion which they could carry with them. These hopes however did not materialize: Transki continued to be exhibited by the government in his golden cage. It was then that Anev, a less well known general but with the garrison of the capital under his command, tried to act.

In Poland the movement of aggregation was directed in the opposite way. Here instead of a potential movement of political dissent waiting for a possible army leader (General Transki) to emerge, the potential leader, and leadership (General Moczar and the partisans) of a possible movement began by advertising themselves. They could be seen during the years 1965–6 putting themselves forward as a potential political alternative to the party.[24] General Moczar, who himself was a veteran partisan, was appointed head of the Security Department after the 'partisans', the right-wing, anti-Russian and anti-Semitic wing of the Polish party, effected a powerful come-back on the political stage of the party in 1960. He then tried to build up his influence outside the party and in the country at large by direct political means. The partisans used the ZBoWid, a sort of official organization of old soldiers and veterans of the Home Army, as a mass organization, which could gradually become an active political organization, and under whose banner further social and political groups could be enrolled. More and more frequent meetings and public gatherings were held in 1966, at which speakers expressed a common nationalistic-conservative attitude. It was expected that participants and onlookers at these meetings or people who heard of them would have an interest in the movement. This is not the place to assess, and even less to forecast, the real strength and the chances of the ZBoWid-organization or of the 'partisan' faction becoming a political force in Gomulka's or post-Gomulka Poland; in any case more will be said about the Polish partisans as a faction in a further section. At this juncture, however, the political phenomenon of the new technique of aggregation through publicity practised by leaders of the army and security police in at least one of the European communist states deserved to be mentioned.

Personalities

Political aggregation around personalities, whether they intended or not to act in politics, has been a traditional phenomenon in East Europe where, perhaps less frequently than in Latin America *personalismo* has been one of the mainsprings of political action. Political parties, factions and groups were often formed around one 'chief', whose name followed by an *-ism* stood for a programme and whose followers described themselves as *-ists*: Horthysts, Bratianists, Stambulyskists, etc.

In conditions of active dissent, unchannelled and unexpressed, there grows the diffuse hope that, from whatever quarter, a personality may emerge who could tell the 'they' in power, how the governed 'we' feel about them, and who therefore might redress some wrongs, or start with some action leading to a change.

[24] See further: 'Factionalism in the parties', p. 228.

In the first period (1945–8) of the bogus-coalition-government in which the communists held the key-positions, the democratic parties were accepted, only for a while, in minor and unimportant departments. It was around some of these representatives of the doomed parties, either bitterly aware or unconsciously optimistic, that the aggregation was taking place. Petkov, Jan Masaryk, Subačić, Zoltan Dobby, or such super-political personalities as, in the case of Poland, the primate, Cardinal Hlond, and in the case of Rumania, where the monarchy survived until the end of 1947, King Michael, were the centres of the opposition's sympathy and hopes. They were believed to have ways and means of winning, after the loss of many battles, the war with the new political conquerors. (This trend continued afterwards, with a new connotation, in the case of some of these personalities who went into exile.) When the darkness of the Stalinist Russian-controlled dictatorship fell on these countries in 1948 – in some of them, and in some sectors of their populations, legends arose of the 'resistance movements' and 'resistance-heroes', around whose real or imaginary names this 'aggregation' continued.

But already in most of the countries, this kind of aggregation was taking place around members of the Communist Party leadership allegedly or really opposed to the 'Stalinist' and 'Muscovite' faction in power, and victimized for their more patriotic and liberal stand. Gomulka, Patrascanu, Kostov, although part of the 'they', were known to oppose the worst excesses of oppression and exploitation. Their activity as 'potential Titos' was followed with special attention, although in the particularly mysterious conditions of communist political life this was not easy.

As time went by, and non-communist forces lost all importance the hopeful expectations were focused more and more on the possible communist 'dissenter'. Three factors encouraged this trend. First, the new, emerging, public opinion, much narrower than the one which had been silenced, was, generally speaking, more familiar with and interested in, the workings and the ways of thinking of the communist party, its wings and its personalities and its policy alternatives. Moreover after the total collapse of political opposition and of the sporadic and local attempts at resistance, it became obvious to anyone still interested in political developments that it was only from within the fortress of power that breaches could henceforth be opened in the 'monolith'.

Finally the rest of the population, politically still sufficiently bruised and disgusted as to be indifferent to the real internal dramas of the communist hierarchy, still felt a curiosity mingled with *Schadenfreude*. This feeling, expressed in such terms as 'let *them* kill each other' or 'when *they'll* start to quarrel it will be the beginning of the end', was and is characteristic of the political mentality of a population reduced by the government to ignorance and hatred.

The aggregation around the dissenting communist personalities operates mostly on the basis of the quest for that man, or that group of men, who would oppose the government on the grounds of its anti-national and anti-democratic purposes. The splits and changes in the world communist movement or in the CPSU are followed with an acute interest and with a characteristic wishful thinking. The death of Stalin was expected, in the entire region, long before it occurred, to be a milestone. Such changes were projected onto the background of the local situation to help to guess 'who will eat whom'. The expectations are directed towards the emergence of one personality from among the thus divided leaders who would defend principles and claims near to those postulated by the population. It is this postulation which starts off the aggregation at national level. This is why in the case, already discussed, of a communist government itself taking a stand against the Russian government and party, with or without 'promises of liberalization' as, respectively in Poland and Hungary in 1956, or in Rumania in 1963, the government itself, and its leaders, benefit from a certain aggregation of popularity.

Then, in a more general way, there was and is a permanent tendency to aggregate around the 'nationalists' as against the 'Muscovites' and around the 'natives' as against the 'foreigners'. (Anti-semitism was operative: none of the leaders from within the communist parties around whose policies or names some aggregation took place were Jews: from Patrascanu to Gomulka, and from Kostov to Nagy.) In the first fifteen years, 1945–60, the national question was uppermost. The wish of the entire populations was that Russia's domination and exploitation should be opposed from within. It was therefore around those who were brave enough to stand against the double forces, of the Russians themselves and of their quislings, that popular sympathy and hopes rallied. For, the people realized that their problems, whether national, political or economic, could be stated in terms of Stalinism versus anti-Stalinism.

The subject is too diffuse, and space here too limited, to allow a more precise examination. But some aspects should at least be mentioned and may lead to further reflections. One is the problem of the efficiency of aggregation. This, of course, depends on two questions: how concentrated must the aggregation be to transform itself into action? and how open must the postulation of motives of dissent be to start off a nation-wide movement of opinion, or indeed of political agitation? In the case of Poland in 1956 it was the workers of Poznan who began, through their anti-communist action, the aggregation around a communist leader: Gomulka, The name of Gomulka acquired in these few months a national popularity. To be sure the die-hard oppositionists, agrarians. catholics or socialists had strong reservations about Gomulka, or indeed any communist leader. They preferred to see the entire regime sink. But the rest of the population took a genuine interest, and active part in the conflict thus narrowed between a Pole and the Russians.

But in the case of East Berlin and of East Germany in 1953 the movement, spontaneously produced and almost instantaneously crushed, remained leaderless. It did not have sufficient strength, or time, to aggregate around, for instance, Herrnstadt, whom Zaisser thought might be proposed as the alternative communist leader to Ulbricht. In the case of Hungary in 1956 the movement again spontaneous, came from outside the party, and chose Nagy, who was reputed to have taken a similar stand within the party, as their centre of aggregation. But some who had joined the movement showed a definite reluctance to accept him, a communist, as their ultimate or even temporary leader. In the case of Patrascanu in Rumania, or of Kostov in Bulgaria, the leadership of the respective parties acted so swiftly against their 'opposition' and crushed them so drastically that even if there was diffuse dissent it hardly had time to be connected with these possible candidates for national popularity. But in any case, at the time, 1948-9, the Stalinist terror was in such full swing that there could be no question of any opposition coming into the open and rallying the people around it. (Patrascanu, however, was kept alive after his dismissal until 1954. After this period of long detention he was then summarily tried and afterwards executed. As his name had slowly, through these years, acquired a certain publicity, one of the reasons for which he was thus suppressed at the time when the issue of a national policy against Russia was in the offing, might well have been the fact that Gheorghiu-Dej and his group feared that the popular reaction against the Russians, would concentrate around Patrascanu's name instead of their own. He was known to have held these views before, and he had the advantage of being free from the responsibility for the worst terroristic years, 1948–53, when he himself had been under arrest. Moreover, unlike Dej, he tinctured his nationalist attitudes with strong anti-dogmatist and liberalistic points of view.)

This leads to, indeed cannot be separated from, the question of the impact, in this otherwise haphazard process, of the strength, stature and character of the personality concerned. In some cases the aggregation is more powerful than the personality. In these cases the personality is, at it were, pushed from behind to positions which he might not have actually wanted, or for which he would have not thought himself a fit competitor. He is made to adopt and express political demands and conditions which he himself would have previously found too categoric and too violent, or at least premature, to put forward or – more to the point – to have a chance to succeed. In the contrary case it is the personality who formulates in advance of the population a coherent criticism of the government and offers an alternative policy. But because of the timidity of public opinion, the connexion between the potential leader and the leaderless public fails to materialize. The potential leader remains lonely and, what is more, unprotected against the rigours of the party and the government which he had frontally attacked.

The first case can be exemplified by Imre Nagy whose withdrawn personality, initially unsure vision and tendency to vacillate made him follow rather than lead the ground-swell of the spontaneous popular aggregation. He lagged behind the particularly rapid postulation of aims and doctrines produced by two characteristic revolutionary factors: rapidly accelerating ambition and the explosive decompression of a population which had been too long and too much disregarded. It is true that Nagy's record in his relations with the party, especially since its coming to power, showed that he had advocated more complex and subtler attitudes not only than the Stalinist ones, but even than the standard

Marxist-Leninist ones. It is also true that, during the two year crisis of 1955–6 he had had time to clarify his thoughts and doctrine in a major publication. Finally, it is true that in the struggle with Rakosi, and afterwards with the Russians, he clarified his own attitude and strengthened his ideas and reactions. But, when all is said, the fact remains that in the Hungarian example the 'chosen' leader was pushed from behind by the growing force of the quickly rallied public opinion. At every stage he tried, because he lagged behind instead of leading public opinion, to satisfy it with compromise solutions which were in any case too late to be effective.

The second case can be best exemplified by Milovan Djilas, a young and ardent Montenegrin who ever since the partisan war had been one of the six people closest to Tito, and had of course a strong following in the League of Yugoslav Communists. He startled Yugoslav public opinion by publishing abroad, in 1956, a book on the *New Class*. The book went to the bitter end of the communist dilemma. The conclusion was, from a political point of view, the need for the institutionalization of other political parties to allow for the control of and opposition against the outgrown Apparat. This would have entailed free elections, but Djilas did not stop at the thought that this might easily have meant the fall from power of the Communist League. Moreover, the ideas to which he was now giving the final twist, had been put into public circulation ever since the Yugoslav-Soviet dispute when the Yugoslav League had crystallized its own doctrine of the withering away of the state as opposed to that of the Stalinist centralistic state.

It could thus have been expected that Djilas's personal authority, intellectual intransigence and political courage would have led the most active sectors of Yugoslav public opinion to aggregate around him. Moreover the regime took the exceptionally drastic step of having Djilas tried and sentenced. Yet, even after this final and provocative publicity, public support for him failed to materialize. The aggregation around his name did not follow the rhythm or assume the proportions which it took in Gomulka's case in Poland, and in Nagy's in Hungary in 1956. Among possible reasons for this was first the fact that Djilas's point of view in 1956 was too much in advance even of reforming public opinion; and on the other hand, that because Djilas had himself been a communist, and even a strong-minded one, those of more established outlook did not 'trust' him enough. One should also bear in mind the fact that general affection and respect for Tito in the influential circles which now formed public opinion were then stronger than the feeling for any of his lieutenants who might contradict or oppose his views. And, finally, the fact that, in 1956, in Yugoslavia, any individual who took, in a period of relative political stability, a stand of open opposition to the regime as a whole rendered himself liable to persecution and pressure from the powerful Apparat. Open opposition in a dictatorship gathers strength and popular support only in moments of acute crisis.

Since then, and in the light of the continuous evolution of the regime itself, and of the national debate, Djilas's theses were more and more often quoted by the increasingly aware public. 'Djilas was right' is heard frequently nowadays. In 1966, *Praxis* and other publications described the political problem of Yugoslavia with direct reference to Djilas's formulations of 1956, and Mihajlov's *Free Voice* was announced as an organ of Djilasism. Thus a new and impressive aggregation seemed to be on the move. This might lead to a reunion between the potential leader and the leaderless opposition. But it may equally be that by now his moment has passed and that new, more administrative and less ideological, more constitutional and less revolutionary-minded leaders will channel the new movement. This will be seen in full clarity from now on, for with Djilas freed from prison at the end of 1966, it is to be expected that his voice will be constantly heard in the debate.

But apart from the aggregation around the major dissenting figures of the party-hierarchy itself – aggregation also occurs around other types of personalities. University professors, like Havemann, who are known to oppose the party for political reasons; editors of reviews, like *Po Prostu's* Lasota in Poland, whose personal popularity as shown in the 1957 elections cost him and his review so much; prelates of the church who use the pulpit to criticize the regime; writers who like Tibor Dery in Hungary, continued to be in open and permanent conflict with the authorities; officers who, like Transki, in Bulgaria are assumed to be opposed to the government; economists of whom like Ota Sik in Czechoslovakia it is learned or rumoured that they are fighting within their own abstruse sphere for economic reform; even artists and cabaret singers who make a habit of being consistently ironical towards the regime, all these might find at some time, or during some periods, that their names circulate among some sectors of public opinion as a symbol, if not a mouthpiece, of dissent.

The Churches, the universities, the reviews, the army, the personalities and all other centres of aggregation of dissent rally behind them groups of followers. These groups can be ephemeral or permanent; small or large; nationwide or limited to some regional or professional sectors of the population; or looser or more compact, according to the intensity of the problem or to the range of attention the chosen issues of conflict can attract. But one point should be made here for the sake of clarity. This is that *these groups* of political or even more so, doctrinal, aggregation of dissent against the policies and ideologies of the regime, are not the same as the interest-groups which exercise the plural checks. They overlap sometimes in action, and very often in membership, but they are not alike. There can be Catholic foremen or farmers who would aggregate around the Church on matters of national policy or especially of freedom of belief, but who would disregard its recommendations on special professional or social issues; or there can be members of the intelligentsia who would act against the government on matters of academic freedom, but with it in matters of, for instance, economic management.

Thus the two categories of groups form different social and political patterns in the communist body politic. To describe them as identical because they both are or are generally animated by the common quest for freedom and institutional order would be misleading. Such juxtapositions and telescoping generalizations lead to the vague notions of 'active political interest groups', 'opposition groups', or, more simply 'groups' supposedly unified in their political resistance to the government's policies. A more careful analysis reveals that the social-functional groups, which check on the government by their very activities within the existing state, do not coincide with the groups aggregated through political or ideological dissent against the state. The coalescence between all kinds of groups can be achieved only at a higher level: that of the factions, which, like the parties, are conglomerates of interests and beliefs. Factions, as will be seen, are usually formed after a period in which the diffuse dissent is *channelled* into the more rarefied spheres of decision-making and finds in those spheres the ways to public expression and representation.

3. CHANNELLING

Factionalism is the greatest sin in communist party-politics; but at the same time it is the only, and indeed, inevitable way in which politics is made inside these parties. 'The party learns its lessons and is tempered in the struggle against factionalism, a new malaise (it is new in the sense that after the October Revolution we had forgotten all about it). Actually it is an old malaise, with relapses apparently bound to occur over the next few years,'[25] said Lenin in January 1921. He then described factions as formed 'from above', that is from within the highest spheres of policy-making, usually the Central Committee, from which more members, or even one single member, starts the factionalist process by putting forward a 'platform' to which other members will or will not adhere. The danger is that this 'platform' can attract and enrol lower organizations behind it or indeed 'go down to the masses'.

This is generally speaking the view of factionalism one obtains when one looks down at it from the centre of power, where consensus (or, rather, monolithic agreement) is believed to be vital. But the process is entirely different if one looks upwards at the formation of factions, starting from the moment in which the diffuse dissent gathers from the vast fringes and peripheries until it is expressed, or ventilated, in the 'platforms' or 'programmes' of some ruling groups. There is a vast difference between the two perspectives. In the first view the 'platform' is handed down from the centre of power 'to the masses' in order to attract the external support necessary to strengthen the fortress of power against internal opposition. In the second view, the aggregating dissent is seen finding its way along the higher 'channels' of policy-making and decision-making. There it is ultimately expressed by one or more of those who can speak in the open and formulate its, or some of its, points as an alternative policy. In the eighteenth century in France the Parlements started to publish their 'remonstrances' against the King. In 1789 the deputies to the States-General brought their own *cahiers de doléances* from the country and the towns. The two

[25] Lenin's *Collected Works*, Vol. 32, p. 105.

trends of dissent were not identical either in importance or in purpose (indeed very often they showed contrary tendencies); but their ultimate result was to amplify and give coherence to the dissent against the power-holder. And when in early American eighteenth century politics, the innumerable 'caucuses', 'cliques' and 'connexions' were all following only their selfish and centrifugal purposes, they were at the same time pushed from behind by growing public opinion, into coalescing into larger factions and to come gradually in the open. This is how the inevitable process of institutionalization always works.

In the European communist states this process of institutionalization through channelling, will be briefly examined in the following pages. It is now rife in all parties because of the broadening of the political process, which is sponsored to a certain degree by the party leadership themselves. The old and permanent phenomenon of factionalism has now a different meaning altogether, for it is possible that the parties themselves will become larger 'debating bodies'. An even more interesting and pregnant phenomenon, however, is the open factionalism in consultative bodies like the local assemblies and indeed the parliaments themselves.

Factionalism in the parties

Every communist party in power in Europe since the end of the Second World War has had constant factional troubles. The most usual cleavage was, up to Stalin's death in 1953, that of 'Muscovites' versus 'natives'. After his death it was that between dogmatists and revisionists, or, indeed between Stalinists and anti-Stalinists. But such a simplified analysis of the problem is far too superficial. Internal ideological conflicts or regional or ethnical incompatibilities, old personal feuds as well as the entire range of functional, professional or social points of view form an endlessly changing kaleidoscope of alliances or antagonisms in the smaller and larger circles of the party. The large currents of thought and motives of dissent seep through every breach and crevice thus opened in the former monolith. The following, taking party by party, is a summary account of the main factional struggles in the past twenty years.

In Poland the deep split within the leadership of the Polish Workers

Party, as it was called since 1942, originated from the fact that it had two separate wings, under different influences and located in different countries. The leadership of the party was formed mostly by people who had never been in Moscow and had not had the special training and indoctrination of Gomulka himself, Zenon Klisko, Marian Spichalski, Wladislaw Bienkowski and others. In November 1943 Wladislaw Gomulka became the first secretary of the Polish Workers Party in Poland. The relations of this wing with Moscow broke down when Gomulka suggested that the Communist Party should join the Polish national resistance. At the same time a new wing of the Polish party was set up in Russia itself. Its leaders were Polish communists who were in Moscow during the war, like Jakub Behrman or Roman Zambrowski, Ochab, Minc, Zawadski, Jedrichowski and last but not least Bierut, who later became the official leader of the Muscovite wing. The membership was drawn from the great numbers of Poles from the Russian occupied territories in Poland who had been deported to Russia. The Russians feared any *rapprochement* between the Polish nationalists and the Polish communists as implied in Gomulka's proposal. The memory of the partition of the Polish territories by Hitler and Stalin, and of the crimes perpetrated by the Russians in their zone of occupation, from the mass-deportations in 1940 to the Katyn massacre in 1941, when the Russian armies retreated from Poland, were too vivid. The Russians rightly thought that further 'nationalist contagion' would turn more Polish communists against them.

These two groups, enlarged by the addition of a small splinter-agrarian group and by Osobka-Morawski's Polish Socialist Party, formed, at the end of July 1944, when the Soviet forces crossed the Curzon line, the then frontier, the 'Polish Committee of National Liberation', better known as the Lublin committee. The relations between the Lublin committee, submitted to Russian control, and the forces of the Polish resistance, or Home Army, which were active in the German-occupied Polish territory, were fraught with deep hostility. The tragedy of the Warsaw rising in August 1944 was the epitome of this conflict. The Soviet command, which did not want the capital to fall first into the hands of the non-communist resistance influenced the Lublin committee to let the nationalistic Poles, who on 1 August 1944 had tried to recapture Warsaw from the Germans, be killed and decimated. After this horrible episode the relations between the Poles and the Russians deteriorated even more. Gomulka's 'native' Polish communist wing was torn in two by this irreconcilable antagonism between the strong feelings of the Polish people and the orders of those who put them in power. Their efforts to find what has ever since been called 'the Polish road to socialism' did not please either the Polish people or the Soviet representatives. The factional struggle within the Party reflected dramatically the conflict between the nation itself and the Foreign Power.

Gomulka's fall from his position as General-Secretary in September 1948, started yet another main factional division within the party. The top-leadership of the party and the government which cut across the 'Muscovite' and the 'native' lines was now divided into the pro-Gomulka group and the anti-Gomulka group, headed by Behrman. For, when Moscow had taken the decision in 1947 to get rid of Gomulka, some of his 'native' friends had turned their backs on him, whereas some of the individual 'Muscovites' wondered whether he might not in the end be proved right. The issues at the time were already very complex. Within the rarefied summit, the main currents of opinion and checks of interest groups clashed on the various social, economic, political or religious issues. This formed a kaleidoscope of alternatives and attitudes, ever changing under the pressures from below. The new lines, on the changing issues, cut across the individuals and groups of the top-leadership.

Two new factions thus emerged and were called after the streets or the houses where they were respectively in the habit of meeting: the Pulawska group, in general more revisionist and liberal-minded, and the Natolinists, the die-hard conservative Stalinist group headed by Zenon Nowak. The clash between these two opposing trends broke out after the events at Poznan in 1956. Although spokesmen of the Natolin Street faction first openly demanded that Gomulka should return, and the Pulawska faction followed suit only later – it was largely on this latter group that Gomulka, Marian Spichalsky and Zenon Klisko who had been removed with him, based their political faction when they returned to the party. When finally, Gomulka re-occupied his position of General-Secretary, vacated by Ochab's resignation, Jakub Behrman and Rokosovsky, the Soviet Marshal, member of the Polish Politburo, disappeared for good from political life. But once installed

Gomulka soon realized that he would have to navigate between the two factions. Thus as early as 1957, when the closing-down of *Po Prostu* occasioned the violent reaction of large sectors of public opinion, Gomulka received the backing of the Natolinist faction, whereas the Pulawska faction supported the manifestations against Gomulka and his new conservatism.

In the sixties a new faction, called 'the Partisans' emerged. It was formed by different categories of people, but generally speaking was an offshoot of the Natolinist faction, yet with a different and new outlook of its own. What happened was that this primarily Stalinist group contained in it a large number of former right-wingers and quasi-fascist elements. The Russians were glad to use, in all the East European countries, such people who by their sheer personal and political vulnerability, would be most obedient collaborators. Many accepted this unexpected offer of membership of the party as a unique chance. But when, after regaining their integrity by their stay in power with the communists for more than a decade, the party freed itself from direct Russian control, the Partisans opposed the 'liberals' on two different accounts. First, they resented the fact that it was the liberals who now had taken the upper hand. Then, whenever genuine attitudes could again be manifested, they fell back inevitably in their old nationalistic ones. The faction made great inroads within party circles, and used a better technique for publicizing itself. It was headed first by Zenon Klisko, but soon General Moczar emerged as the strongest personality. Indeed ever since he was appointed Minister of the Interior in 1964, Moczar linked together the secret faction of the 'Partisans' from within the party, with an, until then, rather inefficient and vague organization of the former combatants and veterans: ZBoWid which was itself formed in 1949 by the union of eleven veteran organizations. Its main purpose was initially to redress the wrongs done to the Polish resistance movement. But under Moczar's chairmanship it became, in a sense like the British or the American Legion, a wide political pressure-group, with nationwide branches, and sharing the Partisans' views about the main political, social and economic problems.

The Partisans' main political role was the drawing together of every aspect of nationalism. They were anti-semitic. Their greatest success and the symptom of their newly acquired power at the top was the removal of Roman Zambrowski, one of the few Jews who remained in the leadership of the Polish Workers Party. They were anti-Russian, for in their rank-and-file drawn mostly from the Home Army many had been persecuted within the party by the 'Muscovites'; but they were also anti-German. It was on this latest issue that more recently the present head of the Partisans, General Moczar, tried to make political capital for his organization. In the conflict between Church and state, ZBoWid took a violent stand against the alleged pro-German attitudes of the Church and organized widespread demonstrations against it. This, of course, could not but be of help to Gomulka and the party. But it was obvious that Moczar's aims were to try to set up a new organization. A faction with popular backing, could provide perhaps, one day, an alternative to the party and become itself a new party.

The Rumanian Communist Party, like the Polish party, had been badly and tenaciously persecuted by Moscow. The Third International constantly changed its leadership which it always considered to be too nationalistic and too lacking in revolutionary spirit. Therefore although the party's weakness during the Second World War and its lack of any serious popular support made it a very different proposition from the Polish party, its internal situation, when it emerged from clandestinity in 1944, was, in a sense, similar to that of the Polish party.

Like the Polish party it had a 'native' faction headed by Gheorghiu-Dej and formed by Chivu Stoica, Gheorghe Apostol, Nicolae Ceausescu, Miron Constantinescu, Ion Gheorghe Maurer, and for a short while, Lucretiu Patrascanu. It also had a 'Muscovite' or 'foreigners' faction, headed by Ana Pauker and formed by people who were either of non-Rumanian ethnical origin, or had spent their war years in Moscow, or both: Laszlo-Luca, Szilagy-Salajan, Petre Borila, Kischinevski and others. According to the now official history of the party, although Gheorghiu-Dej was appointed General-Secretary he was until 1952 the 'prisoner' of the troika of the other three foreign secretaries: Ana Pauker, Vasile Luca and Teohari Georgescu. These three had the upper-hand because the country was under Soviet quasi-occupation, because they were the top local agents of the Soviet secret police and because they were close to Stalin's personal entourage. Thus they prevented the party from even trying to listen to the people's complaints and forged ahead with the simple policy of copying the Soviet model: forcible collectivization, military industrial production, and cultural russification. Such a policy would have enabled Rumania to become, sooner or later, a Soviet Federal Republic.

Both factions, however, united in 1948 for the purge of Lucretiu Patrascanu who was at the time the only avowed nationalist leader of the party, and of his followers. Between these two main factions there was the group of the 'political generals' headed by Bodnaras, who although collaborating more than loyally with the Russian army and security police, had in their pragmatic ways, a sharper ear for the clamour of national indignation than the Stalinist-dogmatists Ana Pauker and Vasile Luca. In 1952, the political generals together with the 'natives' won over Epishev, a former and future army-police man, then Soviet Ambassador in Rumania, and this action precipitated Ana Pauker's and 'the foreigners' downfall. The latter were then made to take responsibility for all the miseries endured by farmers, workers, intelligentsia and generally speaking the entire Rumanian population, in the previous seven years.

Another factional trouble appeared immediately after the Twentieth Congress of the CPSU. The very delegation which represented the Rumanian party, formed by four Politburo members, divided afterwards into two opposing groups: Gheorghiu-Dej and Petre Borila, on one side, and Kischinevski and Miron Constantinescu on the other. Each of these groups, startled by the electrifying revelations made by Khrushchev, then accused the other of 'Stalinism'. This is, at least, what transpired in July 1956 when, taking Khrushchev's purge of the leaders of the 'anti-party' group Malenkov-Molotov as an example to be followed, Gheorghiu-Dej felt that he too could eliminate two 'anti-party' and 'Stalinist' leaders : Kischinevski and Miron Constantinescu. In reality, this was only the settlement of an internal quarrel, for all the leaders of the Rumanian Communist Party had in the previous twenty years been equally Stalinist, with possibly the exception of Miron Constantinescu. This somewhat younger Rumanian intellectual, who had succeeded in the years 1953–6 in inspiring the new intelligentsia of the party with a more nationalistic vision, might well have been the man most likely to ride a genuine anti-Stalinist wave in the party. He was therefore manoeuvred from inside by the powerful Dej. Probably he revealed in the inner circle of power his intention to raise the issue of Stalinism more thoroughly, and soon after the blow fell on him before he could strike himself.

Like all dogmatic parties in power which go through a period of success (due to its economic, diplomatic and ideological nationalistic policies), the Rumanian Communist Party is now less vulnerable to the troubles of internal factionalism. The success and speed of its undertakings, and the feeling of being united against the foreign power unifies the internal groups. But it would be wrong to assume that this is enough to abolish them. There are in the Rumanian party leadership deep ethnic cleavages between the Rumanian, Magyar, Bessarabian and Jewish 'groups' which, under these names, were the 'groups' from which the party was formed in 1921; a permanent hostility between workers and intellectuals (both Patrascanu and Miron Constantinescu were intellectuals); between the old party-apparatchiks and the new experts and technicians; as well as, and still the most important, active distrust of the powerful group of the political generals, old hands of the Russian-MVD and Soviet army in Rumania. As such, these men were formerly in absolute control of the security police which, in Rumania too had been, for the first fifteen years, stronger than the party. They were now annoyed and irritated by the new party leadership, intent on continuing the policy of popular nationalism, and banking on the confidence shown in them by a re-emerging and increasingly nationalistic, public opinion.

The history of the factions in the East German Party, or SED, stems from the overwhelming impact of the Russian occupation, of the aspirations towards German reunification and of the particularly harsh and brutal style of governing maintained by the Ulbricht regime as its only way of remaining in power, even as a quisling-regime, against such formidable odds. As mentioned above, in the case of the first faction, the Zaisser-Herrnstadt group of 1953, it is still a moot point whether it originated at all as an internal party-development or whether it was entirely engineered by Beria from Moscow. The fact is that in previous years Herrnstadt had been one of the few more articulate dissenting members of the SED-leadership and that in June 1953 he succeeded in putting forward a 'Platform' in which neutralism as a way of reunification, and self-management and self-administration as a means of democratization were the main objectives. The faction numbered five full members of the Politburo, and had been supported by Franz Dahlem, purged earlier for similar tendencies. It rightly reckoned on the immediate support of the population. Indeed in the case of East Germany the fact that party faction from within is produced by the over-whelming pressure of the population from without, is easier to detect than anywhere else. In the politics of East Germany the ultimate struggle between the Apparat-State itself, on the one hand, and the population as a whole, on the other, overshadows all internal struggles between the various groups and tendencies of the leadership. Serious as Herrnstadt's, and his faction's, action was inside the leadership – it was only a pale reflection, within the party, of the formidable real movement of the population against it.

The same is true also of another faction which appeared sub-sequently, the Schirdewan-Wollweber group. Karl Schirdewan, a veteran of the German Communist Party which he had joined in 1925, took Herrnstadt's place in the Politburo in 1953. He and Ernst Wollweber, the man who at the same time took Zaisser's place as Minister of Security, then formed, after their return from the Twentieth Congress of the CPSU, as in the Rumanian case quoted above, a new faction. But so limited are the moves on the commu-nist leadership chessboard that the new faction reproduced the pattern of their predecessors. Like Zaisser-Herrnstadt, Schirdewan-Wollweber claimed that the reunification of Germany should be put above all other interests. To Ulbricht's argument that it was the unity of the party which should be maintained against the ubiquitous enemy agents they answered publicly, with a slogan immediately echoed in the country at large: 'Who is the enemy?'. But by the time the Schirdewan and Wollweber 'faction' had been dealt with by Ulbricht, triumphant once again, the action inside the leadership was outpaced by the action outside as already described in two preceding sections.[26]

Afterwards, between 1957 and 1961, when, in August, the Berlin wall was erected, the main form taken by the opposition manifested throughout East Germany was the millions of deser-tions to West Germany of people of all categories: workers, students, intellectuals and farmers thus bleeding the country's economy and society white. This extraordinary movement for which the expression 'voting with their feet' was revived, was to a

[26] See p. 206 and p. 222.

certain extent stopped by the equally extraordinary idea of the Ulbricht regime of building, in the second half of the twentieth century, in the heart of Europe, a primitive cement wall.

Apparent apathy has since fallen on the internal party life of the East German Party. But two resounding 'suicides', that of Lieutenant-General Vincenz Müller, Chief of Staff of the GDR armed forces in May 1961, and that of Dr Erich Apel, the Chairman of the State-Planning Commission and deputy Prime Minister, in December 1963 were dramatic proofs of both the intensity of the internal struggles and the permanence of their causes. Inside the party, and indeed of the entire Apparat, the issues of the reunification with West Germany, for which Vincenz was accused of having tried to find new ways, and those of the exploitation of East Germans by the Soviet Union, against which Apel protested before the signature of a new trade-pact with Soviet Russia, are the focusing points of the insoluble alternatives of this artificial state.

By far the most important development in the policies of East Germany and of its party was the attempted 'dialogue' between the East German party and the Socialist Party of West Germany. But once again the main pressure came originally from the intelligentsia of the party. It soon became apparent that the party was divided between the Ulbricht group, determined to follow the 'hate-campaign' against the West Germans, and other 'groups' and 'factions', mostly of the intelligentsia who press for the view 'that both sides should make concessions . . . after all we are *all* Germans and should therefore be able to understand one another'.[27]

In Bulgaria, the 'native' Traicho Kostov was tried in 1949 for anti-Soviet attitudes and pro-Yugoslav leanings and was afterwards executed. His execution marked the total triumph of the arch-Stalinist and arch-Muscovite Valko Chervenkov, Georgi Dimitrov's brother-in-law and successor, after the latter's death in obscure circumstances in Russia. For seven years the Bulgarian Communist Party, which generally speaking is one of the most pro-Russian and dogmatist in communist Europe, showed signs of internal struggle or factional conflict under Chervenkov's leadership. But in April 1956 Chervenkov was replaced, on Khrushchev's

[27] In a report of the Neubrandenburg Regional executive published in *Freie Erde*, 21 January 1966. See further p. 290.

order, by Anton Yugov, said to be one of his personal enemies. Since then the party split, according to some observers[28] into four factions. They are the Chervenkov faction which contained the greatest number of apparatchiks and had strong dogmatist views and, like the Albanian party, deplored Khrushchev's revisionism and harboured an unforgettable admiration and gratitude for Stalin's Russia; the Zhivkov faction which, on the contrary, was pro-Russian because it had formed new links with and actually drew its influence in Bulgaria from Khrushchev himself; the Yugov faction, which was the personal faction of the Prime Minister because he was Prime Minister, and was ideologically a mixture of 'Stalinism' and 'nationalism'. After Yugov's fall from power, and replacement by Zhivkov, and after Zhivkov had also purged the great Stalinist, Chervenkov, a Yugov faction appeared, which became one of the conservative groups of the anti-Zhivkov Stalinist opposition. Finally, among the progressive groups was that headed by Georgi Chankov, also later purged by Zhivkov. This was a more progressive faction – insofar as it advocated both more independent relations with Russia, even Khrushchev's Russia, and greater flexibility in the economic and political approaches.

Thus Zhivkov navigated between internal dogmatist and pragmatist opposition for his own ill-defined purposes. It was in this atmosphere rife with factionalism that the Anev coup, mentioned above, took place, showing that yet another faction, that of the 'partisans' was advancing on to the dark political stage of Bulgarian communist affairs.

In Hungary the 'native-revisionist'/'Muscovite-dogmatic' factions appeared in the Nagy-Rakosi conflict in a fuller and more dramatic light than anywhere else. This was afterwards transformed, in circumstances of historical dimensions, into the clash between the entire Hungarian people in revolt and the forces of intervention of Soviet Russia as the foreign power. When Kadar took over the Party on 1 November 1965, and then a few days later formed the government, he was well aware, and has remained ever since convinced, that the party could never fully recover from the blows it had received. He also knew that only by treating the social and

[28] See especially J. F. Brown: 'The Bulgarian Plot', *World Today*, London, May 1965.

professional groups, the ruffled public with great discretion could the party be kept alive. This produced slowly, after the first three years, a strange transformation of the Party-Apparat into the Apparat as a whole, which is highly characteristic of the present Hungarian regime. Once this happened, and the entire process has accelerated from 1960 to 1966, the main factionalist activities were diluted, and displaced from the previously 'all-important but progressively less effective centre of power of the Party itself' to the more diffuse and plural centres of power of the Apparat 'state' as a whole. Thus whereas 'the Nagy-wing' of the party was totally liquidated from within the party after its leaders' assassination – its revisionist and anti-Stalinist mentalities flourished in the entire non-party apparat, against the dwarfed party.

The main groups which remained dogmatic within the Apparat were the political police, the old group of managers of heavy industry appointed early on by the Rakosi regime to the executive posts, and the legions of *apparatchiks* of the party, now placed in an intolerable position of inferiority. From these quarters, Kadar and his Politburo group, formed by Kallai, Gaspar, Szirmai and Bisku, received constant warnings that his policy could lead to the total dissolution of the party and of the communist state. In two instances the warnings materialized in opposition to Kadar from within the party itself: that of Imre Dogei who in 1962 was expelled from the party for 'dogmatism', and that, in the same year, of Gyorgy Marosan, the senior officer of the party after Kadar. But in neither case were there new factions behind them. The party-apparatchiks, together with the security police and the old managerial layer formed the main 'dogmatist-Stalinist' faction within the Apparat as a whole. Kadar thus continued to steer his aloof course between this die-hard core, on which his power in the party was ultimately based, and the rest of the Apparat and of public opinion. The latter especially showed a pragmatic, and apathetic attitude towards the regime as a whole – and showed interest mostly in one direction: that of further institutionalization of the legal and political controls over the Apparat. Thus in 1966, this attitude pierced even the party's theoretical review *Tsaradalmi Szemle*.[29] A professor of political science and law, Dr Otto Bihari, asked that the electoral law should be modified so as to allow elections of more candidates for each seat, and that the Parliament

[29] Budapest, August–September 1966.

should be more active. At this point one comes to the main feature which the Hungarian situation has in common with those of Czechoslovakia and Yugoslavia: the way in which the party itself prefers to underplay and, as it were, to hide its own power.

In Czechoslovakia too, the party suffered from continuous factionalist troubles after 1948, culminating in the Slansky-Clementis trials and purges of 1952. These leaders were accused of having created and maintained, within the party, 'factions' directed against the leadership of the party. Antonin Novotny, who was himself the embodiment of the less ideological, more bureaucratic-minded new apparatchiks, followed Slansky as the General-Secretary of the party. In 1953 after Gottwald's death he became the leader of the party. He showed readiness to adopt a less ideological line in the party after the Twentieth Congress of the CPSU – and made this point by expelling Gottwald's brother-in-law, Alexis Cepicka, from the party. Cepicka was also in command of the armed forces and had become the leader of the 'ideological-revolutionary' faction within the party. But after the Twenty-Second Congress of the CPSU, Novotny was faced with another faction formed very near his actual centre of power. Rudolf Barak, until the summer of 1961 Minister of the Interior and therefore in command of the state apparat, who had been one of Novotny's protégés and was considered as his 'Dauphin' was dismissed from most of his posts in 1961. In February 1962, it was announced that he had been arrested, tried as a 'thief and embezzler' and sentenced to fifteen years' imprisonment. The truth was that, like Miron Constantinescu in Rumania, Barak had tried after the Twenty-Second Party Congress to set up revisionist factional attitudes against the Stalinist style and mentality of the party. He presumably received a certain amount of spontaneous support from various sections of the Apparat and the public (unlike Novotny, Barak had an engaging and popular personality).

In April 1963, however, Novotny's troubles started again in the most vulnerable quarters. One of the Czechoslovak Party's gravest problems lies, as with the Yugoslav League, in the 'national factionalism' within the party of the Slovak party, and, to a lesser degree, of the German group. In 1963 under strong pressure from the Slovak population and the Slovak rank-and-file, Novotny was forced to purge Karol Bacilek, First Secretary of the Slovak Communist Party and Bruno Kochler, a German who were both the outstanding representatives of the old Stalinist mentality in the party. Bacilek's dismissal was particularly important. The powerful Slovak dissent which Bacilek had been trying for years to repress by the usual Stalinist methods, spread after his fall to the highest spheres of both the party and the Apparat as a whole. Since then the Slovak party, in turn constantly pressed by the Slovak intelligentsia, which reflects the antipathy of the Slovaks against Prague and its regime, has become, as already noted above,[30] the most active centre of aggregation of general dissent. Thus the Czechoslovak party's main internal troubles were the twin problems of revisionism and regionalism, which together have a dangerous cumulative effect. This is why the Novotny leadership, like the Kadar leadership, has preferred to begin to play down the part and the importance of the party, and in any case to broaden its range and approaches as much as possible. The fact that even before the war the Czechoslovak Communist Party had been a mass party has assisted these attempts to change it from a factionalist and secretive organization, as it had become in the Stalinist years, into a larger 'debating body' in which ideological and national differences of opinion can be ventilated with greater ease.

The Yugoslav League had inspired the Hungarian and Czechoslovak parties with its example as a self-effacing and broadminded party. But it shared with the Czechoslovak party the plight of being divided by permanent national cleavages.

To be sure, none of the other communist parties in power in Europe could rely on a greater internal *solidarity* (as opposed to homogeneity) than the League. This feeling of internal solidarity was based on a number of factors: most of its members had known each other and fought together in the partisan army against the national invader; it had an uncontested leader; already in power, it had to go through yet another test of 'patriotic resistance' against yet another foreign power; it had a deep realization of the danger of national centrifugalism for the new Yugoslav state, communist or not; and finally, on account of all this it had a much lighter hand

[30] See *infra*: 'Federalism', in the section 'The State-Administration and the Party', pp. 121 ff.

in its dealings with broader layers of the population with whom in any case there was good contact through the institution of self-management. To these reasons must be added the fact that its policy was to shed off its party structures and to become as much as possible an all-embracing organism, within the framework of national and social integration, but with the exception of all open activities of political conflict.

As a result, by the sixties, the 'all-embracing organism' embraced so many and such contradictory component groups that it became more and more difficult to make them row together in the same direction. If one tried to draw up a catalogue of the various allegiances of which members of the League, as groups and very often even as individuals feel the pull and with which they might have some links of factional association it should contain at least the following:

From a political point of view: the Ranković wing which believes in the need to rely on the party and the main apparats of the state, army, state administration and security police, at least until the real social integration begins to show more results; the Kardelj wing, with its belief that de-politization should be intensified, and that the party and the state should wither concomitantly with the social and economic integration; the Djilas wing (not under that name, and unable to put forward its views so categorically) believing in the primacy of political reform if the social and economic integration is ever to succeed; the fourth and largest group would be formed by all those sharing permanently or temporarily, one or more points of view, with either of these three viewpoints but who, like Tito, seem to think that ultimate policy is made up of all these alternative ingredients plus the passing of time. The purge of the security police, abruptly announced in July 1966, and Ranković's fall, have meant, from an exclusively political point of view, the defeat of the Ranković at the hands of the Kardelj faction – but with the Djilas faction taking great advantage of the upheaval thus caused.

From a national point of view there were two main groups: on the one hand, the non-Serbians were united against the Serbians, but, on the other, they were divided into Croats, Slovenes, Montenegrins, Macedonians, etc., with the sometimes antagonistic problems of their religious pressure groups: the Orthodox Church, Catholic Church, Muslims, communists and their regional, economic and cultural differences.

From a social point of view there was the large pressure group of the peasantry, which in Yugoslavia had greater economic interests to represent than in other communist states since agricultural production was treated as a separate, non-socialist, operation. There was the awe-inspiring group of trade unions, headed by able leaders, based partly on the revived trade unions themselves and partly on the collective representation of the workers' councils. They were bent on 'showing results' and thus acquired an increasing say in economic and financial matters; last but not least there were the active and ubiquitous groups of the two intelligentsias, technical and creative, which formed in the sixties an inner-circle of influence of their own. The former was composed of the managers and specialists who occupied the central positions in planning and in economic and financial law-making in the sixties. The latter consisted of all professors, journalists, writers, artists and scientists, to be found in great numbers in the League, who coalesced as a pressure group on matters concerning living conditions and intellectual freedom.

Finally there were the pressure groups of the local administration, which in the first five years of the sixties had acquired an ever growing importance and self-consciousness and which acted in two different ways. Caucuses of the institutions of the local administration, of the commune councils, assemblies and the 'neighbouring communities' were formed so as to influence the 'headquarters'; and at the headquarters themselves the powerful lobbies of the various federal and regional institutions carried factional activities within the party, the Executive Council and the National Federal Assembly.

With such a variegated and mosaic-like composition, and with the increasing outspokenness and articulation of each group, it became obvious that the League was bursting under so many pressures. New, less centralistic bodies, were necessary to channel each of these groups' views and interests more comprehensively. Broader 'debating bodies' were sought, the operative word being 'debating'. But what could these new bodies be? In spite of great efforts of ingenuity and imagination, there seem to be only three main ways for achieving a greater political participation, without actually falling into political pluralism. One or all of these three ways have been tried in the European communist states. All these solutions have in common the fact that they lead from the previously exclusive clandestine factionalism in the party, to a new factionalism which cuts across groups of interests and trends of opinions and transfers the debate to more appropriate institutions. These are the Yugoslav attempt to build up a yet broader and less communist-dominated single but national 'Alliance' as a mobilizing debating body; the Polish attempts to legitimize the present bogus multi-party system by letting it acquire some true political substance within the framework of the theory of the 'hegemonic party'; and the attempts in most of these states to use the Parliaments more actively as *the* debating bodies where public opinion can become articulate.

The Yugoslav 'Socialist Alliance'

The 'Socialist Alliance' was until the fifties a 'front organization' which was used in Yugoslavia, as similar bodies under different names such as National Front,[31] Bloc, etc., are used for electoral purposes in most European communist states. But the difference was that in most of the other countries one of the functions of this sporadic front organization was to provide a common electoral list both for the communist or Workers' Party and for the other bogus parties which are allowed a small percentage of token parliamentary representation, whereas in Yugoslavia these bogus parties have now disappeared. There was no doubt that the Alliance was a front organization of the League (party) itself. But in the sixties the League began to reveal two new functional disadvantages. One was the difficulty for a centralistic and 'monolithic' party of including so many interests and opinions. The other was that the population still knew it as the party-apparat which ruled the country during and after the Stalinist years through its zealous *apparatchiks*. The 'Socialist Alliance' thus seemed to the leadership to be more appropriate to the new political aims.

The 'Alliance' was vague enough, and relatively broad; it was apparently not dominated by the League; it seemed thus to offer more scope for consultation and discussion within a single national organization and for becoming an arena or debating body. In this view, the Alliance if properly reconstituted as a more active vehicle of popular representation, could become a second party; not, be it observed, in the constitutional-pluralist meaning of another party

[31] As it used to be called even in Yugoslavia until 1953.

sitting in the precinct, opposite the government party and thus opposing it, but as a larger second party, containing the League within it and as such superimposed on it rather than opposed to it. On the other hand instead of being a static and exclusively debating and legislative body (as Parliaments appear to be to parties in quest of 'mobilization', which believe or claim to believe that Parliaments lead to a further atomization of opinions and attitudes and to more and more centrifugalism of specialized interests) the 'Alliance' would remain an 'oriented' debating body. Its purpose would be to ventilate and discuss fully as many opinions and views as possible before the draft laws and especially the plans, which continue to be considered year after year and decade after decade as the steps in the evolution of the society towards its final integration, are sanctioned by the constitutional organs. This was, actually, yet another of Djilas's ideas. In the article 'League or Party?' in *Borba* of 1954 he said: 'The League of Communists would gradually take on the character of a strong, ideological, widely diffused nucleus, but would lose its party character. It would merge with the Socialist Alliance, and the communists would merge with the ordinary citizenry. Why should that be bad for communists and socialism? On the contrary, the Socialist Alliance would become a truly socialist factor and would not be a self-appointed elite of communists. The role of individuals and personalities would grow, on the basis of their quality and their functions among the masses and not only on the basis of their position in the party committee or administration. The direct political role of the masses would also be increased. The people would decide most political problems by themselves without having leaders and patented formulas forced upon them.'

As it still existed before the Sixth Congress of June 1966, when its future role was discussed with an interest it had never before aroused, the 'Socialist Alliance of the Working People of Yugoslavia' could be defined as 'the political instrument' of all the citizens of the state willing to join forces in a voluntary and democratic union. This 'political instrument' had a national and international purpose, insofar as it might establish relations with other similar parties in the world, although it was not clear whether they were to be mostly socialist parties or, as seems more likely, any other kind of parties. (This question might seem irrelevant at least for the moment, but might become more interesting if and when there is more active collaboration[32] between parties in the different European communist states, and between international political *ideological* organizations other than those of the Communist Parties and world movement.) Finally, the mutual relations between the Socialist Alliance and the League itself were defined as being 'based on each one's independence and co-operation in the realization of common aims and mutual development of initiatives and exchanges of opinions'.

In 1966 the Socialist Alliance numbered 8,126,204 members while the League had a total membership of 1,046,202. Whereas full credit was still given to the League for initiating and projecting the main economic and social plans or laws, its part in their implementation came, in the last few years, more and more under criticism. The 'de-politization' of the work in self-managed or self-administrating units meant in so many words the cessation of interference by the League organizations in their activities. (It is remarkable that the slogan of 'de-politization' was frequently used by such senior League officials as Kardelj and Bakarić, the top personalities of the Croat and Slovene wings.) It became more and more obvious that the League organs and personnel were more often than not opposed to the implementation of the economic reforms, and especially to the real decentralization and autonomy which they entailed. The purge of the security police, which had been denounced as responsible for obstructing at all levels the implementation of the reforms, in reality reflected a further decline in the influence and power of the League, for with the security police the Serbian centralistic wing of the League also fell. It was this wing which had given the League, in the last decade, its sense of remaining the main organism of control in both state and society.

Thus with a reduced number of members, with a shrinking power of control and execution in state and society, and with an increasingly challenged ideological and political primacy, the League must fight hard to remain an active centralistic party. It is difficult to see it become a new broad organism which would mobilize anew the energies and enthusiasm of new generations of Yugoslavs, or for that matter, of Serbs, Croats, Slovenes and Montenegrins. The role which is often recommended to it is that of a kind of ideological nucleus within the Socialist Alliance.

It was this point that was most ardently discussed at the Sixth

[32] See further, 'The other parties' and 'Conclusions'.

Congress of the 'Alliance' in June 1966. The congress, generally speaking, proved to be one more occasion for public opinion to exercise its pressure for institutionalization. It was noticeable that the most effective resolutions were aimed at improvements in matters of information, and of the 'right of the citizens to have a better insight and influence in this sphere'. But two schools of thought were openly opposed on this issue of the future role of the Alliance. The first insisted that it would be worthwhile to make the effort to re-animate and transform the 'Socialist Alliance' into something new and original only if it would quite clearly be entirely different from the League, and entirely safeguarded against the League's possible interference. Behind this attitude lay the justified apprehension that, once more, the omnipotent League would create a new network by which it would maintain its hold on the country and the state. (This more pessimistic view was confirmed by the fact that, during the Mihajlov crisis in August 1966, it was the local organization of the Socialist Alliance in Zadar which held a meeting of protest against the activities of the arrested writer. This showed that the Alliance can be made to work as a front organization.) If it were only to provide the League with yet another, and perhaps better, jumping-off board the majority of the participants at the Congress were not prepared to take the matter seriously.

The other school of thought started from the premise that in any case the League would continue to act as the ideological motor of the Socialist Alliance; and that in any case a long period of transition should be allowed for the merging of the League organizations and membership into the much broader organization of the Alliance. It therefore believed that it would be utopian and unreasonable to think at once of two separate and self-contained units, rather than of two concentric circles. But in reality the clash of views was between those who thought that the Alliance should compete with and oppose the League as a second party, and those who thought that by merging all political activities into a party of 10,000,000 members, the stage of a *non-party* state would be reached in Yugoslavia.[33] For them, the Alliance would be a further

[33] 'Direct democracy is the road to non-party democracy. The Socialist Alliance makes it possible for the single-party political system to be replaced gradually by a non-party system', Aleks Petković: 'The Socialist Alliance – a form of self-management' in *Socialist Thought and Practice*, Belgrade, March 1965.

stage in non-party politics and de-politization. The role of the League itself was amply discussed after the Fifth Central Committee Plenum of 4 October 1966, held after the Rankovic case. Some of the decisions taken, such as the dissolution of the Executive Committee (Politburo), and especially the appointment of commissions with members from inside and outside the party and decision by majority vote, confirmed the liberalizing trend. Indeed the new commissions might easily lead to the formation of a quasi-institutional opposition.

But the debate thus opened did not produce greater clarity on the central issue of the future role of the League itself – and of its conflicting demands for a central political organization and for legalized self-management. The ideas and arguments put forward can be summarized under two main headings. One is what can best be called the theory of the party as a mass organization. Its role would be to discuss 'the deeper aspects of the concrete problems', upon which decisions should be taken by the organs of self-management without the party's interference or indeed participation. Also, and this is perhaps more important, in the debates of this debating body, the minority should be allowed to maintain its point of view, even if defeated, thus creating what was described by the Macedonian leader Cruenkovski as a 'loyal factionalism'. The other theory should be associated with Kardelj's name and growing influence. This is the theory of double responsibility. Communists should be responsible to the League 'in one capacity, but if and when acting in an administrative capacity, or within a state organ, towards those who elected them'. In this theory the independence of the organs of state and society is thus reasserted. The 'representatives of the people have a responsibility of their own.' This might lead to revocation of the mandates, either of the deputies, or of the governments themselves when a majority of the latter vote against them. (A parallel situation arose in Kardelj's own Slovenia, in December 1966. But this will be discussed later.)

Tito seemed to be torn between the contradictions implicit in the existence of a centralistic organ in a self-managing society. When speaking to Yugoslavs he defended the idea of the indispensability of the League as a leading political organization for an unforeseeable duration. 'We talk of the withering away of the state; but the withering away of the League (party) is not to be considered.' But he defended the Yugoslav ideas against what seemed to have been

Brezhnev's and Ulbricht's objections to their dangerous radicalism: 'What some of our friends in Eastern countries say to this effect . . . is not correct'.[34] Thus the Yugoslav ideas about the party, although far too advanced for the rest of the communist bloc, still have to mature in order to clarify themselves in Yugoslavia itself.

Factionalism in a 'hegemonic party' system

In other countries where the national problem is not so acute as in Yugoslavia consideration has been given to the idea of putting more political substance into the bogus multi-party system as preserved from the time of the post-Yalta coalition governments. This is still one of the arguments more seriously discussed. In Poland the main theoretician of the dominant party, around which the other parties are grouped is Jerzy J. Wiatr[35] from whose study 'One party-system' the following quotation is taken.

'In some socialist countries we note an interesting political configuration consisting of the co-existence of several co-operating political parties, one of which, the Communist Party, plays the leading role in the system. The remaining parties share governmental and administrative posts at all levels and participate in policy-making, especially in so far as it concerns the groups or strata represented by them; they shape public opinion by their own propaganda machine, but without attempting to undermine the position of the "hegemonic" party. In Poland, this kind of alliance exists between all three political parties (Polish United Workers' Party, United Peasants' Party and Democratic Party) and three political associations of catholic denomination. Such a system differs essentially from the one-party system *sensu stricto*. Hence it seems proper to suggest the adoption of a different term for it, for instance the "hegemonic party system".

'The hegemonic party system stands midway between the one-party system *sensu stricto* or "mono-party system" as I should prefer to call them, and the dominant-party systems. Under the mono-party system there is no competition for power within the

---

[34] Both quotations from his speech at Bjeljina, on 20 November 1966, quoted in the *New York Times* of 22 November 1966. Brezhnev and Ulbricht had just visited Yugoslavia and according to Press rumours had expressed their distress about the rapid deterioration of the communist doctrinal bases in Yugoslavia.

[35] In Westergaard (ed): *Cleavages, Ideology and Party Systems*, Helsinki, 1964.

system, and no acknowledged opposition. In the dominant party system, a single party secures for itself permanent political leadership, despite the existence of other political parties and groups. All the three systems, i.e. the mono-party, the hegemonic party and the dominant party system share the common trait that political leadership is in the hands of a single party, which acts as the representative of the entire nation. This is true of the evolution of the programmes of all communist parties, as their power increases and society consolidates politically.

'The political consolidation of society on the basis of the programme of the governing party is unable to eliminate all the difference of opinion, which gradually, to a greater or lesser degree, reveal themselves within the party. If this fact is taken into account, the conclusion must be that the political pluralism of a system need not take the form of an outer differentiation into various parties and groups, but may also develop in the inner life of the governing party.

'With respect to the relation between the party system and the principal social forces, the following three situations may be distinguished in the one-party or hegemonic party systems:

'(a) The party system is an instrument of socialist transformations (the Soviet Union, other socialist countries, some revolutionary systems in "new states").
'(b) The party system is an instrument of "modernizing" transformations (Turkey in Ataturk's time, many contemporary "new states").
'(c) The party system is an instrument of conservative or openly reactionary trends, in particular in economically mature countries with strong left-wing trends (Italy and Germany before World War II, Spain, etc.).

'Such widely divergent social goals of mono-party and hegemonic party systems raise the question whether it makes sense to analyse the purely political aspects of these systems while disregarding the essential differences in their social goals. Whatever may be the answer to this question, comparative analysis must take into account the social context of the various systems, and not only the mechanism of their functioning.

'The last issue is partly connected with the relation between the party systems and the pressure groups. The governing party in a one-party system is, of all governing parties in the various systems, comparatively most independent of pressure groups. Theoretically, the multi-party system opens to pressure groups the widest possibilities for action, although it seems that no party system is quite immune to such groups, either on the central or the local level. What these groups are, what methods they use to influence political decisions, and how far they succeed, are all issues of primary importance in a comparative study of party systems. The role of trade unions and other social organizations, of minority organizations, of youth organizations, and – at least in some countries – of the Churches, all these are issues which should be studied.'

Of the parties mentioned by the Polish author there is no doubt that the only independent organization was the catholic group: *Znak*. Unlike *Pax*, *Znak* had kept its political inspiration free from communist subversion or infiltration; if this independent group received guidance from anywhere it came more probably from the catholic hierarchy. The ideological position of *Znak* was clear, both in the speeches of its five deputies and in the publication of the same name which it issued. In the spiritual realm it declared its total incompatibility of views with communist doctrine and policies. In the immediate sphere of practical politics, administration and even foreign policy, it recognized the right, for the time being, of the communist government in power to follow some general lines which were of general national interest. Within this policy, and with these reservations of principle, *Znak* considered itself to be not a party but a group (a clear and honest self-definition) working under the regime of a 'dominant party'. Moreover after the change in the general political climate and the controlled elections of 1961, the *Znak* group lost some of its fervour – and in some instances appeared to be in disagreement with the previous more intransigent attitudes adopted by the hierarchy. But the fact is that *Znak* was, as such, in the whole of communist Europe the only case of a parliamentary and political group which was not under the secret or overt tutelage of the Communist Party and which continued, more or less successfully according to periods and problems, to represent and express within a communist political system, views and sectors of the population which did not hide their ultimate dissent from communist aims and purposes. It was, as such, until 1965 the only case of institutionalized political dissent.

In East Germany, on the contrary, there are two political parties, which not only regard themselves as parties but also maintain their claim to be 'non-socialist'. These are the LDP (the German Liberal-Democratic Party) and the NDP (the National-Democratic Party)[36]. It is true that until 1949 the leadership of the two parties, and especially that of the LDP, have tried to keep to a non-socialist line, and not to follow the main lines of the SED concerning the 'inevitable passage of the DDR through the phase of the bourgeois-democratic revolution to that of the proletarian-socialist revolution'. But this was of no avail as Ulbricht, eager to copy Lenin at least in this respect, made it clear in 1949 that all 'opposition' would be banned and that only forces collaborating in the construction of socialism would be allowed to function. Since then the two parties have acknowledged their mission to be, or act, as 'transmission-belts', with the particular purpose of preparing 'the middle-classes for the "classless society"' and integrating them 'into the new "transformed" social and economic relations'. Their reward is that, at elections, individual candidates considered as representatives of these parties are put on the single list of candidates. But both the communists and non-communist public opinion rightly consider them as anachronisms – and it is very unlikely that it will be through their channel that a rejuvenated public opinion could put pressure on the government.

Of a much greater and different order of significance was another political development in the GDR, the 'dialogue', in 1965–6, between the SED (the German Communist Party in that country) and the SPD, the Socialist Party in West Germany. The 'dialogue' had been made possible from the West German side by the fact that Willy Brandt, the socialist leader, had taken a much more advanced position on the problem of West Germany's relations with Eastern Europe, and especially had recognized that the settlement of the Oder-Neisse line and of other debts and obligations of West Germany towards countries invaded by Hitler should come before the final reunification. The SED, and generally speaking, the German and Russian leadership hoped that the German Socialists

[36] See Harald King: *LDP und NDP in der DDR, 1949–58*, Köln, 1965.

would be lured even further, and that thus a wedge could be driven between them and the rest of West German political opinion. On 7 February 1966 the SED leaders sent 'an open letter' to the delegates, members and friends of the Socialist Party about to meet at its congress in Dortmund. The socialist leaders answered positively on 19 March 1966. But the communists were thoroughly disappointed at the SPD Party Congress in Dortmund in June 1966 when Brandt and the other socialist leaders clarified the issues the SED hoped to be able to blur. Since then the first phase of the dialogue at least has come to a standstill; and the SED and the entire communist press have accused the West German socialist leadership of deceit.[37]

But even this short-lived episode gave birth to at least two new and genuine ideas. One has been taken over by the intelligentsia of the GDR, against the wishes of the party – and the other deserves to be mentioned here if only as a very far-fetched hypothesis. The idea of 'mutual concessions' as a way of achieving a 'dialogue' was taken up by Professor Robert Havemann, who was afterwards punished for his attitude. He insisted that the SED should make some practical proposals – and one of his main points was that if the West German government authorized a Communist Party (now banned) to function in its territory, the East German government should authorize the functioning of a Socialist Party in the GDR. This, of course, entailed the recognition by the East German communist government of an 'opposition party'. But, instead of frightening Havemann this was probably the main point of his campaign: to express the desire of East German public opinion for real rights and competence for their parliament and for some institutionalized opposition. Havemann also openly criticized the SED leadership for having called off the talks so abruptly.

Two important West European communists, Professor Ernst Fischer of the Central Committee of the Austrian CP, and Professor Lucio Lombardo Radici, of the CC of the Italian CP, protested on the screens of West German television, which can be seen in the GDR, against the fact that Havemann had been punished for his attitude. They also criticized the SED for the line it had followed in the question of the talks between the two parties. This provoked another deep reaction in the GDR, which

[37] See Hans Schaul: 'Der Dialog und der Dortmunder Parteitag der SED' in *Einheit*, Berlin, August 1966.

the local communist press tried to cover up by hurling insults at the two foreign personalities. The idea of the dialogue with 'mutual concessions' and of the bringing back of other parties of opposition, had obviously caught on.

The other new idea arising from the abortive dialogue between the SED and the SPD is the practical possibility of furthering institutionalization in the communist European states by their association with international, or European organizations. In the conclusions of this work more will be said about the possibilities offered by such associations.

Factionalism in the parliaments

It is a commonplace to say that if the pressure for the political re-establishment of existing public opinion in the European communist states were allowed to reach its logical conclusion it would quickly lead to the demand for the rehabilitation of Parliaments and their rights. In the late sixties this demand was often made or alluded to not only in Yugoslavia and Poland, where it is openly discussed by various sectors of public opinion, but in East Germany, Hungary and especially in Czechoslovakia where public opinion, for long anaesthetized, was developing as it had in Poland and Hungary in the fifties.[38]

[38] *Reporter*, a bi-weekly of the Czechoslovak Writers Union, published an interview (quoted in *RFE Czechoslovak Press Survey*, No. 1805, 14, June 1966) with Jan Sejna, a deputy and member of the presidium of the National Assembly, which, in some trenchant exchanges, reveals many aspects of the attitude of public opinion, as well as details of the way in which Parliament functions in that country.

Thus: '*Question:* Some of our citizens compare the working of representative bodies abroad to our own national assembly and are rather sceptical when they refer to the critical attitude of our deputies. Have you encountered such views? *Answer:* Yes, I have. This scepticism is most probably the result of the fact that people still visualize parliament in its bourgeois form . . . The work of our parliament is concentrated in committees. It is there that the making of the laws takes place and that the government, the ministries and the central administration are controlled. *Question:* Do you present the views and moods of the electorate accurately in parliament? *Answer:* The deputies talk with absolute frankness . . . *Question:* Nevertheless, it seems that there are differences between the deputies. Some are diffident and make only formal comments. *Answer:* Before answering this question I should like to say that the National Assembly is not in obdurate opposition, so to speak, in principle. The basic party line is binding on the National Assembly, the government and the ministries. *Question:* It is certainly remarkable that not even in the debates in the plenum regarding important laws do we ever hear of a clash of conflicting opinions. Could you explain the source of this unanimity? *Answer:* . . . In their

But it is also a commonplace that for the communist parties in power the re-establishment of a parliament based on a multi-party system and on free elections is inconceivable. For them this would mean more than their immediate fall from power. It would mean the interruption for good, or for a dangerously long period, of the process of 'building socialism', which their ideologists think is in train. This is *the* issue and this is why even the Yugoslav leadership, who have in many respects put their political thinking and action on a more objective basis than selfish party interest, have stopped at this threshold. Only one of their former leaders, Djilas, had the courage to cross it.

In the present section, therefore, we will not consider why it would now be natural to think of the possible rehabilitation of parliaments and why this is still a very doubtful proposition. What will be discussed here is how, within the much more limited framework of the way the political institutions of the European communist states actually work, parliaments might naturally become a more suitable arena for factional activities. In other words, how the different interest and belief groups in a dictatorial state need a political channel which in its turn finds its natural outlets in increased factionalism; and how, in the sixties, this could no longer be contained within the party. Some party leaderships have tried not only to transform the parties into mass-parties with a real 'democratic' centralism, but also to make them 'debating bodies' or, to paraphrase Wiatr, bodies in which different interests and mentalities oppose each other. But this is not enough. There is not enough room, and there is too deep-seated a functional incompatibility in the party, as an apparat, for it ever to be able to contain within itself atomizing pluralistic groups and trends. These, if they are to be contained within the framework of a communist state, that is of a state in which the ultimate power remains with the communist party, must be allowed to overspill into other organs which exist within it.

The organs of forcible consensus, like the local Assemblies or the National Assemblies or Chambers or Supreme Soviets could

districts the deputies gather the views of citizens about new draft laws, but one man cannot find out every opinion. We should make the national committees part of the legislative machinery. In the national committees many views can be gathered, but there is no one to take them up and they just don't get any further.'

not be prevented from becoming, in the sixties, organs of spontaneous conflict. Quickly appearing factions aggregated, either positively for some claims and attitudes which they had in common, or negatively against other factions already formed or in course of formation. Indeed, the catalysis of factions brings with it the emergence of contrary factions, against which yet other loose or unco-ordinated groups and trends coalesce spontaneously. On the other hand, these diffuse reactions are bound to set up a crystallization of attitudes and counter-attitudes, sympathies and antipathies. The more the local 'debating bodies' debate local problems the more they become interested in, and linked with, more general problems. Also, the local groups and factions become progressively aware that they share views and interests with groups and factions across the region or the country. Therefore, although they act as individual 'pressure-groups', their combined pressures create further major cleavages at the centre. A large debate, which only a large debating body can hold, therefore becomes inevitable. This is when Parliaments become, by their functional predisposition, the natural arena for factional consultation.

To be sure most of these Parliaments are not as yet showing any signs of becoming such 'debating bodies'. In Bulgaria, Rumania, Hungary, the GDR and Czechoslovakia, in this respect in order of progress, they are still formal institutions. They meet very rarely, in short and solemn sessions during which laws and decrees are approved retrospectively. When however a discussion is held, it is organized in the manner of a roll-call of deputies who, by regions and districts, or by professions or social classes, are meant to give the approval and observations of geographical or social groups particularly interested in the draft law or plan or in some of its points. This is done with the implicit and explicit assumption that before it reaches final and more often than not unanimous approval by the Supreme Assembly, the law will have been discussed by all local organs and deliberative bodies – and by the commissions of the party and of their opposite numbers the commissions of the Assembly, and thus needs only a final perusing and a solemn confirmation.

On a point of fact, one of the most active 'channels' in the sixties, in some of the European communist states and most notably in Czechoslovakia and Hungary, were these enlarged commissions of the party, and especially of the Assemblies. This is an important distinction, for whereas the party commissions and Aktivs were packed with non-party experts and specialists in order to provide as large consultations as possible, their debates were far less popular than those held in the commissions of the Assemblies by almost the same people on exactly the same topics. Logically, there should not have been a great difference. In the Yugoslav Parliament for instance *all* deputies are also members of the League. The open debates between party members in Parliament, however, were much more hard hitting than those of party members in the party congresses.

It is in such debates indeed that the impact of any political institution, in this case Parliament, makes itself felt on the political processes undertaken through it. Whereas, functionally, the party congress of a centralistic party has to produce an ultimate unanimity and a disciplined consensus, it is natural, almost functional for a Parliament to produce dissenting and minority views. Also, in a party congress the emergence of 'factions' is in principle forbidden and therefore dissenting opinions, even if they originated from factional groups, can be articulated only individually and preferably on individual issues. But in fact in most European communist parties, the factional aggregations within the party had already, in the sixties, spread to entire sectors of the Apparat and of public opinion. Thus, even if the party congress continued to be the place where the secret in-fighting came to a head, it was not the place where the more public discussion could be held. Even if Parliament has no supreme power, and this is firmly located in the party and government organs, its functional characteristics and its atmosphere facilitate the double contact needed for such public discussion. The explicit openness of the debates facilitates contact between individuals and groups who are conscious of the fact that they represent some interests and beliefs of some sectors of public opinion. And the intrinsic publicity renders easier the contact between these groups of 'spontaneous representation' and the public whom they represent.

These features of, as it were, a factionalist parliament are not political science-fiction. They exist already in embryo in some of the European communist parliaments, and are fully developed in others. (Even in the Soviet Union after Stalin's fall, and then after

Khrushchev's fall, the fact that the elites have aquired a new status as the *layer* holding the balance against the personal dictator or the power-holding clique of the Praesidium or Politburo, is reflected in the Supreme Soviet. On the surface, at least, it seems that under Kosygin and Brezhnev the activities and functional techniques of the Supreme Soviet were improved.)

There are two main factors already working towards the functional transformation of the Parliaments into some kind of arena of open factionalism. One is the intense vertical 'processing' of the pressure groups which has gradually built up during the sixties. This process spreads from the innumerable organs of local deliberation to immediately hierarchically superior ones – until the pressures converge on the parliament which acts as a sort of clearing-house for groups and their dissent. The fact that better information now enables people to connect the local and special issue with its general and nationwide background, is the cause of this more effective crystallization of common attitudes. The dissenting peripheral groups of public opinion, which gradually acquired a greater cohesiveness, systematically over-emphasize the connecting link between the special and the general issues precisely because by doing so they increase their chance to participate in, and to influence, debates held at a higher level. The other factor is that although both in the party congresses and in the Parliaments all 'representatives' are party members, there is a fundamental difference between the kinds and categories of party members who sit in these two different forums. In the party forum the selection of the individual delegate is based on the criterion of activism within, and devotion to, the party and therefore the Congress as such is the elite of the 'apparatchiks'. On the other hand in the Assembly forum (and here this is taken to mean both local and central Assemblies) the selection of probably the majority of the party members representatives is made on the criterion of their activity within the community as a whole and of their popularity with the public and with the various, local groups of public opinion. Therefore whereas party members attending a non-party Assembly are, from the point of view of party life, generally speaking mediocre and useless – the trusted apparatchiks are, in the non-party assembly, suspected of acting on the party and government's orders.

This leads to yet another process. The apparatchiks once thus isolated within the broadening arena increasingly become a faction on their own, even if indeed a formidable and over-powering faction. They become the government faction against which, as in the history of all factions and Parliaments, the rest are bound to catalyse by reaction into a non-government faction – or opposition. But with this we come to a summary and somewhat conjectural analysis of the main factional differentiations which emerge in a communist parliament as a result of its characteristics and methods.

The Polish and the Yugoslav Parliaments being the most advanced and developed, are the obvious models,[39] for a more general view of the differentiation within a communist parliament at work. Moreover, for two reasons, the Yugoslav Parliament (Skupcina) is probably more relevant. The first, general, reason is that, the Skupcina has in the sixties been more active and more dynamic than the Polish Sejm, which had its more active period in the late fifties. Since 1961, the Polish Sejm, although showing greater consistency in legislative action (an outstanding example was its critical attitude towards the government's project for a new criminal code which caused it to be sent back with heavy amendments) has been much less a forum of crystallization of new attitudes and trends of opinion. If anything the new attitudes and trends of opinion, having found the parliamentary channels blocked once again, have opened other ways, as described above, through the pulpits and mass-demonstrations. In other words even in the very limited range, and rarefied atmosphere, of communist parliamentary activity, a lack of receptivity towards the trends and pressures of public opinion will force the latter to find 'safety-valves' in extra-parliamentary means of expression. (The increasing apathy of the *Znak*-group was, in the sixties, a symptom of the slow sclerosis of the Sejm.)

[39] The expression *model* is used here deliberately in the sense that the Yugoslav parliament seems to be more of an inspiration to other European communist states in which the up-to-now exclusively solemn 'Parliament' or 'Assembly' might be changed into what is called here a functional factionalist parliament. Thus in Czechoslovakia 'insofar as foreign experience is influential in this respect it is not that of the Soviet Union, or even of Poland, which arouses most interest, but of Yugoslavia. One Party intellectual argued that in Poland there had been a more or less abortive attempt to create a real Parliament. Yugoslavia was thought to be more interesting than Poland "because it doesn't pretend to be a multi-party system" but tried nevertheless to allow pressure groups to express themselves.' A. Brown: *Pluralistic Trends in Czechoslovakia*, loc. cit.

The second, more special reason, is that the Yugoslav Skupcina, because of its own characteristically complicated structure which is changed with every new constitution, and forming as it does a pattern of intricate, and in many respects, contradictory rules, comes nearer to the model of an ad-hoc factionalist parliament. Here vertical and horizontal groups and factions form a mosaic of inter-actions and inter-relations in which, however sporadically and with the same persons very often changing allegiances and loyalties, every group is delimited by the sphere of interest, or belief, which it 'represents' on different issues. In Poland, on the contrary, as the above-quoted Czechoslovak opinion confirms, the Sejm is still too much based on bogus political parties. These are not only restricted but, on the contrary, with the exception of *Znak* are intended by the party to work as 'transmission-belts' for different social layers[40] and classes which they should help to 'integrate'. Thus the Polish Parliament which had the glory, in 1957, of being the first genuine Parliament in the communist world, lost more and more of its reality. But, from an analytical point of view, if one wants to visualize the activities of a developed communist Parliament one should imagine a combination of the Sejm of the fifties with the Skupcina of the sixties. They both show the watershed where pressure groups have become factions but factions cannot become parties. It is then that the main inter-relations of dissent and conflict become more easily detectable – and, indeed, real.

The first factional relationship within the Parliaments, and by far the most important, is that between the government and the non-government – between those who carry the responsibility and the initiative and those who, for pragmatic reasons of the value of their advice and sponsorship, and for constitutional reasons of

[40] The fourth plenum of the Supreme Committee of the ZSL (The United Peasant Party) of June 1966 provided further proofs of this trend. It was stated that peasants formed the bulk of the party's members, 70·2 per cent; the second biggest group are teachers, national-council and co-operative employees, agricultural engineers and technicians. Czeslaw Wychech, the Chairman said that: 'We want to be, above all, a peasant party, an agrarian party and we should, first of all, gather in our ranks peasants and the intelligentsia working in rural areas, as well as urban intelligentsia working in institutions such as the national councils, agricultural co-operatives and associations. But it would be incorrect and not in compliance with our tradition if we encroached in our activity on spheres of the economy which are not connected with rural areas and with agriculture and thus weaken our efforts.' Summary of World Broadcasts, BBC, Second Series EE/2180, 7 June 1966.

procedures, must be consulted, and must approve of, the legislation or administrative projects. This, for obvious reasons should not be assimilated, by over simplification, with the usual distinction – party and non-party. On the one hand, as already mentioned, all deputies are also party members and therefore, at least semantically the distinction is irrelevant. On the other hand, in both countries, but in Yugoslavia more than in Poland, the party is dissolving somewhat into coherent factions, which coalesce internal groups of interests and beliefs. But the relation between government and non-government in the Skupcina is institutionalized in the constitutional relations established between the Federal Assembly (the Parliament) and the Federal Executive Council (which is in reality the Council of Ministers but which is elected by the Assembly as a sort of Political Committee for the duration of four years[41]). The increased trend in this direction led in the sixties to a greater influence of the five chambers of the Federal Assembly in the legislative process, and, generally speaking, in the decision-making processes. More and more of the draft laws and plans were initiated in the sixties in the Assembly – and in any case none of the projects initiated by the Council were merely rubber-stamped by the Assembly. They were on the contrary submitted to long discussion and heavily amended. Joint working commissions were set up between the Federal Council and the Federal Assembly to prepare drafts after preliminary consultation with both bodies.

This new attempt towards self-assertion of the, as it were, legislative against the legislative-executive body (because this is what it finally amounts to) was facilitated by two other characteristic features of the Skupcina. One is the fact that it was already divided into different and selective chambers which thus formed within it larger units of professional-corporatist specialization. The other is the fact that the individual deputies, because they belong to one or other of these chambers, have been stimulated to

[41] 'It is a long time now since the general conception of a government holding both executive and administrative power has been abandoned in Yugoslavia. Executive power is now divided into what is usually called the executive political function on the one hand and the administrative function on the other. The first is entrusted to a permanent political committee of the Assembly, called the Executive Council. This is the executive organ of the Assembly which also permanently controls the activities of the administrative organs and of the administration itself.' Jovan Djordjević, *The Anatomy of a Society in Transition*, loc. cit.

show greater competence and interest in the special projects of law and plans which were sent to the respective chambers from the joint Commissions of the Assembly, of the Federal Council (of Ministers) and last but not least of the League-Party.[42] A double selectivity is thus operated. First, at the level of the appointment, if not election, the man who goes from the local, or professional sphere of activity as a deputy to the Assembly and within it to one of the special chambers is, or should be, chosen objectively for his competence. Second, at the level of Parliament itself, the man who succeeds in amending the draft (and as such in checking the initiative of the government) makes his name by his interventions and by the support which he can rally, either by way of factional association or by way of spontaneous aggregation within the precincts of the chamber.

The first massive example of such a legislative resistance to the executive's initiative was the discussion of the draft of the 1965 economic plan. Here the organization in depth of the resistance could be seen in its continuation at three different levels, each successively influencing the following one in the procedural phase of the passing of the bill. Centred on the nettling issue of investments-versus-personal consumption, which is also the main bone of contention between the workers' councils and the central administration, the 1965 plan was widely criticized for giving too

[42] This double process of quasi-corporatist and individual specialization and responsibility was noticeable also in the other European communist Parliaments, and especially in Rumania and Czechoslovakia (although otherwise the general political trend was contrary in both these countries, Czechoslovakia advancing rather, towards the Yugoslav kind of self-effacement of the party, whereas in Rumania the trend was towards a new self-assertion of the party). Thus, in Czechoslovakia, to quote once more from A. Brown's excellent study on the 'pluralistic trends in Czechoslovakia': 'No one I spoke to in Prague thought that the National Assembly had functioned effectively in the past. But there unanimity ends. Of the several different views expressed, the most important distinction is between those who think (or say) that everything is now alright and those who think that the necessary reforms are only just beginning.' The latter view: 'could be summarized as follows. The shortcomings of Parliament are well-known and attempts are now being made to bring about their improvements in the following two ways: 1. Members have at their disposal experts, and there is an attempt to provide them with more expert assistance so that they are not at the mercy of ministry and party departments. 2. Members should be more connected with a "branch of life". Some people favour a change from territorial to an occupational system of representation, or having at least part of the Assembly elections in that way. This, it is argued, is because the existing political parties are not equipped to reflect "the real (and conflicting) group-interests that exist".'

much preference to investments and capital expenditures. The criticism originated first from the workers' councils, or, more precisely, from the workers in the enterprises. In the second phase, the trade unions, as a body to be consulted before drafts are submitted to the Assembly, rejected it at the end of December 1964. When, after this rough passage, the draft, amended and modified by the government so as to obtain a 'smooth consensus', arrived at the Assembly, two of the Chambers, the Federal Chamber which is in reality the kernel of the Assembly and the corresponding Economic Chamber, inflicted on it another fifty-two amendments which were carried through eleven other revisions. The twelfth revised version was afterwards adopted by the Assembly (but still continued to be criticized from trade union quarters).

Since then the participation of the Federal Chamber in the formerly exclusive responsibilities of the Federal Council, the preparation of laws and plans, has, by all accounts, increased. Moreover it has also provoked some characteristic secondary measures of institutionalization within the procedures of the Assembly itself. These as far as such things can be detected in the *chiaroscuro* of the politics of a communist state, can best be described as three differentiations which may be created. The first of these is the institutional differentiation between the executive and the legislative which throws open once more the question of the principle of the unity or separation of powers.[43] Then there is the functional-institutional differentiation found to be feasible between the government faction and the rest, the former, as already mentioned, being formed by the men under direct command of and with overwhelming vested interests in, the government in power – the latter ultimately aggregating all those who are not directly involved in the first category. This is a natural and classic pattern of formation of an opposition. Indeed, opposition appears in political history mostly as the grouping of

---

[43] See Brown, *Pluralistic trends*, loc. cit. In Czechoslovakia 'the view that the Deputy Chairman of one of the Committees of the National Assembly put to me was that "in recent times all the necessary measures have been taken and the weight of the National Assembly has increased". He emphasized that the concept of the division of powers was rejected but he would not deny the need for control. In his view the problem of countering Stalinism could be solved by elected bodies having real power, and in this way "subjective decisions" could be avoided.'

those who are not of, and ultimately are driven to take a stand against, the government's or the King's party. In other words it is because there is a party in power, that the opposition itself takes the form of a party.

The third detectable differentiation is that within the factions in the government party itself. Within the League, the increase of the power of the Federal Assembly, as different from, and therefore opposed to, the Federal Council, was advocated in the sixties by the powerful faction headed by Edward Kardelj, who was then opposed to the Ranković faction entrenched in the 'executive', in the security police, the central state administration and the other apparats. It remains to be seen, after the fall of the Ranković faction, whether the Kardelj faction will continue to press for further emancipation of the Assembly, or on the assumption that the 'Federal Council' has thus been 'democratized', whether it will take a more conservative view of the advantage of having a stronger executive. But even if the former view prevails it will not solve the main political problem of the self-assertion of its independence by the Assembly, or Parliament, under the pressure of public opinion. This is part of a general problem, affecting not only the Yugoslav party factions and their crystallizations, but the self-assertion of Parliaments in all dictatorial states. It is recognized by political historians as inherent in the process of institutionalization which has its own impetus and its own *perpetuum mobile*.

The factional debate is also facilitated by the quasi-corporatist organization of the Yugoslav Federal National Assembly into five different chambers. These are the Federal Chamber, which controls the political legislation and actions of the Federal Council – and which contains among its 190 deputies the 70 appointed members of the Council of Nationalities of which more will be said presently; the Economic Chamber; the Educational and Cultural Chamber; the Social and Health Chamber and the Political-Administrative Chamber. The Federal Chamber must always approve of a law, or bill, or plan in conjunction with one of the four other Chambers. The Federal National Assembly as a whole is called in plenary meetings only for solemn occasions. The approval of at least the Federal and one other chamber is sufficient for the legislative procedure, but more often than not there are more than two interested in an important law. This informal differentiation produces yet another parliamentary aggregation and channelling because the local assemblies, at a low level, are also usually divided into three, four or five chambers, according to the size of the basic assembly. A vertical contact is thus established between the local, say, Economic or Social and Health Chamber and the corresponding one at Assembly level. This contact makes the intervention of the government and of the party more difficult and, in any case, less direct. The pressure groups can thus more easily open their own channels of pressure, and the vested interests are often quickly able to judge how far their influence extends across the country. But further factionalism is also produced within these vertical five channels of the five chambers. Within them the more specialized interest-groups and the more self-conscious beliefs-groups are further differentiated by spontaneous or permanent associations with kindred groups from the other chambers. Thus the action of, say, the trade unions, or the intelligentsia associations or unions, or of the representatives of the farmers – or in another context of catholics, or liberals, or partisans – is much more strongly and rapidly crystallized in these specialized assemblies.

The strong, and, in the case of Yugoslavia, determining influence of national, or regional, factionalism is increased in the Assembly not only through the mechanism of the five specialized chambers in which, whatever the issues, the Croats, Slovenes, Montenegrins, Macedonians or, indeed, Serbs, are bound to aggregate together but also because of the institutionalization of the Council of Nationalities. This is a body of 70 deputies appointed by the Federal Republics themselves in which the high dignitaries of the Republics are not only permitted, but obliged to stand – in spite or because of the fact that they occupy a special administrative function. The Council of Nationalities is only a pale reflection of the former fuller sovereignty of the Federal Republics which, as seen above, was curtailed through the further measures of national integration.[44] But within the Assembly itself, thus strengthened and diversified, the Council of Nationalities as a centre of factional aggregation plays two important roles. It can, and does, act against the Federal Council in cases in which this council falls into more centralistic, Serbian, hands, as the responsible body for the regional and national opposition against the

[44] See *supra*: 'The Party and Local Administration', pp. 120 ff.

Serb dominated or biased central government. And it acts, within the Federal Chamber itself, and by contacts with the other chambers, as the centre of the legislative dissent or consensus of the six main nationalities to be found in Federal Yugoslavia. These national factions thus channel their particular views and requests to their representatives in the different Federal Chambers, vertically through the local and republican specialized chambers or Assemblies, and horizontally across the Federal Assembly itself, through the rallying of all the Croat, Slovene, Montenegrin, etc. deputies around their main representatives sitting in the Council of Nationalities.

This is not the place, and neither is there space, to continue a more detailed analysis of the diverse factionalisms, and factional institutionalization which takes place more naturally and with a greater openness within even the 'formal' parliaments of the communist states. But the main conclusion which can be drawn, is that in the period of the broadening of the Apparat which all the European communist states, with the obvious exception of Albania, have reached, because of their level of economic and other development, the process of 'broadening' takes the political activities themselves beyond the competence of the party. This is true simply in terms of location. The enormous buildings, with secret corridors and guarded doors, of the Central Committee, however ramified in commissions and committees, cannot be the setting of a permanent deliberative body. And the congresses or conferences are too solemn and too fraught with the emotions of potential political clashes and crises, and too short in time, to provide the atmosphere of an institutionalized debate. This must be held in conditions and settings which would be suitable for and conducive to the atmosphere of a discussion. In other words another institution is needed for these functions than the party.

Again, the broadening trend takes political activity beyond the party because this activity must start from non-partisanship. The most advanced communist parties (in Yugoslavia, Hungary and later in Czechoslovakia) tried to achieve this anti-*partiinost* precisely in order to attract the skills, talents and numbers required for the administrative 'mobilization'. The participation of the plural groups and forces in the 'mobilization' cannot, however, fully succeed in the system of one-way transmission-belts; it must be based on some kind of a two-way system, in which the effects of the plural checks can be felt on the formerly monolithic centre of command. In other words pluralization goes together with decentralization, and the Parliament, even in a communist state, is the best organ for decentralized consultations and exchanges.

Finally, the institutionalization of plural checks and of public exchanges cannot but shake the loyalty and the blind submission of the party members. As in India,[45] with its dominant Congress Party, the factionalism of interests and groups within the communist parties caused by the articulation and development of the pluralistic society, shakes the former single loyalty and devotion of the pre-revolutionary members. This change in mentality and attitude is fostered by two changes in personnel. One is the change in generation, of which more has been said above, with their different conceptions and habits; the younger, as in India, being much more pragmatic and *blasé* than were the generation of pre-war members or of those who belonged before the party came to power. The other is the direct change in personnel which must be made for obvious political and administrative reasons.

In Yugoslavia, where the ingenuity of the political leadership was always seeking ways of avoiding political elections, much has been made of the institution of *rotation* of personnel (whereby the same persons cannot indefinitely hold a position in the state ad-

[45] In the different contexts of India's political life and of the Indian Congress Party the following similar trends were noted by Paul R. Brass in his important work on *Factional Politics in an Indian state* (University of California Press, 1965): 'It has been argued here that, despite internal factionalism and in some respects because of factionalism, the Congress Party organization in Uttar Pradesh is a strong political organization, with considerable resiliency. Yet a certain reservation about the underlying stability of the Congress organization must be stated. This reservation relates to the question of party loyalty, what F. G. Bailey calls a "moral" committment on the part of party workers and voters to a political party. Bailey has argued of this committment that it reflects the failure of the parties (and of the Legislative Assembly in which they function) to achieve legitimacy in the society. As long as the parties lack legitimacy, a strong element of political instability exists. It is probable that loyalty to the Congress organization has declined since Independence. Certainly, the younger generation of Congressmen lack the same attachment to the Congress which the pro-Independence leaders felt. For pre-independence Congressmen nationalism was their religion and the Congress represented their nationalism. For many Congressmen the Congress symbolized a way of life. Few of the younger Congressmen have this feeling of attachment of the Congress. For many now, participation in the Congress organization is purely "rational" activity, in the sense that calculations of personal advantage predominate over other motivations.' This phenomenon *mutatus mutandis* can be found also in the European communist states and parties.

ministration) as a means of rejuvenation of the cadres. This rotation does not only mean that the representative assemblies have to re-elect half of their members every two years, and that the members of the Executive Council (which, as seen, is considered as the political committee of the Assembly) can have their mandate revoked by the Assembly before the end of the legislature. Even more significantly, it means that no holder of a public office of a higher status can hold it for a longer period than four years, nor can he be re-elected to it.

It is this measure which is considered by Yugoslav consti-tutionalists as an innovation of considerable importance, since it is bound, in their view, to foster a quest for new and more qualified people for the functions thus open to competition; and because it is a continual reminder to office-holders that they cannot maintain their positions by political favouritism or by nepotism. But rotation can have different effects in different political climates. If it is obvious that the League, or any internal ring of power-holders, directly and exclusively controls appointments or elections, rotation will only make the precariously appointed personnel fear the power-holders more. If, on the contrary, it takes place in conditions of open participation of public opinion, rotation will stimulate the appointees to show greater independence in their work so as to build up their reputation for further appoint-ments. (It is characteristic that in Bolingbroke's England the idea of 'rotation' was, in 1730–40, the basis of a compromise between government and opposition.)

It was inevitable that Yugoslavia should be the first country where a communist government was overthrown by the adverse vote of a communist parliament. On 6 December 1966, the government of Slovenia, Yugoslavia's most emancipated republic, was put in a minority on the vote for the new social security bill. Eleven votes went for the government and forty-four against. Although the Slovene government could have avoided resignation, it preferred to draw the consequences. Already in November the Yugoslav Federal Assembly had been drafting new standing orders specifying the cases in which the Federal govern-ment would be able to submit its resignation. It dealt with the new situation arising in government-parliament relations, and established the rule that it is within the competence of the Assembly to replace the government collectively, or its members individually. Less than a month later the case presented itself – but in a slightly different form since the procedures did not cover the case of a government choosing to resign because of a minority vote.

Le Monde made on the occasion a comment which is fitting also for the conclusions of this chapter. 'Sooner or later,' it said, 'such a crisis was bound to occur in one of the Yugoslav republics. If the regime goes on saying that the League of Communists has ceased to be the leading party, and that the Parliament is really the holder of the national sovereignty, the deputies will try to test their power. For a long time now heated discussions have taken place in the commissions' meetings and at that level Ministers found themselves in difficulties. Then the criticism passed from the commissions to the plenary meetings of the assemblies. And besides, could a deputy who voted against a draft of a bill, change his position when the Bill was then submitted to the Chamber? . . . This is not a systematic opposition because these deputies vote for some bills and reject others. But until now the opposition was always in minority. At Ljubljana it found itself in a majority.'

Beyond factionalism

Generally speaking, all the factionalist activities within the political life of the communist European states analysed here are factionalist precisely because they take place within the claustrophobic non-electoral political system. They have a restricted sphere of action and draw on a restricted reservoir of people.

This brings us back to the problem of elections, that is to the double problem of elections. The first is the question whether a communist political regime can ever be made to accept political elections as the means of representation – and therefore to accept political pluralism as the inevitable consequence. The second is whether even if it accepted political elections (and, as repeatedly seen in the pages of this book there is a permanent confusion about this point in the communist constitutional interpretations) the regime would allow elections to be held according to procedures and in conditions of legality which alone would render them effective.

Indeed, the electoral laws of different political systems and of different countries even in the realm of the constitutional-pluralist states vary from, for instance, the British system of majority representation to the proportional representation of Italy. But in matters of elections there is no substitute for legal freedom: elections without free choice remain a non-sense. To be sure, both in Yugoslavia and in Poland, the party has tried to experiment with means of obtaining greater electoral freedom, yet without endangering its ultimate stability in power. All these attempts were variations on the theme of the single-lists; in Poland mainly by adding the names of representatives of other parties pledged to acknowledge the PCP as the dominant, governmental party, and with some pre-ordained percentages in the allocation of seats; in Yugoslavia by having the members of the local organs of voters' meetings propose party or non-party candidates, from which afterwards the communal assemblies nominated the final candidates for the District, Provincial, Republican and Federal Chambers. Both in Poland and in Yugoslavia there were sometimes more candidates for elections than seats and this gives a certain play, within safe majorities, between candidates. This is very useful as an indication of the quest of the regimes for new ways and very different from the practice in the other communist countries where the rigid single-lists, with the number of candidates exactly equal to that of seats, is still the rule. But obviously it is still not enough. Yet there is no logical reason why a communist government should accept really free elections whose declared aim is the replacement in power of one party by others.

With the increased and rapid pluralization which is taking place in these states, and with all the accompanying effects which this book has tried to describe, it might happen that one day in one of these states the communist government will find that, even in the very restrictive conditions which it applies to elections, the largest sectors of the population will use the occasion of elections to demonstrate against the government. But, first, this would still be a demonstration – and there are other, perhaps more efficient ways of demonstration in order to dislodge a dictatorial government in power. And, secondly, it would change overnight the character and structure of the political system, which as a communist political system defines itself by its refusal to acknowledge political representation and political opposition.

PART FOUR

TWO IRREVERSIBLE TRENDS

This analysis of the political societies of the European communist states has concentrated on the study of their present realities. If one were to attempt to forecast their future one would do so by singling out the two features which have shown such a basic continuity in these realities that they might be considered as two irreversible trends. The first is that the pluralization and the reinstitutionalization which follows from it will continue to lead to the dissolution of the Apparat. The second, which cannot be discussed without considering together with the internal problems of these countries some basic elements which belong to the field of international developments, is that the European communist states will in the future become more European than communist.

The studies of 'communist Eastern Europe' have for the last twenty years been focused more specially on their future course. This was partly due to the importance of this question for the wider problem of East-West relations, the 'cold war', etc. Most of these studies were undertaken as operational prognoses. But it was also partly due to the fact that from both sides, the communist and the non-communist, the anti-communist and the anti-anti-communist, the European communist states were looked at as intrinsically transitional, and their trajectory was considered more worth study than their substance itself. (Hence the noticeably transitional headings of many such studies: bolshevization, satellization, sovietization and Stalinization or de-bolshevization, desatellization, desovietization and de-Stalinization, or relaxation, liberalization, democratization, disintegration or the usual metaphorical headings of 'thaw' or 'tightening of the screw'.) In communist political interpretation these states are phases in the evolution towards the apolitical classless societies, or society, of the future. In non-communist political interpretation they are intermediary, amphibious, political forms destined to fall ultimately either into the category of totalitarian states or into that of liberal-democratic states.

That these political societies are in transition, intermediary or amphibious no one will dispute. But a distinction should be made at some point between a transitional and an established political society. For, if not, all political societies, even less precarious and with a longer duration in history than the twenty years of the European communist states, could ultimately be described as intermediary or amphibious since they all move between a past and a future form. All political societies go from phase to phase, by evolution and reform, as well as by revolutions and counter-revolutions. The distinction might best be made perhaps, at the point where, or rather when, the amorphous transitional forms harden enough to show some distinct and original features of their own. It is this intrinsic originality of a certain political institution or structure which is worth study. This is why communist political studies continue to explore such short lived institutions as the French commune of 1870 or the Russian Soviets of 1905 – and non-communist political studies examine the Swedish Riksdag or the Polish Liberum Veto.

It is a fact that some of the political situations and institutions created in the twenty years of adjustment of the Soviet-type Apparat-state to the societies of Eastern Europe were and are much more thought-provoking than anything that could be detected under the thick ice of the glacier of Stalinist and post-Stalinist Russia. This is not a judgment of value. Originality and bold experimentation have occurred more easily in the European communist states for at least two reasons which rendered life more difficult for their communist rulers. One is that they had to face, and to compromise with, more alert and resilient societies than Russian society. The other is that if the smaller powers and the secondary parties indulge in experiments, the risks of contagion during the experiment and of total collapse in case of failure are less than if the experiment were to be tried at the very centre. But this being said, the fact remains that the European communist states are ahead of Soviet Russia in their dramatic attempts, if the expression can be coined, to continue socialism by other means. It was not an accident that in 1955 Stalin's successors had to apply to his country some of Tito's Yugoslav conceptions; that in 1956 they had to bow in Poland to Gomulka who had suffered Stalin's wrath in the Soviet bloc itself; and that many of the anti-Stalinist conceptions stemming from Eastern Europe are now officially integrated in the ideology of the European communist bloc, as opposed to Mao's Asian communism, itself a magnified version of Stalin's political philosophy.

It was for these reasons that an attempt was made here to study the European communist states as they actually are, in the sense in which Leopold von Ranke's phrase said about history: that it should reconstruct the past *wie es eigentlich gewesen*. But even, on this basis, one can at least deduce what are the main trends of the present towards the future. The first trend is that the dissolution of the Apparat continues under further pluralization.

Such concepts as democratization, liberalization or even 'thaw' are, on the one hand, mostly political and, on the other, lay the stress on the power-holders themselves. It is they who are presumed by the few optimists, or not presumed, by the legion of sceptics, to take measures which would set in motion or push forward liberalization or democratization, presumably by means of revolution from above or enlightenment. But pluralization (although yet another transitional noun) is an objective process which accompanies the process of economic, social and political development. The more a society develops the more pluralistic it needs to become on these three planes together. This is one of the premises of the present study and was confirmed by it. The same is true of the assertion that once the point is reached in the economic development of a society when, after the initial simpler phase of absolute growth obtained by all means and especially by speedy but costly industrialization, it is efficiency which is sought above all, then the question of how to foster the participation of the people engaged in production and administration replaces that of how to coerce people into massive but indiscriminate work.

From the analysis undertaken in the preceding pages it has been seen that the Apparat, which was erected by the parties in all these countries, under Soviet inspiration, and as a means of direct control and active interference in all the activities of the societies, is now, in practically all seven of them, dissolving under pressure from outside and from within. This is because all seven states are faced with immediate and direct economic problems which lead to a questioning of the viability of the system itself. This is why the quest for popular participation in production and administration is the main object. From the inside this is taking the form of a genuine effort to *broaden* the Apparat so as to make the participation of non-apparat people as easy and as genuine as possible.

Indeed this time the intention of the power-holders cannot still be to put up only a façade of attendances at meetings and a lip-service in indifference and under constraint. What is sought is spontaneity both in participation in the effort to be undertaken and in the ideas on how it could be best undertaken. It is no longer claimed even that the central ideas should originate with the party, or that they should reproduce and follow the initial ideas which it put forward. It is only suggested that the new ideas thus solicited, should show themselves ingenious and practicable. The Apparat, and especially its main apparat: the party-apparat, is aware of its urgent need to be fertilized with ideas and energies. It is therefore not only prepared, but anxious to establish a two-way collaboration with the productive sectors of the population, and to drop the previous *sine qua non* condition that the control and command of the operations should be exclusively and explicitly recognized as belonging to the party.

Of course, the parties of the seven countries vary substantially when they deal in public, and in their different doctrines, with this subject. At one end of the spectrum there are the Communist League of Yugoslavia and the Workers Party of Hungary which take endless pains to erase the self-projected image of the Party as the monolithic, omniscient and ubiquitous leader of society. At the other extreme the Rumanian and the East German parties believe that the reassertion of the importance of the party is, on the contrary, timely and necessary. But it is hoped that the study made in this work of the *real* attitude of all seven parties, as opposed to their public and ideological one, has shown that all of them, under different postulations are now eager to use ways of consultation and of collaboration with the plural forces of the society, which could not but lead to the broadening from inside of the Apparat and to the sharing of its previously exclusive power of decision. This broadening could, in their eyes, not only go together, with, but reinforce, the political primacy of the party as the single or hegemonic political organization. ·

But can it? The parties are faced now with the coming to a head of the basic contradiction which was contained from the very beginning between their doctrine and their practice and moreover between their constitutional framework and the actual network of power in their states. The constitutional framework was based on the idea of self-administration and self-management of the society. But for a half-century in Soviet Russia and almost a quarter of a century in the European communist states, administration and management were carried out exclusively by a prolonged and unauthorized proxy, the party. When the parties thus entered, from the rough seas of revolution, into the long and narrow straits of consolidation and of adaptation to the overwhelming tasks of running the state and maintaining it in existence – it became clearer and clearer that this could not be done unless they restored some of the power which they had assumed. In this process, administrative, economic and political elements are indivisibly mixed, and cannot be separated. What is demanded now from the parties is that they should relinquish through further institutionalization, or, as shown, *re*institutionalization, an increasing part of their monopoly of decision. In a sense the wheel has now come full circle from the moment when Lenin found that the party should take over the Soviets, organs of self-administration, through its own Apparat. What is demanded now is that the organs of self-administration should take over the Apparat.

The expression Apparat used in this book as a concept for the analysis of a special political system should therefore now rejoin the vernacular sense in which it is used in the communist countries themselves. There it now polarizes, especially when it is used to designate the personnel of the Apparat, the *apparatchiks*, the antipathy of the populations against the system: to oust the arrogant apparatchiks from within the articulations of the state; to abolish control by the apparatchiks; to regenerate the people's participation in the functioning of the system as it is described in the constitution, above or even without the Apparat. When, as in Slovenia in December 1966, a government is put in a minority by a vote of the Parliament, this means that in the communist political societies of today the point has been reached where the Apparat's power is held in check by the newly separated constitutional powers.

To be sure, in the vernacular sense, the expression Apparat actually means, in the communist countries, the party. This is so for two reasons. First the main Apparat, and the apparatchiks who staff it, belong in these countries to the communist party and it is the party which holds the central power and command. To speak of the Apparat means therefore to speak of the party. But, secondly, there is a nuance in doing so which makes the denunciation of the Apparat not only less direct and therefore offensive than that of the party but also, in some respects, more palatable to some sections of the party itself. This is the fact that denunciation of the 'Apparat' implies a denunciation of the bureaucratization of the revolution which the party has not been able to prevent. The growth of the state of the apparatus and of its mechanics of coercion as well as the prolongation of its existence without any 'withering away' in the foreseeable future can be denounced as a betrayal of the revolution which should have led, after a brief period of dictatorship of the proletariat, to the classless society. How to abridge and put an end to this over prolonged 'period of transition', and how to enter into the new and lasting 'state of the whole people' this is what the *official* political debate is about now. This is what is discussed in public, at least.

This may be but a fiction. Moreover it may well still be the fictitious language in which a political debate is initiated between power-holders, already too shaken in their self-confidence and only too aware of the imminent alternatives with which they are faced – and an opposition still too frightened by the memories and the present dangers of repression, and still too torn between previous beliefs, allegiances and vested interests, and the unknown future it wants to bring about. After all, all revolutions have gone through a shorter or longer initial phase during which discussion centred on the reform of the regime and the way to bring it back to its initial purity.

It is of course only common sense to say that the ultimate debate in the European communist states will be carried on between the partisans of the yet unproven direct democracy and those of the well-tried parliamentary institutions and procedures. But before this issue is settled, the debate, and the experiment, will probably go through many phases. Some of these phases may give rise to certain forms and organs of adaptation to new political-social situations which might afterwards remain in use for longer periods. After all, planning, now a common feature of both socialist and non-socialist states, raises in all countries alike constant problems of readjustment of the old political structures to the new functions of the state. In France, and now in Britain, a great deal of thought is devoted to the means of adjusting traditional parliamentary representation to the institutions of planning. This does not imply that because problems arise from planning in the parliamentary countries of Europe, and because similar problems face the communist-Apparat states of Europe, a 'convergence' is taking place between these two otherwise distinct political systems. This author has expressed elsewhere his critical views on the theory of 'convergence'[1] and more will be said on this subject later, when the problems of the political evolution of the European communist states are projected on to the evolution of the continent to which they belong. But if one had to select one particularly fitting example of the new institutions and mechanisms which might arise as a result of the new experiments in administration required in any case and everywhere by the functional development of industrial societies, one might think of some forms of 'public corporations'. What is meant here by public corporation is the large and autonomous public authority to which the state delegates, by charter, the right to manage one or more sectors of social and economic activity, for a shorter, or more probably longer period, and for some specific or more general assignments.

Public corporations, taken in this sense, are more and more often thought of, when the future of administration is envisaged. This is so, because they seem to unite the greatest number of economic and political prerequisites which are needed by the developed societies and expanding markets of today, and which cannot be held together within centralistic structures. They can and should be aimed at public service. They can and should achieve a control, if not a monopoly of an entire range of economic and social activities. They are under the state's ultimate supervision, but they act independently once the mandate is given to them. They create their own, vertical, form of internal representativeness, and at the same time they achieve more quickly and

[1] *The Breakdown of the Soviet Empire in Eastern Europe*, loc. cit., pp. 163-4.

efficiently a horizontal collaboration with other similar administrative units. Moreover, they are best suited for cutting across regional and continental subdivisions and achieving a functional concentration at the continental level. But this takes us to the second trend, in which the influence of the small European countries on the continent of Europe, and of the emergence of the continent on the future of these countries must be examined.

The second irreversible trend is: that the European communist states will become more European than communist.

More than other states the European communist states are subjected to the double influence of developments within their own society and within the international sphere. All states, even great powers or super great powers are nowadays more sensitive than previously to the impact of world affairs. Medium and smaller states are even more sensitive in this respect because the relationships of the super or great powers affect them directly and indirectly, according to their geographical situation. The medium and small states of Eastern Europe belong to a part of the world traditionally vulnerable to these relationships – and which was the cradle of two world wars. Except for the short interlude of the period between the two world wars they were, together or separately, under the influence of one or more great powers, usually struggling between them to get the upper hand in this 'zone of influence'. Although, for reasons explained at greater length elsewhere,[2] East Europe is by now only one of the regions of escalation in the conflict which opposes the super powers over the entire world chessboard, and not even the most important from a strategic point of view, it is nevertheless true that the states in this area have been for the last twenty years under the direct supervision of a super power. Not only their sovereignty, but their constitutional and political systems are conditioned by their relation with Soviet Russia as the dominant power in the region –

[2] For this and most of the main points only conjured up in this opening paragraph see 'A note on the importance of Eastern Europe' in my *Breakdown of the Soviet Empire*, loc. cit. The international, or intercontinental aspects of the political evolution of the European communist states are treated here only very summarily.

and in consequence by her relations with the other powers of the world.

In this relation of causation it is the international development which is the primary cause and the national developments which are the direct or more indirect effects, traceable or not. For neither would the political systems of the European communist states have been established and maintained without the overwhelming factor of Soviet Russia's domination of the region after the Second World War. Nor, on the other hand, would the discontent and opposition of the people or peoples of any of these states be sufficient, as the case of Hungary in 1956 clearly showed, to overthrow any of the governments. In a way, too concisely expressed to be accurate, it could be said that the international relationships give the tone to the internal relationships. When the cold war was at its height, the opposition from within in all the then 'satellite' countries was exacerbated by the severity and brutality of the demands made by the Russian-controlled administrations. Salvador de Madariaga's drastic formula, which he addressed to the Western governments in these years: 'in such times if you help the governments you are the enemies of the peoples, and if you want to help the people you must be the enemies of their governments' was not merely a metaphor. On the other hand it is *not* merely a metaphor to say that in the period of co-existence, of which Europe benefited more than other parts of the world, external co-existence has proved conducive to the progress of internal co-existence too, and the acceptance of pluralism in the world at large makes for a pluralistic vision at home as well.

This dual causality had among other effects also that of dividing most of the interpreters, and especially forecasters, of Eastern European developments into two opposite schools of thought. For some, probably the majority, the solution was to be found only in a change to be brought about in Soviet Russia's position in the world in general and in that part of it in particular. This as a premiss is reasonable. But it does not lead so necessarily as it was and still is believed to the conclusion that 'liberation' was the only way of obtaining the only change which counted, that is of forcing Soviet Russia, by means of political or military pressure, to relinquish her control of one or more of these countries. The other school of thought, centred around the concept of 'liberalization', believed, on the contrary, that the changes effected by the present leadership in the internal regimes of the communist states, with or without Soviet Russia's encouragement, would alternate the differences between them and the Western democratic political system (the theory of 'convergence' is only a variation on this theme). The 'relaxation' thus obtained would reduce the internal tensions in each of these countries, and this, in turn, would lead to the reduction of tension between the two camps intrinsically opposed by their contrary political doctrines and regimes.

By now both theories are obsolete. The theory of 'liberation' did not, even during the secretaryship of its architect, John Foster Dulles, materialize as a policy. The theory of 'liberalization' might now be succeeded by the more objective assessments of pluralization and institutionalization. The analysis of the social, economic and political processes shows that the communist governments do not *liberalize* but try to adjust their initial political structures, behaviour and mentalities to these more complex and more sophisticated processes. But new conceptions, with new criteria and more sophisticated analysis have not been slow in appearing. They differ in many respects. But they have in common precisely the basic inter-relation which they establish between the evolution of the international, and especially European, situations, and the internal evolution of the communist, and especially European, states. Moreover it is on the dynamic mutual influence of these two developments together, which acquire thus a further momentum, that some of the solutions ultimately depend.

The importance of the fact that these two evolutions are taking place in Europe cannot be overestimated. To be sure, the entire *rapprochement* which is observed between, to use in this context the more appropriate names: the Soviet bloc, led by Russia, and the Western camp, led by the United States is a political-diplomatic development with unforeseeable consequences. It has as its background three motives which could only become more and more operative in the future. One is the technological attraction which the West, and especially America exercises and will continue to exercise upon Russia and the European communist states. Another is the clear realization of the by now assuaged and matured communist leaders of the 'contradictions' in their own social-political systems, economies and ideologies; and of the fact that it is inconceivable, since the Cuban confrontation of 1960, that these grave internal troubles of communism could be solved by some major international victories. The third is the profound split in the communist bloc itself between the bloc of the parties from developed countries led by Soviet Russia and that from the hungry under-developed countries over which China is trying to assert her leadership. This development too is not likely soon to be brought to an end. On the contrary the gulf proves wider and more irreparable with the passage of time. It is, in the particular context from which it is looked at here, one of the strongest catalysers of what can be called the 'Westernization' of the Soviet communist bloc.

On the other hand many of the difficulties and obstacles which the US administration might have encountered when and if they tried to adopt more flexible and dynamic policies towards the Soviet bloc, from the strong political and economic anti-communist pressure groups, seem to have been overcome by the Johnson administration. This enables it to announce the policies of 'bridge-building' and 'peaceful engagement'. The Vietnam War, for all intents and purposes, should be a major obstacle in the way of this *rapprochement*. But, still, one should give more than a passing thought to the question of whether it is not a great advantage for Soviet Russia to have its two major rivals on opposite sides, the United States and China, engaged in a more and more active conflict?

But whereas all this is to the good and could lead only to beneficial results if and when such trends set in in earnest, there remain permanent stumbling blocks in the way of these trends. After twenty years of constant discussion everybody knows how the East-West 'question' or 'crisis' *could be solved*, and also why *it cannot be solved*. It is undeniable that in order to solve the main European problem, of which the Berlin wall is the more than symbolic signpost, one should first remove the larger causes of misunderstanding. The first is that of unilateral disarmament; next comes that of European security; within this one is included that of the German question; which in turn contains that of relations between Eastern and Western Europe as a whole. In each of these problems and especially in that of international disarmament and the German question, the old positions and oppositions have hardened to the point where only a major change in either the Western or the Communist policies could bring something new. This has led to the situation when each side waits for such a change to be brought about in the other camp.

This awareness both of 'what should be done' and of 'why it cannot be done' has also divided political circles and public opinions, openly in the West, and less detectably in the East, into the two camps of the hopeful and dynamic and of the sceptic and static. Of late, the European policies, proposals and initiatives have become much more dynamic. This has happened for many reasons but also because there are essential differences in the ultimate result to which such policies can lead, according to whether they are initiated by the two *blocs*: Soviet and Atlantic, or whether they are initiated by the countries of Europe alone – including Britain but excluding the Soviet Union.

What is suggested here has very little to do with either the theory of the third force, or with that of European neutralism, or with the old fashioned theory of 'disengagement'. The point concerns only the difference in the stimulus of the initiative and the novelty of the results, according to whether they originate from the blocs respectively led by the two super powers or from the European countries themselves. Whereas, in the former case, the worst coming to the worst, a more consolidated more flexible and yet more lasting *status quo* could be acceptable if not recommendable, in the latter it is precisely the *status quo* of the general relation between Europe and the two Super Powers which is questioned. It is the modification of this *status quo* which would lead to a new vision of a European, and implicitly, international reorganization.

That this is not vain speculation is shown by the special interest raised in Europe by General de Gaulle's initiatives. The Yugoslav, Polish or Rumanian moves towards direct intercontinental relations, on the other hand, are also considered with special interest, precisely because it is not clear whether these moves were approved, or frowned upon, by Soviet Russia. It is the fact of the initial absence or presence of the respective super power in the proposal, move or project which makes a special impact on the European circles to which they are addressed. Large international projects, launched or sponsored by the super powers, meet in European circles with a weariness caused by the constant failures of their previous versions and by the inherent suspicion that they would lead only to a more lasting consolidation of the *de facto* situation created in Europe after 1944. Small, practical, intercontinental agreements, or series of agreements are believed to be immediately feasible, to lead functionally to new situations and vistas, and to lead ultimately to a change in the status of Europe in which European people have undoubtedly a great, emotional but also practical, interest. No one can forget, to be sure, that the main snag in any such Europe-without-super powers or Europe-of-the-Europeans projects is in the difference of geographical positions and indeed distances from the super powers. The United States is separated by the entire Atlantic Ocean from the territories which it is ultimately pledged to protect, while the Soviet Union can send its tanks rolling at once over a frontier of 'lines' and small rivers. The withdrawal of the American forces from Europe only increases, relatively and absolutely, Soviet power and influence over the continent. And this might well be the reason for which General de Gaulle's proposals might raise the hopes of the Soviet bloc as a whole.

But whereas this argument is very difficult to answer when disengagement or European security are discussed, it is much less relevant when what is conjured up is the slow and empirical progress of what could be best described as European functionalism. The technological and economic evolution in the European countries is now very rapid. This creates a situation of flux on the one hand, in the institutions and systems of both the Western and the Eastern European countries, and, on the other, in the intercontinental relations themselves. From this point of view the very ambiguities of functionalism can best fit the ambivalences of these two, interrelated, evolutions. What is meant here is not that functional arrangements or approaches can, one day, to the surprise of one, or the other, or both 'camps' or 'blocs' alter the basic premisses, tip the balance one way or another, or loosen the deadlock from within so as to open it for good. What is meant is that it is more probable that, in a situation of double flux, changes recorded in the *internal sphere* of each country of a 'camp', and of the camp itself, would reverberate more effectively on the process of integration itself. And that all changes in the collaboration *at the continental level* between countries of the camps would reverberate more effectively on the process of internal, economic, social and political evolution of the countries involved. It is indeed proven that many 'insoluble' questions of a more local character have been

solved as it were, in the wake of solutions of a more general character. Measures of federal or regional integration have always also
served to solve implicitly secondary problems attached to them.

There are four different fields in which such measures with ambivalent, continental-internal and internal-continental impact can
have direct consequences; in the field of communications, in the
field of administration, in the field of economics and in the field of
politics.

Nothing new or original could, for instance, be added to the
truism that increased communications help international understanding. Intensified exchanges of the media of information:
written matter, radio or television, and especially through some
intercontinental agencies which produce common works or programmes, cannot but speed up the spreading of knowledge and
of mutual understanding. It is also a truism that the impact of the
spreading of information is greater in the countries in which, in any
case, the volume and diversity of information is inferior to that
obtaining in other countries. A special point was made in this book
of the re-emergence and of the new awareness of public opinion in
the European communist countries. The increase of communication, with the hoped-for establishment of some permanent continental centres of organization and dissemination of information,
are obviously of great advantage to public opinions in quest of more
information.

In the field of administration many of the vexing and loaded
problems arising from territorial or national litigation have been
solved by quasi-federal or regional arrangements. From this point
of view all signs pointing to further regional integration in either of
the two 'camps' of European countries could not but help ultimately towards the progress of continental integration. The
rumoured reopening of the discussion for some plan of Balkan
Entente, or Union, or Federation between Yugoslavia, Rumania
and Bulgaria (which was promptly and healthily replied to by a
Hungarian proposal for a 'Danubian' Entente, or Union or Federation) is a good example of the kind of thinking which is going on
now in the communist 'camp'.

The communist plan for a Balkan union undoubtedly conceals
some intentions which render it palatable even to the USSR. But

one has to weigh this more distant possible goal against the probability that a federalization in the Balkans would produce in fact a further loosening of the ties of all these countries with the USSR. One should weigh it also against the probability that once they begin to think in terms of a regional unit the governments of these countries would naturally find more problems and interests in common with the other Balkan countries, and ultimately with the other countries of Europe, of which the Balkans are a sizeable region. At the end one comes to the conclusion that such a move would draw these countries closer into the European orbit, and further away from the Soviet orbit.

This brings us to the field of economics. There are already as mentioned before and as a matter of general knowledge, many signs that in spite of the pattern of the communist economies and in spite of the alleged bonds with COMECON (of which more will be said in these paragraphs) the communist governments of Eastern Europe have thought and are thinking of economic collaboration with Western Europe. The evidence is of two kinds. Some indications point to the collaboration between the communist governments and different international agencies. Yugoslavia's membership of GATT is a good example of open-mindedness on both sides. The participation of the communist governments in the work of ECE in Geneva has changed character very much in the sixties. They no longer use it as a forum for propaganda tirades approved by the Soviet delegate. If anything, each of them tries to use ECE to get better contacts and to further its bilateral trade-agreements with non-communist countries. Poland, Czechoslovakia and Yugoslavia have concluded minor agricultural agreements with the Common Market. And most of the East European countries participate in the Kennedy tariff negotiations. Some other signs point to the idea of establishing joint enterprises between some industrial concerns or even branches of industry in the communist countries and similar concerns in the 'capitalist' countries.

To be sure, none of these 'economic agreements' have reached the point where they can be compared with the effective, successful and expanding bilateral trade agreements and relations which the European communist states have entered into with practically all Western European states. Indeed one might well say that until now the attempts at economic collaboration between states of command

and states of free economic systems have shown how widely incompatible they are. But, again, this is only a very recent development. It will naturally take long. But what drives, and what has driven, the communist governments into thinking of such ways and devices is their clear realization that their major bonds with the economy of the USSR, and their system of excessively centralistic planning leads their own economies to obvious slowness and to the frequent dangers of deadlock. Their respective public opinions press these points upon them. The fact that in Poland and Hungary in 1956 the economists were a leading group of the opposition to the Stalinist regimes, and that in Rumania since 1960, and in Czechoslovakia since 1964, it is the Planners from within the Apparat who have advocated the reforms, which led to new policies, shows how public opinion works in such matters. Finally, the success of European integration itself shows the possibilities of a future reunion of the two artificially severed parts of the continent.

It is here that the concept of 'public corporations' acquires another, continental dimension. (The better known term 'community' has not been used here, because for the time being it describes the three units formed by the six Western European countries.) What attracts the communist elites or rather the elites in communist countries to the West is certainly its technological advance. A technological corporation for Europe would be of the greatest interest to countries like Czechoslovakia, Rumania, Hungary, Poland, etc. Would they in the present changed circumstances get over a possible Soviet 'veto', which in 1947, prevented them, almost at the last moment, from accepting the invitation to join in the Marshall Plan?

Mention of the Marshall Plan brings immediately into the picture the difference of approach and of mentality between what the Western governments thought it best to do in 1947 and what they should do twenty years later. In 1947 Europe needed American help and protection above all. The Marshall Plan was a plan of reconstruction, based on massive American economic and financial aid. It was extended also to the Eastern European countries which needed reconstruction. But their refusal was to be expected, given the political circumstance. The success of the Marshall Plan underlined in two ways the separation between the two zones. It accentuated the difference between the prosperity of the Western economies and the misery of the East. It helped for a while to bring the East European economies under the tighter control of Soviet

Russia: COMECON was created in 1949 and the years 1947–57 were the worst for East European countries from all points of view.

Twenty years later Western Europe, and specially the European Community, have progressed and extended almost unbelievably. On the Eastern European side, also due in part to their progressive emancipation from Soviet control and to the increased trade exchanges with the West, the situation has also improved. The economies of these countries have achieved some flexibility and may show more in the future. The disenchantment with the Soviet Union as an economic model and partner is accentuated; the attraction of the West more felt. Finally, the Soviet Union cannot act with the severity with which it did in 1947. What is thus now expected of the Western European governments, instead of anything reminiscent of the American Marshall Plan, is a genuine European economic plan, based on the idea of regional or continental communities, in which the renascent economic and social forces from both sides of Europe could unite their means and energies. Here the goals would no longer be reconstruction and viability – but increased efficiency, productivity and development through the increased effort of the united forces. Here, from a first point of view the stress falls therefore on the idea of an economic plan for the continent. And from a second point of view, because of similarity of size, of demographic, social and economic conditions, and because of the obvious geographic closeness, the accent falls on the European factor, taken again in the sense of a community of neighbour states of which none is a super power.

In this respect it must be pointed out that nothing would be more opposed to this purpose than to start with the idea of bringing together, and even of initiating negotiations between the two so-called 'economic organizations'; the European Community and COMECON.[3] There are several fallacies in the alleged similarity between the two organizations. And because of these fallacies, negotiations started on their basis would lead either to nothing or to the result of putting the Soviet Union in a dominant position in the European economy as a whole. The fallacies are as follows. The Common Market is working fully as an integrated and

[3] This author was profoundly surprised by the naive approach of such a profound student of the East European communist economies as Jan Marcziewski when in a study (*Preuves*, November 1966) he took as the basis of his speculations on the future collaboration between West and Eastern Europe the COMECON-Common Market negotiations.

integrating economic community; COMECON is still and only at the 'functionalist' stage of bringing together some of the activities and institutions of the member-countries. In the Common Market the supranational command exists; in COMECON it does not. The working of the Common Market is showing beneficial results for its members; COMECON does not.

But the greatest difference of all, and indeed perhaps the cause of COMECON's lack of success and of viability is this. Member countries of the Common Market are homogeneous in size: West Germany, France, Italy and the three smaller ones united under the name of Benelux are, with obvious differences, of equal calibre in the sense that none of them is a super power. In COMECON the difference of calibre between one of the two world super powers, the USSR, and the less developed and smaller East European countries, smaller even than the Western ones, explodes the entire framework. The Common Market would not have worked, or would have been something entirely different, if the United States had been a member. The presence of the USSR transforms COMECON into a grouping of small and under-developed economies around the economy of a protective great power, with whatever colonial analogies this can and should call to mind. Soviet economists and politicians, have often defended the right of the USSR to be considered as a great power in the economic family of the socialist countries, self-sufficient and self-contained both for production and consumption. But this fact of life should also be taken into consideration, and especially in the West, when COMECON is proposed as a good analogy to the Common Market. From this cardinal point of view the two organizations are not only not analogous: they are absolutely opposed to each other.

To think therefore of some future European integration, by means of the inclusion of the East European countries *grouped under Comecon* in some of the present and specially of the future corporations or even communities would only hamper the efforts. The East European countries would from the beginning have to ask for the consent of the Soviet Union at each stage of the discussions. They would have to weigh her interest in joining in some of the projects as against theirs, and these interests, as shown, are for natural reasons more often than not different. They would have to enter, in view of the future participation with her and under her leadership, into some further integration with her economy – of which most of them are apprehensive and against which they defended themselves until now with great courage. The original wishes and ideas of some of the smaller countries, which are more imaginative and more flexible than the Soviet Union, would be lost in the official answers given, with her approval, in the negotiations. Further streamlining of the internal economies of the East European countries so as to increase their ideological homogeneity as a bloc, would have to be expected. This would be the price that Soviet Russia would think worth asking for letting them increase the collaboration with the unholy capitalist economies. Finally, faced with the enormous weight and impact of such a formidable member as is the Soviet Union in any sort of European economic community or association, the West European countries would probably have no other solution than to invite the United States to join on the Western side so as to counter-balance it. This would be of course a great progress as far as general international economic collaboration goes. But very probably it would water down the entire project to the perennial and inconclusive vast economic international agreements always discussed, never concluded. And it would not be European.

Finally, coming to the mutual effect that the parallel inter-continental-national processes might have on each other, perhaps the most important of all will turn out to take place on the plane of political representation.

The European communist states participate in the work of different Parliamentary unions and international associations to which they send delegations. This communist participation in discussion of real parliamentary affairs and prospects is from many points of view unwarranted and irrelevant. But, now the meaning of Parliaments acquires a much greater importance in the politics of some of the European communist states. The fact that in one communist state one government has already resigned because of an adverse vote of the Parliament adds considerable weight to the argument that the reinstitutionalization taking place in such states as Yugoslavia, Poland or Hungary has its own impetus. This impetus might be intensified by the continental trend of further institutionalization and enlargement of the European parliament or of the supranational parties which have been nominally formed within it. A gradually greater participation of East European parliaments, and parties, in these European institutions might have the long term effect of increasing the weight and importance of their national parliamentary life; of improving their internal selectivity for reasons of representation abroad; and it might also help towards the further crystallization of groups and parties within the national parliaments, which would have their hand strengthened by the fact that they would belong, even if formally at the beginning, to an international group of kindred parties, or to some supranational party. Thus better forms of internal political representation could be attained through the participation in continental or regional organizations and deliberations.

The same is true of one of the ideas which was discussed in the course of the East-West German 'dialogue'. This is the idea that if the West German government would allow the functioning of a Communist Party within its constitutional political life (from which it is now banned) a Social-Democratic Party would be allowed to function in East Germany. Put in this light, this idea shows its great importance not only, as it is mainly regarded, as a new channel of reunification between the two German states, which is important enough. This proposal came to nothing for the time being. But it continues to be discussed. It might remain only a fiction. Or it might be circumscribed by so many and so perverse conditions by the East German communists that it would, or should, become inacceptable. But, on the one hand, there is now a new German government, in which the socialists Willy Brandt and Heinz Wehner, sponsors of the projects for political reunification between the two Germanies, are in charge of West German foreign policy. On the other hand it is known that in East Germany the opposition from within the party presses for further contacts and 'mutual concessions'. If for some international or inter-continental reasons, the East German communist state would accept, as a 'mutual concession', exception to the rule that the communist (SED) party should control from within and directly all other political parties, the political situation in East Germany would be functionally changed. A genuine political opposition could thus be institutionalized. In the spirit of these concluding thoughts, these kinds of changes are those which matter most when the future of Eastern Europe, and of Europe as a whole, is considered.

BIBLIOGRAPHY

ALMOND, Gabriel A., 'A comparative study of interest groups and the political process', in *American Political Science Review*, no. 1, 1958.

ALMOND, Gabriel A., and COLEMAN, James S. (Eds.), *The Politics of the Developing Areas*, Princeton, 1960.

ARENDT, Hannah, *The Origins of Totalitarianism*, Cleveland, 1951.

ARON, Raymond, *Sociologie des Sociétés Industrielles* (roneotyped), Sorbonne, Paris, 1958.

—— *Dix-huit leçons sur la société industrielle*, Paris, 1962.

—— *Démocratie et totalitarisme*, Paris, 1965.

—— 'The dead end of the monolithic parties—a discussion', in *Government and Opposition*, vol. 2, no. 2, January 1967.

ASPATURIAN, V., *The Soviet Union in the World Communist System*, Hoover Institution Studies, Stanford, 1966.

BARGHOORN, F., *Politics in the USSR*, Boston, 1966.

—— 'Soviet Russia. Orthodoxy and Adaptiveness', in *Political Culture and Political Development*, Princeton, 1965.

BAUMAN, Zygmunt, 'Struktura Wladzy Spolecznosci Lokalnej', in *Studia Socjologiczna*, Warsaw, 1962.

BECKER, Rudolf, 'Die sozialökonomische Funktion der Produktionsberätungen', in P. C. Ludz (Ed.), *Soziologie Der DDR*, Köln, 1965.

BELL, Daniel, *The End of Ideology*, Glencoe, 1959.

BENTLEY, Arthur F., *The Process of Government*, Bloomington, 1935.

BERGERON, G., *Fonctionnement de l'état*, Paris, 1965.

BERLIN, Sir Isaiah, *Two Concepts of Liberty*, New York, 1958.

BIRCH, A. H., *Representative and Responsible Government*, Toronto, 1964.

BRASS, Paul R., *Factional Politics in an Indian State*, Berkeley, 1965.

BRITISH TRADE UNION DELEGATION, *Report of Trade Unionism in Yugoslavia*, London, 1964.

BROGAN, D. W., and VERNEY, Douglas V., *Political Patterns in Today's World*, New York, 1963.

BROWN, A. J., 'Pluralistic Trends in Czechoslovakia', in *Soviet Studies*, April 1966.

BROWN, J. F., *The New Eastern Europe: the Khrushchev Era and After*, New York, 1966.

—— 'The Bulgarian Plot', in *World Today* (London), May 1965.

BRZEZINSKI, Z. K., *The Soviet Bloc*, rev. ed., New York, 1967.

BRZEZINSKI & HUNTINGTON, Samuel P., *Political Power: USA/USSR*, New York, 1964.

BURDEAU, Georges, *Traité de Science Politique*, vol. vii, *La Démocratie Gouvernante*, Paris, 1957.

CLAUSEWITZ, Karl von, *On War*, London, 1908.

CONSTANT, Benjamin, *Oeuvres*, Paris.

CRAIG, Gordon A., *The Politics of the Prussian Army: 1640–1945*, New York, 1955.

CRICK, Bernard, *In Defence of Politics*, Chicago, 1962.

—— *The Reform of Parliament*, Gloucester, Mass., 1964.

DAALDER, Hans, *The Role of the Military in the Emerging Countries*, New York, 1962.

DAHL, Robert A., *A Preface to Democratic Theory*, New York, 1963.

—— *Who Governs?*, New Haven, 1961.

—— *Political Oppositions in Western Democracies* (Ed.), New Haven, 1966.

DAHRENDORF, Ralf, *Class and Class Conflict in Industrial Society*, Stanford, 1959.

—— *Gesellschaft und Demokratie in Deutschland*, München, 1966.

DEUTSCH, Karl W., *The Nerves of Government*, New York, 1966.

—— *Nationalism and Social Communication*, Cambridge, Mass., 1953.

DJILAS, Milovan, *The New Class*, New York, 1957.

DJORDJEVIC, Jovan, 'Le système de plannification en Yougoslavie', in *Revue de Science Financière* (Paris), 1966.

—— 'Political power in Yugoslavia', in *Government and Opposition*, vol. 2, no. 2, January 1967.

DRU, Jean, *De l'état socialiste*, Paris, 1965.

DUNLOP, J. U., *Industrial Relations Systems*, New York, 1959.

DUVERGER, Maurice, *Political Parties*, New York, 1954.

—— *De la dictature*, Paris, 1961.

—— *Sociologie politique*, Paris, 1967.

EASTON, David, *A Systems Analysis of Political Life*, New York, 1965.

EISENSTADT, S. N., 'Problems of emerging bureaucracies in developing areas and new states', in Bert F. Hoselitz and Wilbert E. Moore (Eds.), *Industrialization and Society*, New York, 1963.

FAINSOD, Merle, *How Russia Is Ruled*, Cambridge, Mass., 1963.

FETSCHER, Irving, *Der Marxismus*, Frankfurt, 1966.

FINER, S. E., *The Man on Horseback: The Role of the Military in Politics*, New York, 1962.

FISCHER-GALATI, Stephen (Ed.), *Eastern Europe in the Sixties*, New York, 1963.

FISK, Winston M., and RUBINSTEIN, Alunz, 'Yugoslavia's Constitutional Court', in *East Europe* (New York), July 1966.

FOORD, A. S., *His Majesty's Opposition (1714–1830)*, New York, 1964.

FREUND, J., *L'essence du politique*, Paris, 1965.

FRIEDRICH, Carl J., *Constitutional Government and Politics,* New York, 1937.

—— *Man and His Government,* New York, 1963.

FRIEDRICH, Carl J., and BRZEZINSKI, Z. K., *Totalitarian Dictatorship and Autocracy,* rev. ed., New York, 1966.

GADOUREK, I., *The Political Control of Czechoslovakia,* Leiden, 1953.

GELLNER, Ernest, *Thought and Change,* Chicago, 1965.

GOOCH, D. C. F., *Frederick the Great,* London, 1947.

GOZSTONY, P., 'General Maleter', in *Problems of Communism,* March–April 1966.

GROTTIAN, Walter, *Das Sowjetische Regierungssystem,* Köln, 1965.

HABERMAS, Jurgen, *Studenten und Politik,* Neuwied, 1961.

—— *Strukturwandel der Offentlichkeit,* Neuwied, 1962.

HANGEN, Welles, *The Muted Revolution,* New York, 1966.

HARTZ, Wanda, 'Opinions and demands upon local authorities', in Ostrowski and Przeworski (Eds.), *Local Political Systems in Poland,* Warsaw, 1965.

HAZARD, John N., *The Soviet System of Government,* Chicago, 1964.

HERSCH, Jeanne, *Idéologie et réalité,* Paris, 1955.

HINTZ, O., *Staat und Verfassung,* Leipzig, 1943.

HISCOCKS, Richard, *Poland, Bridge for the Abyss?* New York, 1963.

INKELES, Alex, and BAUER, R. A., *The Soviet Citizen: Daily Life in a Totalitarian Society,* Cambridge, Mass., 1959.

INSTITUT EDRUSTVENIH NAUKA, *Radnicko Samoupravljanje,* Belgrade, 1963.

IONESCU, Ghita, *Communism in Rumania, 1944–1962,* New York, 1964.

—— *The Breakup of the Soviet Empire in Eastern Europe,* Baltimore, 1965.

JACKSON, George D. Jr., *Comintern and Peasant in East Europe,* New York, 1966.

JANICKE, Martin, *Der Dritte Weg,* Köln, 1964.

JELENSKI, K. A., 'A Window on the future: the story of *Po Prostu',* in *Encounter,* 1957.

JOUVENEL, Bertrand de, *On Power,* Boston, 1947.

—— *Sovereignty,* Chicago, 1963.

—— *Pure Theory of Politics,* New Haven, 1963.

—— 'The Means of Contestation', in *Government and Opposition,* vol. 1, no. 2, January 1966.

JOVICIC, Miodrag, 'Representation', paper presented to the International Political Science Association Roundtable in Warsaw, 23–24 September 1966.

KALKOWICZ, Roman, 'Die Position der Sovjetarmee vor und nach dem Sturz Chrustchows' in *Osteuropa,* no. 10, 1966.

KASER, Michael, *Comecon,* New York, 1965.

KHRUSHCHEV, N. S., article in *World Marxist Review,* September, 1962.

KING, Harald, *LDP und NDP in der DDR,* Köln, 1965.

KORBONSKI, Andrezej, *Politics of Socialist Agriculture in Poland, 1945–1960*, New York, 1964.

KOTOK, V., 'Representation', paper presented at the International Political Science Association Roundtable in Warsaw, 23–24 September 1966.

KOTT, Jan, 'Les dix années que je viens de vivre', in *Les Temps Modernes*, February 1957.

KUHN, Heinrich, *Der Kommunismus in der Tchecoslowakei*, Köln, 1965.

LABEDZ, L., 'The Soviet Intelligentsia', in Richard Pipes (Ed.), *The Russian Intelligentsia*, New York, 1961.

LANE, R., *Political Ideology*, New York, 1962.

LAZAR, A. J. von, 'Class struggle and socialist construction: the Hungarian paradox', in *Slavic Review* (New York), vol. XXV, no. 2, June 1966.

LEBED, A., *Pudgotouka i vaspredelenje Rakovodyashchikh Kadrou SSR*, Institute for the study of the USSR, Munich, 1965 (roneotyped).

LENIN, *Collected Works*, 32 vols., London, 1965.

LÉVY, Yves, 'Police and Policy' in *Government and Opposition*, vol. 1, no. 4, July 1966.

LIPSET, S. M., *Political Man*, New York, 1959.

—— *Party Systems and Representations of Social Groups*, New York, 1961.

LIPSET and BEREDAY, George Z. F. (Eds.), 'Student Politics', special issue of *Comparative Education Review* (New York), June 1966.

LOEWENSTEIN, Karl, *Political Power and the Governmental Process*, rev. ed., Chicago, 1965.

LOWENTHAL, Richard, *World Communism: The Disintegration of a Secular Faith*, New York, 1964.

LUDZ, B., *Soziologie der DDR*, Köln, 1965.

LUKACS, Georg, *Geschichte und Klassenbewusstsein*, Berlin, 1923.

MACRAE, Donald, *Ideology and Society*, New York, 1962.

MAJKA, J., 'What is Polish-Catholicism like?', in *Znak* (Warsaw), March 1966.

MARCUSE, Herbert, *Soviet Marxism: a Critical Analysis*, New York, 1958.

MASON, Edward S. (Ed.), *The Corporation in Modern Society*, Cambridge, Mass., 1960.

MEISSNER, Boris, *Sowjetgesellschaft im Wandel*, Stuttgart, 1966.

MEISTER, Albert, *Socialisme et autogestion, l'experience Yuogoslave*, London, 1965.

MERLEAU-PONTY, M., *Humanisme et terreur*, Paris, 1951.

—— *Les aventures de la dialectique*, Paris, 1953.

MICHELS, Robert, *Political Parties*, with an introduction by S. M. Lipset, New York, 1962.

MITRANY, David, *Marx against the Peasant*, Chapel Hill, N.C., 1952.

MONTESQUIEU, *Oeuvres*, Paris.

MOORE, Barrington J. Jr., *The Dilemma of Power*, Cambridge, Mass., 1950.

NIKOLIC, Pavel, 'Notion and classification of the systems of power in the modern state' in *Annals of the Faculty of Law of Belgrade*, January–March 1966.

NORTH, Robert C., *Chinese Communism*, New York, 1966.

OPPENHEIM, L., *International Law*, ed. H. Lauterpacht, vol. I, New York, 1955.

OSIPOV, U. V. (Ed.), *Industry and Labour in the USSR*, London, 1966.

OSTROWSKI, K., and PRZEWORSKI, Adam, *Local political system in Poland*, Warsaw, 1965.

PALMER, R. R., *The Age of the Democratic Revolution*, Princeton, 1964.

PALOCZI-HORVATH, George, *Mao Tse-Tung*, London, 1964.

PARETO, Vilfredo, *Trattato di Sociologia Generale*, Rome, 1923.

PARSONS, Talcott, *The Social System*, Glencoe, Ill., 1951.

PETHYBRIDGE, R., *A Key to Soviet Politics*, New York, 1962.

—— *The Development of the Communist Bloc*, Boston, 1965.

PETKOVICS, Aleks, 'The Socialist Alliance: a form of self-management', in *Socialist Thought and Practice* (Belgrade), March 1965.

PYE, Lucian W., & VERBA, Sidney (Eds.), *Political Culture and Political Development*, Princeton, 1965.

RAJOVIC, Radosin, *Process stavarnja opstirskih prahvnih propisa*, Belgrade, 1963.

RAPAPORT, David C., 'A comparative theory of military and political type', in Huntington, Samuel P. (Ed.), *Changing patterns of military politics*, New York, 1962.

RICHER, H., *Macht ohne Mandat*, Köln, 1965.

RIGBY, T. H., 'Selection of Leading Personnel in Soviet Russia', unpublished thesis, University of London, LSE, 1958.

RIKLIN, Alois, & WESTEN, Klaus, *Selbstzeugnisse des SED Regimes*, Köln, 1963.

ROBERTS, Henry L., *Rumania: Political Problems of an Agrarian State*, New Haven, 1951.

ROBSON, William A., *The Governors and the Governed*, Shreveport, 1964.

ROSENBERG, Hans, *Bureaucracy, Aristocracy and Autocracy: The Prussian Experience, 1660–1815*, Cambridge, Mass., 1958.

ROSTOW, W. W., *The Dynamics of Soviet Society*, New York, 1954.

SARTORI, Giovanni, *Democratic Theory*, Detroit, 1962.

SAUVY, Alfred, *L'opinion publique*, Paris, 1956.

SCHAPIRO, Leonard, *The Origin of the Communist Autocracy*, Cambridge, Mass., 1955.

—— *The Communist Party of the Soviet Union*, New York, 1964.

—— *The Government and Politics of the Soviet Union*, New York, 1965.

SCHAUL, Hans, 'Der dialog und der Dortmunder Parteitag der SED', in *Einheit* (Berlin), August 1966.

SCHUMPETER, J. A., *Capitalism, Socialism and Democracy*, New York, 1942.

SEMYONOV, V. S., 'Soviet Intellectual and White-Collar Worker' in G. V. Osipov, *Industry and Labour in the USSR*, London, 1966.

SETON-WATSON, Hugh, *Pattern of Communist Revolution*, London, 1955.

—— *Neither War nor Peace*, New York, 1960.

SHILS, Edward A., 'The Intellectuals in the political development of the new states', in John Kautsky (Ed.), *Political Change in Underdeveloped Countries*, New York, 1962.

—— *Political Development in the New States*, The Hague, 1962.

—— 'Opposition in the New States' in *Government and Opposition*, vol. 1, no. 2, January 1966.

SKILLING, H. Gordon, *The Governments of Communist East Europe*, New York, 1966.

SOVIET-Yugoslav Dispute, R.I.I.A., London, 1948.

STALIN, J., *Problems of Leninism*, London, 1940.

STERNBERGER, Dolf, *Grund und Abgrund der Macht*, Frankfurt, 1962.

STURMTHAL, Adolf, *Workers Councils*, Cambridge, Mass., 1964.

SYME, Ronald, *Roman Revolution*, London, 1939.

SZCZEPANSKI, Jan, 'The Social Structure of Polish Society', in *Kultura*, 29 December 1963.

TATU, Michel, *Le pouvoir en URSS*, Paris, 1967.

TÖNNIES, Ferdinand, *Community and Society*, Lansing, 1957.

TOWSTER, Julian, *Political Power in the USSR*, London, 1948.

ULAM, Adam B., *The Bolsheviks*, New York, 1966.

VÁLI, Ferenc A., *Rift and Revolt in Hungary*, Cambridge, Mass., 1961.

VLADISLAVJEVIC, Sivko, *Saveti Narodnih Odbora Organizacija i Funksionisanje*, Belgrade, 1963.

VRATUSA, Anton, *The Communes in Yugoslavia*, in *Socialist Thought and Practice* (Belgrade), 1965.

WEIL, Eric, *Philosophie politique*, Paris, 1966.

WESTERGAARD (Ed.), *Cleavages, Ideology and Party Systems*, Helsinki, 1964.

WIATR, J. J., and PRZEWORSKI, Adam, 'Control and administration in the People's Democracies', in *Government and Opposition*, vol. I, no. 2, January 1966.

WILES, Peter, *The Political Economy of Communism*, Cambridge, Mass., 1962.

ZAKAZEWSKI, Witwold, 'Representation', paper presented at the International Political Science Association Roundtable in Warsaw, 23–24 September 1966.

INDEX OF NAMES

INDEX OF SUBJECTS